Vulcan's Fury

VULCAN'S FURY

Man Against the Volcano

Alwyn Scarth

Yale University Press
New Haven and London

Copyright © 1999 by Alwyn Scarth

Set in New Baskerville by Best-set Typesetter Ltd, Hong Kong
Printed in Hong Kong through WorldPrint Ltd

Title page illustration: Etna lava flow

Library of Congress Cataloging-in-Publication Data

Scarth, Alwyn.
 Vulcan's fury: man against the volcano/Alwyn Scarth.
 Includes bibliographical references and index.
 ISBN 0–300–07541–3 (cloth: alk. paper)
 1. Volcanism—Social aspects. I. Title.
QE522.S294 1999
363.34'95'09—DC21   98–37547
                                                                      CIP

A catalogue record for this book is available from the British Library.

10 9 8 7 6 5 4 3 2 1

A mes amis français

Contents

Preface

This book is about an unequal contest. It describes human reactions to volcanic eruptions: what the people saw, what they did, and how they survived, or how they died. Volcanic eruptions are among the most spectacular events in the natural world, but they are far more varied than is generally realized, and their victims have faced swirling hot ash, huge blasts, mudflows, and great sea-waves as well as lava-flows. Through the ages, too, fear, fascination, religious fervour, awe, enterprise and courage have been amongst the equally varied human reactions – and they have hardly ever changed, for all the recent advances in technology.

These accounts range across a wide geographical and historical spectrum, beginning with the annihilation of two cities and ending with a timely evacuation that saved thousands of lives. The narratives are based, wherever possible, on eyewitness or contemporary accounts, many of which appear here in English for the first time. I have used available translations from Dutch and Icelandic, but the translations from Latin, French, Spanish and Italian are my own. A prudent return to the original sources not only reveals the thrilling stories, but also helps to disperse the cobwebs of myth and misinterpretation and sheer inaccuracy that have distorted accounts of too many famous eruptions. At the same time, the latest research has been used to reappraise several eruptions in the past. But this is not a technical book about the causes of volcanism, for there are plenty available on that complex topic. It is addressed, instead, to all those who would simply like to know how humanity has tackled some of the most severe environmental problems that it has ever faced.

The choice of the eruptions described depended both upon the availability of suitable source materials, and upon the varied kinds of eruption and the human reactions to them in different areas and cultures at different periods of history. Some eruptions were so famous that they could not possibly be omitted, while many others that are equally fascinating have been included because they deserve to be better known. In the end, however, any choice of examples has to be personal and limited to the number allowed by an indulgent publisher.

I gratefully acknowledge the assistance of (in alphabetical order) Juan-Carlos Carracedo, Phyllis Forsyth, John Grattan, Anthony Newton, Jean-Claude Tanguy and Thorvaldur Thordarson in the preparation of this book. Amongst the friends who have always offered help, stimulus and encouragement, I should particularly like to thank Gareth Partington and Jean-Louis Renaud, who kindly read the manuscript and offered their invaluable comments, and Pat Michie, who developed my modest word-processing talents with tactful and unfailing patience. Any errors are my own. If you enjoy reading this book as much as I have enjoyed writing it, then my own efforts – and yours – will have been worth while.

Alwyn Scarth
Paris and Dundee, 1998

Acknowledgements

The author and publishers would like to thank the following for permission to make use of copyright material in this book.

Harvard University Press and the Loeb Classical Library for Letters 16 and 20 from *Pliny the Younger: Letters and Panegyricus*, translated by Betty Radice (1969), which were used as the basis of quotations in Chapter 3.

The Icelandic Institute of Natural History for quotations from 'The Öraefajökull Eruption of 1362' by S. Thórarinsson, in *Acta Naturalia Islandica*, vol. II, no. 2 (1958), pp. 1–98, which were used in Chapter 6.

Ministerio de Educación y Cultura de España and the Archivo General de Simancas, Valladolid, Spain, for quotations from the *Gracia y Justicia, Legajo 89*, which were translated and used in Chapter 7.

Thorvaldur Thordarson for permission to quote his translations of eye witness accounts and for other information contained in 'The eruptive sequence and behaviour of the Skaftár Fires (Laki) 1783–85, Iceland', T. Thordarson, Master's Thesis, University of Texas at Arlington, and 'Volatile release and atmospheric effects of basaltic fissure eruptions', T. Thordarson, PhD Thesis, University of Hawaii at Manoa, which were used in Chapter 8.

Barry Voight of Pennsylvania State University, and Elsevier Science Ltd, Oxford, for quotations from 'The 1985 Nevado del Ruiz volcano catastrophe: anatomy and retrospection', B. Voight, *Journal of Volcanology and Geothermal Research*, vol. 44 (1990), pp. 349–86, which were used in Chapter 14.

Elsevier Science Ltd, Oxford, for quotations from F. Le Guern, E. Shanklin and S. Tebor, 'Witness accounts of the catastrophic event of August 1986 at Lake Nyos (Cameroon)', *Journal of Volcanology and Geothermal Research*, vol. 57 (1992), pp. 174–84, which were used in Chapter 15.

And I beheld when he had opened the sixth seal, and, lo, there was a great earthquake; and the sun became black as sack-cloth of hair, and the moon became as blood; and the stars of heaven fell unto the earth, even as a fig tree casteth her untimely figs, when she is shaken of a mighty wind. And the heaven departed as a scroll when it is rolled together; and every mountain and island were moved out of their places. And the kings of the earth, and the great men, and the rich men, and the chief captains, and the mighty men, and every bondman, and every free man, hid themselves in the dens and in the rocks of the mountains; and said to the mountains and rocks, Fall on us, and hide us from the face of him that sitteth on the throne, and from the wrath of the Lamb: for the great day of wrath is come; and who shall be able to stand?

Revelation 6:12–17

1

Introduction

Volcanoes are fascinating, glamorous and exciting, often beautiful, and sometimes threatening. They inspire awe and reverence, fear and dread, as well as respect, or even – sometimes – endearment. Their often unpredictable behaviour gives them personalities that no other features in the landscape can equal, for their eruptions rank with the most spectacular displays in all the natural world.

Volcanoes have a reputation as dangerous killers which they do not entirely deserve. Most eruptions kill not a single soul, and it is only the outstanding and reported disasters that have given volcanoes their bad reputation. In the past two centuries, for example, these notorious eruptions have claimed about 225,000 victims throughout the world, but, during the same period, earthquakes killed almost as many people in Calabria and Sicily alone; some three-quarters of a million died in the few minutes after the Tangshan earthquake in China in 1976. And, *every year*, cars and cigarettes can kill many more than that.

The real fascination of volcanic eruptions, then, lies not primarily in their macabre role as death-dealers and headline-makers, but in their great variety and in the enthralling human reactions that they have always inspired as these crises unfolded. The challenge is to describe what people saw, what they felt, what they did, or what they failed to do; to explain how and why victims died; how farmland, forests, homes, and even whole cities were destroyed – but also to describe how tragedies might have been avoided: and how the survivors coped with some of the most acute environmental problems that humanity has ever faced. And, just as volcanic eruptions are varied, so human responses to them through the ages have varied.

Fear of the unknown, social customs, religious beliefs or the declarations of soothsayers have coloured reactions to eruptions much more than real scientific knowledge. In general, as events at Parícutin, Etna or Lanzarote illustrate, ordinary people have followed their instincts and sought consolation in talismans, traditional folk tales, rituals or religion. Indeed, if some reactions to recent events at Lake Nyos and Nevado del Ruiz are anything to go by, then science still has a struggle to gain the upper hand even now. To find a religious explanation for natural wonders of the world has always been an instinctive reaction. Of all natural disasters, eruptions provided the clearest vision of the flames of Hell for the Christian world. Thus doomsday, damnation, hellfire and brimstone have been the leitmotifs of many a volcanic crisis. It was commonly understood that sin provoked the Divine fury that unleashed eruptions. The guilty victims – the supposed sinners – undertook prayers, confessions, repentance, votive offerings, processions of revered saints and holy relics, self-mortification, sacrifices – and even marriage – in desperate attempts at expiation. In several cases, such religious reactions may well have been all the more fervent because priests were not only community leaders, but also the sole 'intellectuals' who were in touch with the ordinary people whom the eruptions were threatening most closely.

Almost all those facing a volcanic emergency have shown greater faith in ministers of religion than in ministers of government – or, of course, in scientists. On the other hand, although some collaboration between earth scientists and public administrators has, at times, helped to reduce damage and death tolls, it has also provided many examples of human errors, misconceptions and mismanagement. They should not, however, be condemned out of hand, but judged with due humility in the light of the still puny – but praiseworthy – achievements of modern volcano management. Triumphs in the fight against eruptions have been modest: a few relatively docile lava-flows have been diverted; some efficient evacuations from danger zones have been carried out; and some threatened populations, especially in Japan, have been trained to avoid possible disasters. The major triumph, so far, has been the well-staged, efficient evacuation of a large population from the flanks of Pinatubo, in the Philippines, in 1991, which must have saved at least 20,000 lives. But not a single volcanic eruption has ever been stopped.

Individual reactions to eruptions are as varied as corporate responses. It comes as a surprise to those inhabiting calmer environments that many threatened populations find it hard to perceive that an eruption might be dangerous until it is too late – even if they live at the foot of the volcano. Sceptics find it hard to imagine incandescent clouds of ash careering down their High Street at 500km an hour. Such things only happen in other countries or in sensational books. These sceptics suffer from disaster myopia, like motorists who drive fast in fog. Deaths have often resulted from such flawed perceptions. This proved to be the fate of the Pompeiians in AD 79 and the citizens of Armero, in Colombia in 1985, for instance. But, in many other cases, fatalistic resignation makes people cling to their homes, even when molten lava arrives on the doorstep. In fact, they often have little alternative except to keep on hoping until the last moment, because their homes are all that they possess in the world. Their assets are not transferable. Even the richer members of society, too, often feel compelled to guard their premises or their safes. At the other end of the spectrum, many people panic at once. As so often happens in a crisis, they flee to the apparent safety of the nearest town – or run off in the first direction that enters their heads. An unnamed

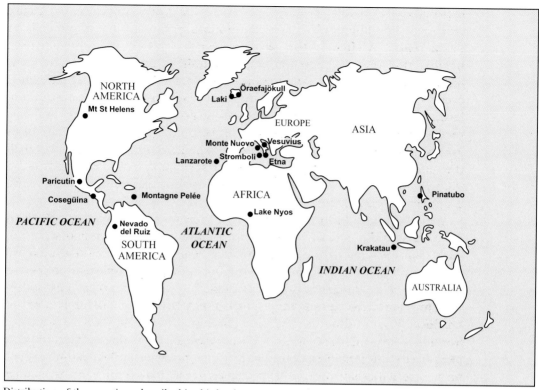

Distribution of the eruptions described in this book.

correspondent vividly described the exodus from the slopes of Etna as molten lava began to gush forth in 1669.

> [As] the Earth began to open in several places, and to threaten them with inevitable ruine, they fled with much trouble and amazement to this City [Catania]. These shakings of the Earth [were] so frequent and violent that the people went reeling and staggering, with much difficulty supporting one another from falling . . . what with their want of sleep, the pains they were forced to take in travelling, and the great terrors imprinted on them by what they had seen and suffered, they appeared at their arrival in this City as so many distracted People, wholly insensible of what they did.

And this was only a quite moderate eruption which killed nobody.

It is in such conditions of acute emotional distress that rumours have played their most vital role. The product of vivid imaginations and wagging tongues, rumours always seem to travel faster than the truth. They flourish particularly well when a great eruption causes chaos. Rumour stands for fact until the truth arrives. Early human responses to any eruption may be based at least as much on rumours as on reality. Pliny the Younger, for instance, complained about those who claimed that half of Misenum had been destroyed in AD 79; and, during the eruption of Cosegüina in 1835, some affirmed that whole tracts of Central America had vanished. Most rumours provoke extreme, or crazy, reactions because they can be so wildly exaggerated. But this is not always the case. Ironically the citizens of Armero in 1985 and of Saint-Pierre in 1902 died because the predominant rumours tranquillized them and encouraged them to remain at home, directly in the path of two of the most lethal volcanic weapons unleashed in the twentieth century. In fact, if the rumours had been wilder, they could well have caused more panic, which might have provoked early flights to salvation – just as they seem to have done in Pompeii.

One of the most striking features of an eruption crisis is how powerless and isolated the victims often are. Eruptions bring already slow communications to a complete standstill. In the ensuing chaos, people are commonly left to their own devices and have to fend for themselves. They have no technical knowledge to alleviate the disaster, no fast transport to escape, and no cheques to cash in faraway banks. Their survival depends on the speed of their reaction, upon what the volcano hurls at them, or upon sheer luck. They suffer terrible physical and psychological isolation, perhaps only surpassed by the immense traumas produced by great earthquakes. Those who then declare that the world is ending are scarcely dramatizing their plight. The catastrophes of Vesuvius, Montagne Pelée or Krakatau provide ample illustrations, but the reactions at Etna or Nevado del Ruiz also show that eruptions do not always have to be large to be terrifying.

The problems that loom up during eruptions can be extremely complicated. As a result, the social and scientific context must be a paramount consideration when assessing reactions to any volcanic crisis. Behind every human response to past eruptions, the fundamental question must be: with the knowledge available to them at the time, what else could they have done?

Science might have provided the indispensable supportive crutch in many an eruptive crisis, but the earth sciences were still in their infancy when most of the eruptions described here took place. Volcanology has only really developed its relevant analytical tools during the second half of the twentieth century. These tools enable scientists to inspect the past behaviour of the volcano much more closely. They can try to isolate the signs that herald an eruption, and thus try to forecast what the volcano might do next, so that they can warn both public administrators and the threatened population. Until a few decades ago, there were no such benefits. What are now recognized as warning signals were often there, but, in those days, they were not measured, and they were usually not even perceived as portents of the disaster to come. Indeed, in many cases, the earthquakes that often preceded an eruption terrified the people more than the ash that was swirling about their heads – and sometimes even led them to fear a massive earthquake at least as much as an eruption.

However, in spite of all these warning signs, volcanoes can also surprise even the most rational and well-informed of beings. For example, intelligent people, who were conversant with the established scientific facts of the day, averred that Montagne Pelée presented no real danger to Saint-Pierre in 1902. They were wrong for what seemed the right reasons: Montagne Pelée devastated the city with a volcanic weapon which science had not yet identified.

Unfortunately, there is a common popular assumption that volcanic activity is always the same. But eruptions come in all sorts and sizes, ranging from hissing gas to gushing molten lava, and huge explosions of ash and dust; and their side-effects can produce great sea-waves, mudflows, brilliant sunsets, fires and famines. These many kinds of eruptions occur when hot materials, similar to molten rock, and containing gases and steam, rise up from the nearly molten layer which lies under great pressure below the cool and solid crust of the earth. They reach the surface via chimney-like vents or along fissures that crack the crust. Specialists have spent their whole working lives arguing about exactly how this happens. Basically, as the mass approaches the surface, the pressures acting upon it are reduced and the gases and steam can separate out. When the materials are fluid and hot – at about 1,250°C – the gases and steam can hiss out fairly easily to the surface. Most of the molten material runs across the land as lava-flows, although mild gas explosions can shatter some of it into ash and cinders that pile up as little volcanic cones usually rising less than 250m above the chimney. This kind of activity, with small variations, is described in the accounts of Stromboli, Etna, Lanzarote, Laki and Parícutin, where the keynote of human reactions was largely the struggle against encroaching lava-flows.

On the other hand, the rising materials can often be much more viscous and perhaps as cool as 800°C. In this case, the steam and gas cannot easily escape as the pressure reduces. They form bubbles that honeycomb and weaken the molten rock until it becomes a stiff, frothy mass. Suddenly the multitude of bubbles explodes with enormous violence. The molten froth shatters into an infinity of small pieces which are thrust into the air, where they cool to dust, ash or pumice. Sometimes, these fragments form huge, incandescent clouds – or nuées ardentes – which can race down a volcano at 500km an hour, burning everything in their path. This was the fate reserved for Pompeii in AD 79 and Saint-Pierre in 1902. Even more frequently, however, violent eruptions hurl colossal, billowing, grey columns of gas and fine fragments into the stratosphere. Vesuvius, Coseguina, Krakatau, Mount St Helens and Pinatubo, for instance, all displayed this superb spectacle. Often the cloud spreads widely and blots out the sun so that ash rains down in total darkness all around the volcano. The finer particles and the gases sometimes form aerosols that can be blown round the world in about two weeks. They produce beautiful sunsets, but they also tend to act like a parasol and stop some of the sun's heat from reaching the earth's surface. The result – sometimes, but not always – can be abnormally cold winters for the two or three years that the aerosols linger in the stratosphere. Meanwhile, the coarser ash, cinders and pumice fragments accumulate around the volcanic chimney, and some small lava-flows may emerge when the power of the explosions is spent. Repeated

eruptions pile up layer upon layer of varied volcanic materials which eventually form impressive and beautiful cones, often well over 1,000m high. Many
cones rise high enough to be decorated with ice-caps. This makes them more
dangerous, because further eruptions melt some of the ice and generate
glacier-bursts, as at Öraefajökull, or lethal mudflows, as at Nevado del Ruiz.
At times, too, eruptions damage the volcano itself. In 1980, for instance, the
rising molten rock made part of the northern flank of Mount St Helens
collapse in a vast landslide that precipitated the eruption. Even more cata-
strophically, no less than two-thirds of the island of Krakatau foundered into
the Soenda Straits on one eventful morning in 1883. The giant sea-waves, or
tsunamis, which followed ensured that, rather paradoxically, most of the
victims of Krakatau were drowned.

However, knowing *what* erupts is only half the battle. From the human point
of view, it is also vital to know *when* it is going to happen. In fact, active volcanoes are not usually in a constant eruptive turmoil, and Stromboli, off Sicily,
is one of the very few that erupts nearly all the time. The smaller volcanoes,
formed by relatively moderate outbursts, are usually active for only a few years
before they become extinct. Monte Nuovo, active for a week, and Parícutin,
active for nine years, illustrate the extremes of their normal life-span. In

Contemporary woodcut of the eruption of Monte Nuovo, 1538.

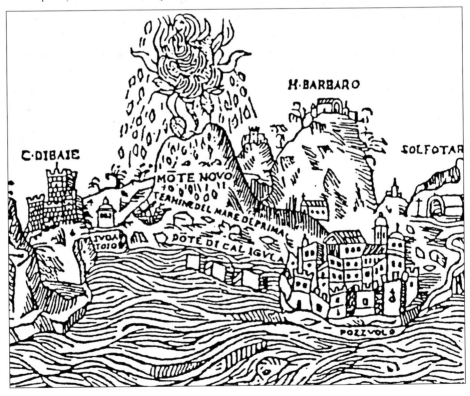

contrast, the more violent volcanoes can keep up their vigour for hundreds of thousands of years. However, the cataclysmic outbursts that give them their notoriety are commonly limited to a few tempestuous days separated by years or centuries of repose. These volcanoes are usually dormant throughout most of their active lives. Indeed, nobody can quite be sure whether many of them are really active, or dormant, or actually extinct. These long intervals of calm can then become very dangerous because they lull people into a false sense of security. They encroach upon the flanks of the cone, building towns and cultivating the fertile, weathered volcanic soils. Great then is their surprise and horror when the volcano springs back into action. Pinatubo caused one such surprise in 1991; Vesuvius will eventually cause another.

It can save lives to know how each individual volcano behaves, because the danger that it presents depends on what it erupts. It is obviously far easier to combat slow-moving lava-flows than blasts of incandescent ash travelling at 500km an hour. All those who live around active volcanoes should be made thoroughly aware of the threats that they may ultimately face.

In fact, most volcanoes behave fairly consistently and their eruptions also follow a fairly consistent pattern. Indeed, 'once a crook, always a crook' is a maxim that applies better to volcanoes than to humans, because – so far at any rate – no volcano has yet been rehabilitated. The potential crook has always to be watched.

In the past, most eruptions came like bolts from the blue. Nowadays, the volcanoes that are apparently the most dangerous are very closely studied. The details of their past behaviour are brought to light through studies of their geological history; and close and continual monitoring reveals all their pre-monitory rumblings. The warning signs that molten rock is rising into the volcano might include: volcanic earthquakes that are centred under the cone, slight swelling of the mountain, or escaping gases such as sulphur dioxide or hydrogen sulphide. As it reaches the surface, the molten rock might also heat the groundwater to steam and thus cause explosions which shatter a small part of the volcano into fine, but *cool*, fragments that are thrown out of the crater. These warnings are good, but, unfortunately, not infallible hints that an eruption is on the way. Matters become altogether more serious when the molten rock itself starts exploding from the crater. Then, all doubts are removed – the real, and usually much more powerful, phase of the eruption has begun. It is time to take evasive action – if it is not already too late . . . In the past, warnings have often been misinterpreted, or have gone unheeded. The stories of Pinatubo, Nevado del Ruiz, Mount St Helens and Montagne Pelée, for example, show how threatened populations perceived and reacted to these warnings, and what happened to them when their awesome crisis came.

Nowadays the volcano warns the experts, who warn the authorities, who warn the threatened people. In principle. But these are not days of cool, Olympian calm: they are days of fear and turmoil. Total darkness, hot, falling ash, shaking ground, approaching lava-flows – or rumours of much worse – have always fanned anxiety to the point of panic and terror. People have yearned for consolation, comfort, and for scientific and social guidance, which has often been conflicting, wrong, or absent altogether. This is partly because an eruption frequently exaggerates major divergences in basic interests and opinions that already exist between scientists, public administrators and ordinary people. These differences make crisis management very difficult. For each group, doubts and disagreements about the future course of events mean very different things. For scientists they imply more discussion, more research, more publications, and perhaps even promotion. For public servants, who revere civil stability, they presage disorder, disaster and dismissal. For the ordinary people they mean certain anguish, a desperate search for food, shelter or help, or, quite possibly, the prospect of a swift, nasty and unnatural death. Imperfectly linking these three groups are journalists, who could publicize explanations, forecasts of likely events, or evacuation plans. But scientists are often trapped in their own technical jargon, and do not always explain the problems involved as clearly as they might. Their cautious technical pronouncements make neither good copy nor striking sound-bites. Moreover, even now it is hard to say exactly when a volcano will erupt. After all, the great explosion of Mount St Helens in 1980 killed the geologist who was monitoring the volcano. Ordinary people do not understand the complexities of volcanoes. They can quite happily, or resignedly, attribute eruptions to the handiwork of an angry God. They require clear guidance from the experts, not a technical catalogue splattered with provisos. In the end, the general public finds it hard to decide between the cautiously expressed views of experts and the much more confident-sounding pronouncements of 'eminent personalities' or 'local characters', whose ignorance of the wiles of volcanoes is matched only by the dogmatic silliness of their forecasts. The destruction of Armero in 1985 encapsulated the tragic consequences that can then result. Comparable uncertainties, no doubt, also resounded through the streets of Pompeii and Herculaneum. At least, events at Pinatubo in 1991 swung the balance a little way in the other direction.

Even if an adequate crisis strategy could have been formulated, communications were so slow until the twentieth century that administrative instructions almost invariably reached the disaster area too late to have been of any use. Isolation thus weakened the public authorities. They were – and are – often further hamstrung by rigid, hierarchical government structures, and can also be unduly influenced by commercial, industrial or even military interests. In truth, the authorities have a more difficult practical task than the scientists in a volcanic emergency. They have to comprehend the scientific forecasts, deal with a terrified population, and perhaps to pander to unforgiving, autocratic rulers as well. To evacuate the threatened people or not to evacuate them: that is often the vital question. Not *anywhere*; not at *any time*. The administrators have to prepare refuges, and have to time an evacuation so accurately that it is completed just *before* the devastation starts. They are at the mercy of the experts, who are required to predict the advent of menacing eruptions virtually to within a day. This is much easier said than done. It is indeed possible to forecast when a lava-flow might overrun a village, but it is far, far, harder to forecast the more violent, more dangerous and more widespread volcanic outbursts. If the authorities evacuate the population too early, then there is unrest, as at Pozzuoli in 1984. If they evacuate the people too late, then they might be held responsible, rightly or wrongly, for thousands of deaths. However, when the authorities and scientists co-operate effectively, they can save many lives – as they did when Pinatubo erupted in 1991. But administrators have often had a thankless task. They need the quicksilver intelligence of classical Athens, and evacuees need the iron discipline of Sparta. These attributes have frequently been sadly lacking . . . Even when the Mexican authorities efficiently evacuated and rehoused the villagers from around Parícutin volcano, they ran into all manner of social problems afterwards. Moreover, like any crowd, a population terrified by an eruption often behaves irrationally. People are not always keen to act upon good advice even when they do get it. For example, they do not relish leaving their comfortable homes for distant tents. Their viewpoint does have a certain logic: they find it much easier to imagine that their unprotected houses will be looted than that they will be damaged by an eruption. Some knowledge of crowd psychology should perhaps be added to the qualifications of the decision-makers.

Most of the eruptions described here are seen, wherever possible, through the eyes of witnesses, whose accounts often conjure up vivid pictures of the course of the crises. This will be clear from the English extracts quoted, and will perhaps also come through in my own translations from the original Latin, French, Italian or Spanish, many of which now appear in English for the first time. With the stupendous exception of Mount St Helens in 1980, most of the eye-witnesses had neither cameras nor sketch-pads to illustrate their descriptions. Instead, they had to rely on acute observation and hearing, a wide and precise vocabulary, and sometimes on talented prose that might have caused Edward Gibbon a twinge of envy.

The older reports, in particular, share many drawbacks that are the bane of historians everywhere. Observations are incomplete, haphazard, and often tantalizingly brief. Errors are repeated when they are not, indeed, magnified. Facts are commonly twisted to fit preconceived notions. Myths and legends proliferate. Descriptions are exaggerated. The Devil, gods and saints of all kinds assert themselves. Flights of fancy abound. By the standards of our 'scientific age', explanations are bizarre. On a more mundane level, too, the common historical problem persists that few witnesses ever seem able to agree on the dates of events, let alone on their exact timing. And yet . . . and yet . . . many observers were also remarkably perceptive. This is nowhere seen to greater effect than in the oldest surviving detailed narrative of a volcanic eruption – Pliny the Younger's masterly relation of the great outburst of Vesuvius in AD 79. Recent research shows that the events he described can be corroborated by the layers of volcanic fragments that Vesuvius expelled. Thus the good story is also a fundamental scientific document.

Careful analysis of many of the old descriptions, however, also shows how many exaggerations, misconceptions, mistranslations or errors have crept into accepted views of these events and have then become sanctified in the subsequent literature. For example, it has commonly been held that the lavas of Etna destroyed Catania in 1669; and that only two people survived the nuées ardentes from Montagne Pelée on 8 May 1902 – and some have gone so far as to claim that one of them was a murderer. Both tales are false. They are not alone. Perhaps the myths stuck so tenaciously in accounts of eruptions because volcanologists have naturally been more concerned with unravelling the mechanisms of activity than with the details of its brief impact on human society, whilst historians have preferred to study political, religious, social or economic developments rather than the natural disasters of the past. In recent years, on the other hand, expert volcanological research has enabled reappraisals of the influence of the eruptions of Cosegüina, Laki and Vesuvius, for instance.

The past was a quiet place. Before the twentieth century, the most common noise that people noticed was probably the sound of bells, and the loudest noises heard would be claps of thunder and gunfire. When an eruption occurred, witnesses turned to familiar sights and sounds for their comparisons. Thus did Sir William Hamilton, with thirty years of volcano-watching behind him, describe the eruption of Vesuvius in 1794:

> It was a mixture of the loudest thunder, with incessant reports, like those from a numerous heavy artillery, accompanied by a continual hollow murmur, like that of the roaring of the ocean during a violent storm; and added to these was a blowing noise like that of the going up of a large flight of skyrockets, and which brought to my mind the action of the enormous bellows on the furnace of the Carron iron foundry in Scotland, and which it perfectly resembled. The frequent falling of huge stones and scoriae [cinders] . . . contributed undoubtedly to the concussion of the earth and air, which kept all the houses in Naples for several hours in a constant tremor, every door and window shaking and rattling incessantly, and the bells ringing. This was an awful moment! . . . The murmur of the prayers and the lamentations of a numerous population forming various processions, and the parading in the streets, added likewise to the horror . . . I recommended to the company [in the house] . . . who began to be much alarmed . . . to go and view the mountain at some greater distance.

Such narratives open small windows on history, and many offer brief, illuminating insights into the ways of the past as well as into the behaviour of volcanoes. They illustrate the attitudes, fears, prejudices and beliefs of both the ordinary people and the elites as they tried to cope with crises that were often well beyond their experience. The stories are thrilling in themselves and the observations of the witnesses add a certain spice to the pictures. Some of the source materials used for this book had almost vanished into the mists of time. They spring from official reports, administrative instructions, requests for help, the diaries of clergymen, letters, and the observations of sharp-eyed peasants and old compilations of eye-witness accounts – but sometimes also from articles in contemporary and modern learned journals. Used with discretion, these narratives seem to give the most reliable versions of the course of events, and perhaps the closest approximation to historical truth. They often bring out the character, the resourcefulness, the ingenuity and the courage of the participants in these tragedies, the stupidity or the scientific acumen of a few, and the religious fervour of many.

In their stark isolation, some terrified victims watch helplessly as lava swallows their homes. Some shovel away the ash as fast as it falls. Some impede advancing lava-flows with rubble. Some try to outpace hot blasts. Some hide in the cellar. Some wander about in shock. Some simply pray. Some ring church bells. Some bang drums. Some let off fireworks. Some sacrifice virgins. Some panic. Some collect their goods and their families and flee into the stifling darkness. Some try to help their neighbours. Some take warnings seriously. Some dismiss them as myths. Some follow pundits and false prophets. Some react with intelligent forethought and prescience. Some execute efficient plans. Others run around like headless chickens. Just as they always will. To witness a great eruption closely is an awesome privilege. To survive is a bonus.

2

Stromboli

Stromboli is unique amongst the world's volcanoes because it has been in virtually constant activity for at least 3000 years. Stromboli gives a spectacular display of eruptions of ash, cinders, and the occasional lava-flow, safely viewed from the summit many times a day.

Stromboli is the best place in the world to go to be sure of seeing a volcanic eruption. But it is something of an unsung hero, for its eruptions are *usually* never violent enough to attract the attention of the media, and *usually* nobody is killed. Yet it is one of the wonders of the natural world. No volcano on earth has erupted so often, or so consistently, during the past 3,000 years at least. Stromboli is the northernmost of the Aeolian Islands that lie off the northern coast of Sicily. It rises to a height of 926m above sea level, but, in fact, the volcano is much larger than it looks, for two-thirds of it lie below the Tyrrhenian Sea. It began life about a million years ago, some 2,000m down on the sea-bed, and seems to have been in pretty constant activity ever since. Stromboli is really about as big as Etna and over twice the size of Vesuvius.

Homer had a few ideas about Stromboli. In Book X of the *Odyssey*, he said that the island was surrounded by 'an unbroken wall of bronze' – a clear reference to the dark-grey cliffs of solidified lava all around Stromboli. He also called it the 'floating island of Aeolia, the home of Aeolus, the God of the Winds'. It is possible that the Ancient Greeks were tricked by the ash and pumice that might, indeed, have floated around the island after one of the volcano's bigger outbursts. For instance, on 18 November 1887, an unusually large eruption scattered floating pumice all over the sea to the east of the volcano. Homer also revealed that Aeolus and his family were much given to riotous partying and perhaps the idea of the noisy festivities, at least, came from the constant roar of the eruptions at the summit.

The Ancient Greeks also called the island Strongylê, which means round. They cannot have looked at it too closely, because it is shaped like the Great Pyramid of Cheops in Egypt. What they could not avoid seeing, however, were the continual eruptions, and they called Stromboli the 'lighthouse of the Mediterranean'. But, like many a lighthouse, Stromboli has remained remote, and even today, access is slow and the few villages on the island are tiny. The island did not even become popular after Rossellini made the film, *Stromboli*, in 1949, which starred Ingrid Bergman. Even then, the volcano had no luck. Once again, it was to remain an unsung hero. Ingrid Bergman took all the

Stromboli in eruption.

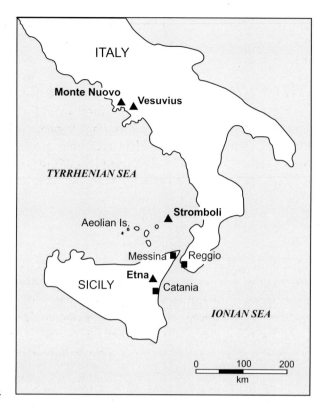

The Volcanoes of Southern Italy.

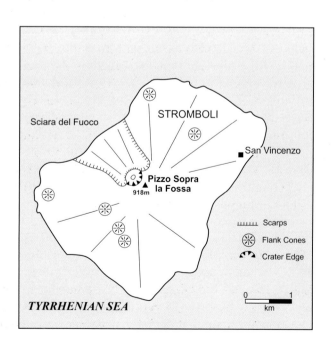

Stromboli.

attention, because she had just caused a sensation by leaving her husband for Rossellini. Alas, the passionate affair did not inspire the famous neo-realist director, and his portrayal of a Strombolian eruption was, in fact, far from realistic.

The main settlement, San Vincenzo, is only a cluster of white houses on the eastern shores of the island. They face on to the islet of Strombolicchio, the remnant of an old volcanic chimney, plugged with solidified lava, that is set like a die in the blue waters. The volcanic action on Stromboli goes on almost out of sight, and usually out of mind, high up on the crest of the mountain. But the spectacle is well worth a closer look.

The Climb

The climb up to the summit is not strenuous. It is best to make the ascent on a windless evening, preferably with the prospect of clear moonlight later, to light up the return. What is an imposing show during the day becomes a spectacle of neck-tingling beauty when night falls. The reward for the two or three hours' effort is the most consistently impressive natural firework display in the world – a Fourth, or Fourteenth, of July on every day of the year – and many times a day, or night, at that!

The show is not to be missed; and a well-worn path leads from San Vincenzo to the summit. The path passes the corner of the Punta Labronzo, where, in 1930, one of the fiercest eruptions of Stromboli ever recorded destroyed the old observatory. Then begins the zigzag up from the northern shore towards a rocky bastion overlooking an enormous smooth slide of black-grey scree that stretches steeply from the crest of the volcano right down into the sea. This is the Sciara del Fuoco, the 'Scar of Fire', the toboggan run for the lava-flows that sometimes cascade straight into the water. High above, the regular eruptions of threatening puffs of black smoke and reddish rocks, like distant gunfire, irresistibly draw the climber towards the craters on the upper rim of the Sciara. Eventually, the stunted, wind-battered bushes give way to the bare, mineral world of jagged rocks, ash and cinders that covers the whole crest of Stromboli. The craters cluster on a kind of landing, 300m across, between the top of the Sciara del Fuoco and the summit of the volcano. It is not wise to venture onto this landing. It is hot and dangerous. There is a much better, and much safer, natural viewpoint – the summit eyrie called the Pizzo sopra la Fossa, the peak above the abyss.

The Programme

Stromboli usually erupts about every twenty minutes or so. Sometimes the intervals are shorter, but they are rarely any longer. It throws out small, red-hot fragments of molten rock from several craters grouped just below its

Stromboli's cone and, lying below, San Vincenzo.

summit. Most of these eruptions are quite moderate and modest, and they are all the more beautiful for being visible – in safety – at close quarters.

Between three and six craters usually operate together. The molten rock rises up a cluster of chimneys inside the volcano and explodes out at the surface as a hot, stiff fluid at a temperature of around 1,000°C. As the molten rock, or lava, nears the surface, the pressures on it are reduced, and the gases contained within it begin to separate into bubbles, in the same way as champagne, or beer, froths out when the bottle is shaken and uncorked. Then the bubbles burst with a raucous roar in a multitude of explosions. As the gas explodes, it shatters the molten rock into small fragments and hurls them into the air.

The more powerful the explosions, the more the molten rock is shattered, and the finer the fragments that are produced. Some are as minute as dust particles; bigger fragments form ash; some are the size of walnuts; and others are as big as a human head and as knobbly as clinker or cinders. The wind blows the finer particles away, often showering the spectators, and occasionally spreading the fragments all over the island. But most fragments fall back to earth, cool down, solidify, and accumulate as cones of ash or cinders, which have a bowl-shaped crater at their summit marking the top of the chimney. During the eruption, the crater forms the open mouth of the chimney, but as soon as activity stops the molten rock solidifies and plugs the top of the

Stromboli in eruption.

chimney, which forms the base of the crater. At Stromboli, the craters are never sealed for long.

The Show

The Pizzo sopra la Fossa is the dress circle. The stage is on the landing, about 500m away and nearly 200m below. Soon the ground begins to shudder and tremble, and a dull, vibrating, rumbling stirs in the crater. One crater often just gives off a blue flame of burning gas like a Bunsen burner. The others explode molten lava fragments. In the darkness, the red glow of the rising molten rock shows up the position of the chimneys. Sometimes the chimneys hiss, sometimes they chug away like old steam engines, rumble like thunder, or explode like shells. Soon the escaping gases roar upwards, shattering the molten rock into red, vermilion, and even yellow, clots and droplets of lava. They soar in graceful curves high up into the air, a constellation of glowing splashes and sparks like a gigantic firework. Gas and steam swirl around the chimneys, half reflecting, half masking, the glow. The molten fragments are thrown as much as 200m or 300m into the sky before they lose their impetus, seem for a moment to hesitate in mid-air, and then fall back to the cones that each new explosion is making just a little larger. The smaller glowing embers cool where they have fallen, but the larger clots slide slowly down the cone and come to rest towards its base. After several minutes of these eruptive spasms, the roar of the explosions fades to a low groan, the last cinders expelled crash, echoing, down into the chimney. The vermilion glow of the embers deepens to blood red before it dies and the cones and their gaping chimneys vanish again into the darkness. Clouds of steam swirl about the craters, especially if the weather is damp, and an acrid odour of sulphur wafts across the summit for a while. Then silence. Stromboli is such a reliable performer that there is usually only a short interval before the next act.

Lava-flows erupt much less often and are less dangerous for the spectator than the fragments. Normally, they would solidify in rugged, black tongues in the valleys on the flanks of the volcano, but the lie of the land at Stromboli directs all of them down the Sciara del Fuòco, well away from the Pizzo sopra la Fossa. Most of the flows break out near the top of the Sciara, but they are often too small to reach the bottom. Some are hard to detect because they flow in tunnels down the scree. The steepness of the Sciara causes other flows to break up into large chunks and slide, hissing and steaming, down into the sea.

Sometimes, after a few years of constant effort, Stromboli rests for three or four days. But, unlike on other active volcanoes, this is certainly no time to make an excursion to the craters. This is when Stromboli is at its most dangerous. The pause is often a portent of an unusually powerful eruption – by Stromboli's rather modest standards. When it comes, the solid plug of lava is shattered: red-hot ash, and even the occasional big lump of lava, can shower down on half the island.

There have also been times when nuées ardentes – glowing clouds of ash, steam and fragments – have rushed down the volcano and approached San Vincenzo. The most recent of these more spectacular eruptions took place on 11 September 1930. The whole island lifted up by a metre just beforehand, as the molten rock invaded the volcano. A plume of ash and steam soared 2.5km into the air, and a glowing avalanche of hot ash and steam careered down the northern flanks of Stromboli, burnt crops, singed orchards and destroyed several buildings on the north-eastern coast. Ash fell over Calabria. But such drastic impulses happen only two or three times a century. For decades at a time, Stromboli never disturbs the tranquillity of its coastal villages, preferring, perhaps, to keep in good voice for a few more centuries . . .

But, for all its diligent work, Stromboli never achieves the enormous blasts that have made Vesuvius a byword for volcanic violence. Nobody is quite sure why Stromboli has behaved so modestly for such a long time, because volcanoes that erupt in that way usually tire themselves out after a few years, leaving behind an extinct cinder-cone about 200m high. Stromboli already rises 3,000m from the sea-bed, and, it seems, the show must go on, and on, and on . . .

SOCIETATI REGIÆ LONDINI
GULIELMUS HAMILTON
·BALN·ORD·EQUES·
D · D · D ·
CIƆIƆCCLXXIX·

3

Vesuvius, AD *79*

Vesuvius is altogether more vicious than Stromboli, and is not to be viewed at close quarters when it erupts. The famous eruption in AD *79 was perhaps the most violent and destructive ever described in Europe. It was also one of the most useful because it preserved part of the Roman world for posterity; and recent research has thrown new light on the terrible fate of the victims. Pliny the Younger's account of the catastrophe is a masterpiece.*

Emperor Titus:
More than his wont, fearsome Vesuvius has erupted glowing rivers from his mouths, he has shaken the rocks, and has filled the nearby city with ruins and all the lands around it. The hapless people are still fleeing, but those that the fire has spared are now laid low in penury. Let this gold help repair the distress of all these victims. This, Romans, is the kind of Temple that I would wish.

Libretto by P. Metastasio and C. Mazzolá for W. A. Mozart, La Clemenza di Tito, *Act I, scene iv*

A Glorious Setting

Vesuvius is the most glamorous volcano in the world. Few volcanoes have been painted and photographed so often, or stand in such a beautiful position; none has made such a wonderful contribution to history; and only its Sicilian rival, Etna, has a longer recorded biography. But Vesuvius far outstrips Etna in violence, for it is the nastiest active volcano in Europe. That sleek and graceful cone adding such distinction to the Bay of Naples is a lethal volcano, with a history of violent outbursts stretching back many thousands of years. A famous Italian proverb suggests that there is no need even to try and find a more beautiful landscape than the Bay of Naples: 'Vedi Napoli, e poi muori' ('See Naples and die'). And Vesuvius has always added a shudder of apprehension to the scene . . .

Vesuvius has had at least 200 powerful eruptions during the past 2,000 years. Time after time, crops, farms, vineyards, houses, hamlets, and even cities have been destroyed, and thousands of people have perished. The volcano stayed quite calm in the Middle Ages, but awoke with a huge and sudden outburst in 1631. From then on, until 1944, Vesuvius was in almost continuous activity; its mightier spasms made everyone in the district seek protection from a favourite saint and drove sinners rushing to confession.

Eruptions of Vesuvius, from *Campi Phlegraei*, 1779.

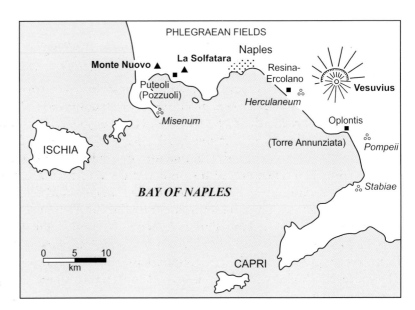

The location
of Vesuvius.

Vesuvius has always been rather lucky in those who have written about it. Pliny the Younger gave it immortality in the classical world; and Sir William Hamilton, grandson of the third Duke of Hamilton and British Ambassador to the Kingdom of Naples, produced *Campi Phlegraei*, the most beautiful book ever written on volcanoes. He also described the eruptions of Vesuvius during the last thirty years of the eighteenth century in perceptive detail in a series of letters to the Royal Society of London.

But by far the grandest of all the eruptions of Vesuvius in the past 3,000 years took place in August, AD 79, when Pompeii, Herculaneum and many other smaller settlements around the volcano were buried under a thick blanket of pumice and ash. There they remained for 1,700 years or more. Paradoxically, their volcanic destruction caused their archaeological preservation. Burial meant immortality, for the towns and their contents were – and are still being – excavated. They form some of the world's richest and largest archaeological sites, where Imperial Roman culture has been laid bare.

This invaluable catastrophe was described a few years later by Pliny the Younger in two letters to his friend, the historian Tacitus. In comparison to all the other descriptions of eruptions in antiquity, which vary from tantalizingly brief to poetic or plain crazy, Pliny's account stands out like a beacon of clarity and accuracy. It was not just a good story. As he told Tacitus, 'I have described in detail every incident which I either witnessed myself, or heard about immediately after the event, when the reports were most likely to be accurate'. Pliny never mentioned Pompeii and Herculaneum in his letters because he stayed in and around Misenum, 32km to the west, during the catastrophe. But, although he was only 17 years old at the time, he has proved a very reliable witness – and few eruptions have been favoured with such an intelligent observer.

Pliny the Younger was an aristocrat. Aristocrats, of course, did not live in small towns like Pompeii. They had spacious summer villas out to the west in delightful surroundings along the shores of the Bay of Naples, 'where the winter is sweet, and the summer fresh'. The Pliny family lived right out at Cape Misenum, overlooking the naval base, not far from the mansion once owned by Julius Caesar. The head of the family, Gaius Plinius Secundus, Pliny the Elder (AD 23–79), was not only Commander of the Roman Fleet, but also one of the foremost intellectuals of his time and the author of a famous *Natural History*. At the time he was fifty-six, rather overweight, and starting to suffer from breathlessness. His sister was also spending the summer in Misenum, together with her son, Gaius Plinius Caecilius Secundus, Pliny the Younger (AD 62–113). His uncle had just adopted him and taken charge of his education. To occupy the young Pliny's summer leisure, his uncle had set him plenty of work on Livy's *History of Rome*. History, of course, was right on their doorstep – in more ways than one . . .

Portrait of Sir William Hamilton by David Allan, 1775.

Pompeiian frescoes: (*above*) A Fight in the Ampitheatre and (*right*) Terentius Neo, the baker, and his wife.

In AD 79, the Roman Empire was looking forward to continued stability. Memories were beginning to fade of the antics of the Emperor Nero, who had died in AD 68. In AD 69 there had been civil chaos and no fewer than four emperors, Luckily the fourth, Vespasian, had brought peace and prosperity. Vespasian had died on 23 June, AD 79. His son, the new Emperor Titus, seemed to be quite as sensible and able. After all, he had renounced his beloved Jewish princess, Berenice, for reasons of state. Titus himself probably visited Herculaneum about a month before the eruption, and may also have gone on to inspect the fleet under Pliny the Elder at Misenum. In August, AD 79, prospects were also looking rather better in the district. A great earthquake in AD 62 had ravaged much of the area around the Bay of Naples, but, little by little, the more important buildings were being repaired. Nobody had the slightest idea that Vesuvius was soon going to change all that.

At that time, the chief centre in the region was Neapolis (Naples), with a population of about 50,000. Pompeii lay 10km south-east of Vesuvius. It was a busy town covering an area of 1,500m by 1,000m and had a population of about 20,000. The streets were laid out in the usual grid pattern, and its main

Vesuvius, from the Forum at Pompeii.

arteries were 8.5m wide, well drained and well paved with black lava slabs and high pavements.

Pompeii had all that a vibrant Roman provincial town might hope for: temples, taverns, tanneries, textile workshops, bakeries, banks, pubs, cabarets, cabinet-makers, groceries, greengroceries, fishmongers, drapers, flour-millers, schools, markets, jewellers, laundries, two theatres, an amphitheatre seating 12,000 spectators, a gymnasium, public baths, public toilets, and several brothels tastefully decorated with helpful murals.

Like present-day Naples, Pompeii was a town of public, as well as private, passions. The municipal elections of AD 79 had brought forth a mass of inscriptions and graffiti. Twenty years earlier, a contest between gladiators from Pompeii and nearby Nocera had caused a battle royal between their supporters that resulted in many deaths and injuries. It was 'characteristic', sneered Tacitus, 'of these disorderly country towns'.

Many of these boisterous and passionate souls lived in brick, one- or two-storey houses, often built around courtyards. Some were sumptuous dwellings, with marble colonnades, gardens. fountains, statues and mosaics. The House of the Faun, for instance, had a fabulous mosaic of Darius and Alexander at the Battle of Issos in 333 BC. Many houses, too, were decorated with wall-paintings of mythological and rural scenes as well as portraits. One of the finest portraits to survive is that of the baker, Terentius Neo, and his wife, who now stare rather apprehensively out at their admirers in the Naples museum. But some of the wealthier citizens must have left the town after the earthquake in AD 62. Some ruined buildings had been abandoned or shored up. One mansion had been turned into a tavern run by a freed slave called Sextus Pompeius Amaranthus. Some of the poorer ruined houses had been knocked down altogether and transformed into orchards and market gardens, growing cherries, almonds, peaches, cabbages, onions, beans, chick peas, walnuts and hazelnuts. There were pigs and poultry too. The main public open space in Pompeii was the Forum, 142m long and 38m wide, bordered by impressive temples and marble colonnades. Here the Pompeiians could talk untroubled by noisy chariots rumbling over the lava-paved streets. From time to time, they might also have glanced up beyond the Temple of Jupiter, ruined in AD 62, towards the cone of Vesuvius, standing 10km away, alone on the northern horizon.

There was an even better view of Vesuvius from Herculaneum, for this prosperous seaside town stood on a low headland, 20m above the beach, and only 7km due west of the mountain. Legend has it that Hercules himself had founded the town, and, like Naples, it had certainly been a Greek settlement. It was much smaller than Pompeii, with a population of about 5,000, although it had similar urban facilities. Overall, Herculaneum concentrated on craft industries such as marble-working, mosaic-making, spinning and weaving as well as some fishing. Its villas and public buildings were at least as rich as those in Pompeii. Here Julius Caesar's father-in-law had lived in a house that, in AD 79, contained a fabulous collection of Egyptian papyri. Another house contained a room with a cross, and may have been used by a Christian converted by the Apostle Paul when he had landed at nearby Puteoli (Pozzuoli) in AD 61. A more surprising relic is a graffito, found in the lavatory of the House of the Gem, revealing that Apollinaris, the Emperor's doctor, had had a very satisfactory bowel motion during his visit a month before the eruption.

There were many other settlements around Vesuvius at that time, including Oplontis, near the present town of Torre Annunziata, and Stabiae, near Castellammare. Opulent villas, farms and vineyards also covered the fertile lower slopes of Vesuvius. Although nobody then realized it, the settlements within a 15km radius of the summit were built on volcanic rocks that Vesuvius had erupted in the distant past. They were all soon to be its victims.

Of all the settlements that Vesuvius buried beneath its blanket of ash and pumice, only Pompeii and part of Herculaneum have been extensively excavated. Many Roman settlements have not even been found, and little, apart from a few villas, has been dug up at Stabiae or Oplontis. Vesuvius is still clutching most of its victims and hiding their archaeological treasures.

Reawakening, AD 62–79

In AD 79, Vesuvius had been calm for many centuries, although some scholars recognized that it was a volcano. Strabo (64 BC–AD 25), the Greek geographer, described Vesuvius:

> surrounded by beautiful farmlands and dwellings . . . A considerable part of the summit is flat, but all of it is unfruitful, and looks ash-coloured. Its rocks are soot-coloured, with holes like pores, so that they look as if they had been eaten by fire. Thus it can be inferred that this district was on fire in former times and had craters of fire which were quenched only when the fuel supply gave out.

The first inkling that Vesuvius might be about to spring into life came when a large earthquake rocked the area around the back Bay of Naples on 5 February, AD 62. The destruction in Naples was slight, but many buildings were thrown down nearer Vesuvius, especially in Pompeii. The aftershocks continued for several days; repairs continued for several years. When Pompeii was buried seventeen years later, the public buildings had been restored and the Forum had regained its former majesty, but parts of many private houses had not always been rebuilt. In AD 64, the Emperor Nero, artist and fiend, had just delighted his dutiful subjects with his lyrical debut in the theatre in Naples, when another earthquake threw the building to the ground. Nero took it as a mark of Divine respect that none of the spectators had been killed. Other, smaller earthquakes may have shaken the ground during the early months of AD 79, but there was no reason – then – to suppose that the earthquakes could be indicating that molten rock was making its way towards the surface of the earth. There had, after all, been plenty of earthquakes before, and none had ever caused an eruption so far as anybody knew.

Morning, 24 August, AD 79

There were more earthquakes for several days before the eruption started. People shuddered in a moment of fear, and then shrugged their shoulders and went about their business when they saw that they were safe. These frequent tremors were only a small price to pay for living in one of the most dazzling areas in the whole Empire. Nobody could have imagined that one of the most violent volcanic eruptions in Europe during the past 3,000 years was about to shatter the calm of that idyllic place.

It all began on the morning of 24 August, when noisy explosions showered the slopes of Vesuvius with fine ash. Sir William Hamilton gave some idea of what it might have been like when he described the start of a very much smaller eruption of Vesuvius on 19 October 1767.

> I heard a violent noise within the mountain . . . [it] split . . . and, with much noise . . . a fountain of liquid fire shot up . . . in an instant, clouds of black smoke and ashes caused almost total darkness; the explosions . . . were louder than any thunder I ever heard, and the smell of sulphur was offensive . . . My guide, alarmed, took to his heels; and I must confess that I was not at my ease. I followed close, and we ran near three miles [4.5km] without stopping, as the Earth continued to shake beneath our feet . . . I thought it prudent to leave the mountain, and return to my villa, where I found my family in a great alarm at the continual and violent explosions . . . which shook our house to its very foundations.

This was just an opening gambit in AD 79. The eruption was to get far, far worse. Soon.

In the first of his two letters to Tacitus, Pliny the Younger described how they first saw the beginning of the violent phase of the eruption that lunchtime, from a distance of 32km:

> My uncle was at Misenum in command of the fleet. On 24 August, about one in the afternoon, my mother pointed out a cloud with an odd size and appearance that had just formed . . . From that distance it was not even clear from which mountain the cloud was rising – although it was found afterwards to be Vesuvius. The cloud could best be described as more like an umbrella pine than any other tree, because it rose high up in a kind of trunk and then divided into branches . . . Sometimes it looked light-coloured, sometimes it looked mottled and dirty with the earth and ash it had carried up. Like a true scholar, my uncle saw at once that it deserved closer study and ordered a boat to be prepared. He said that I could go with him, but I chose to continue my studies.

Pliny the Younger's decision might have saved his life. It also suggests that he was more intellectual than adventurous – or perhaps he was just afraid, for the enormous column of gas and ash must soon have been roaring 25km into the sky.

Pliny the Elder's Journey to Stabiae, 24 August, AD 79

Just as [Pliny the Elder] was leaving the house, he was handed a message from
Rectina, the wife of Tascus, whose home was at the foot of the mountain and
who had no way of escape except by boat. She was terrified by the threatening
danger and begged him to rescue her.

This was Rectina's fatal mistake. She would have been well advised to leave
home with her messenger. He reached the safety of Misenum. She almost certainly died during the eruption.

He changed plan at once and what he had started in a spirit of scientific curiosity, he ended as a hero. He ordered the large galleys [quadriremes] to be
launched and set sail [probably about 2 p.m.]. He steered bravely straight for
the danger zone, which everyone else was leaving in fear and haste, but he still
kept on noting his observations.

The quadriremes, for all the muscle-power of their unfortunate oarsmen,
could not move faster than 15km an hour. They would travel much more
slowly as soon as they entered the 'danger zone' where hot ash was blowing
southwards from Vesuvius. Pliny the Elder, therefore, would probably take
about three hours to approach the coast near Oplontis, some 28km from
Misenum. Pliny the Younger continues:

The ash that was already falling became hotter and thicker as the ships
approached the coast, and it was soon superseded by pumice and blackened
burnt stones shattered by the fire. Suddenly the sea shallowed where the shore
was obstructed and choked by debris [floating pumice] from the mountain.
He wondered whether to turn back as the Captain advised, but decided
instead to go on. 'Fortune favours the brave,' he said; 'take me to Pomponianus'. Pomponianus lived at Stabiae across the Bay of Naples [17km from
Vesuvius and 8km from Oplontis]. It was not yet in danger, but would be
threatened if the danger were to spread. In fact, Pomponianus had already
put his belongings into a boat to escape as soon as the contrary, onshore wind
changed. This wind, of course, was fully in my uncle's favour and quickly
brought his boat to Stabiae [probably about 6 p.m.]. My uncle calmed and
encouraged his terrified friend and . . . was cheerful, or at least pretended to
be, which was just as brave.
   Meanwhile, tall, broad flames blazed from several places on Vesuvius and
glared out through the darkness of the night. My uncle soothed the fears of his
companions by saying that they were nothing more than fires left by the terrified
peasants, or empty abandoned houses that were blazing. He went to bed and
apparently fell asleep, for his loud, heavy breathing was heard by those passing
his door.

Meanwhile Pliny the Elder's sister and nephew had dined and started to sleep fitfully at Misenum. There was no such rest at Pompeii and Herculaneum.

Pompeii, Afternoon and Evening, 24 August AD, 79

Pompeii was in the very eye of the storm, where hot ash and pumice, blown by the northwesterly wind, were showering down most thickly. It was soon accumulating at a rate of 12–15cm an hour, and roofs were starting to collapse under the weight. It was pitch dark. The ground was shaking. A fearful rumbling was coming from Vesuvius. The Pompeiians faced a daunting choice. They could shelter in their cellars or in well-closed rooms until the eruption abated. Or, they could gather up some of their more valuable possessions and struggle to safety through the hot and suffocating ash and pumice that was already a metre deep in the streets and was still falling as thickly as before. But which way should they run?

Sir William Hamilton described what happened when a mere 2.5cm of ash fell on Naples between 19 and 22 October 1767:

> The confusion at Naples cannot be described . . . the churches were opened and filled, the streets were thronged with processions of saints . . . [and] various ceremonies were performed to quell the fury of the turbulent mountain . . . the prisoners in the publick jail attempted to escape . . . but were prevented by the troops. The mob set fire to the Cardinal-Archbishop's gate because he refused to bring out the relicks of Saint Januarius [San Gennaro, the patron saint and protector of the city] . . . The oldest men declared they had never heard the like, and, indeed, it was very alarming; we were in expectation every moment of some dire calamity.

The Pompeiians can hardly have been any calmer, since much more ash and pumice had been showering upon them all afternoon. But, given the horror of the situation, the thickly falling ash could have been a blessing in disguise. As it turned out, those who panicked at once and fled probably survived. If they had the luck to run southwards, or took a boat westwards, they gave themselves the best chances of escaping. The baker, Modestus, was one of those who did not apparently hesitate for long. He decamped, leaving eighty-one loaves in his oven, where they remained, overcooked, for more than 1,800 years. Perhaps three-quarters of the population of Pompeii took their chance and left while they could, on the afternoon of 24 August.

Those who hesitated were lost. The situation got worse. After 8 p.m. the eruption became still more violent. Amidst the ash, fist-sized chunks of grey pumice began to clatter and thud down onto the city. An indication of what Pompeii suffered can be gained from Sir Willian Hamilton's description of the effects of a small pumice fall on Ottaviano in August 1779.

During the tempestuous fall of ashes . . . and stones . . . the inhabitants dared
not stir out – even with the vain protection of pillows, tables, winecasks etc. on
their heads. Driven back, wounded or terrified, they retreated to cellars and
arches, half stifled with heat and dust and sulphur . . . Through 25 minutes this
horror lasted, then suddenly ceased, and the people took the opportunity of
quitting the country, after leaving the sick and bed-ridden in the churches.

Twenty-five minutes! At Pompeii, the infernal deluge lasted for eighteen
hours . . .

Herculaneum, 24–25 August, AD 79

The Pompeiians could not even see what was going on. The people of
Herculaneum could see only too well. At first, theirs was a visual terror. The
citizens watched the billowing column rise, roaring, over 33km into the sky
above the crater of Vesuvius. After nightfall on 24 August, the red-hot ash and
pumice in the column glowed menacingly and lightning flashed and
crackled. But Herculaneum was lucky to be lying upwind, so that less than a
centimetre of ash sprinkled the town. The terrified citizens realized that salvation lay to the west, across the Bay, and they made for the boats. Many fled
past Pliny the Elder as his quadriremes tried, in vain, to approach the pumice-
choked coast. Hundreds might have reached safety in Naples, and settled in
what became known as the Herculaneum quarter.

By midnight, scarcely a dozen people remained in the town itself, and there
were no stragglers in the streets. But several hundred people were still waiting
to embark from the shore. They had assembled near the brand-new suburban
baths, in front of the large arches beneath the Sacred Area along the coast.
This is where they died.

At about 1 a.m. on 25 August, the column rising from Vesuvius lost its vertical impetus for a moment. Its lower part collapsed like a crumbling pillar of
fire and formed a nuée ardente of hot gas, glowing dust, ash and pumice that
swept down the western flanks of Vesuvius at a speed of well over 100km an
hour. Straight onto Herculaneum. No one could escape. In less than four
minutes, the hot and lethal cloud engulfed the town, sweeping between the
houses, ripping off roofs and balconies, and surging fastest of all down the
streets leading to the sea.

The people waiting anxiously on the shore would not have seen the nuée
ardente until the very last moment. When it suddenly fell upon them, they
turned and clustered desperately under the arches, crowding as far inside as
possible. They died in the space of a few choking breaths, huddled together,
sometimes embracing their loved ones, always striving to protect their faces
with their hands. They died burnt and suffocated. About an hour later, a faster,
hotter and much bigger nuée ardente surged over the pathetic remnants of

The excavated old shore at Herculaneum, with Vesuvius in the distance.

the town, carbonized the woodwork, smashed down all the surviving upper storeys, dumped the rubble on the beach and boiled the sea. Four more nuées ardentes were to sweep over the town within the next eight hours, but by then there was hardly anything left to destroy. The hot clouds penetrated every nook and cranny of Herculaneum, sealing the town in a fuming blanket, 20m thick and adding a strip of new land, 400m wide, to the coast.

The hundreds of victims who died on the shore were not unearthed until 1982. Many more may be discovered when the excavations are extended along the coast. Only a few bodies had ever previously been found in the town itself. A man and a woman had died together in the men's baths. Two men who were probably sick had been left in their beds. A boy was lying on his bed in the House of the Gem-Cutter, and a baby had been abandoned in its cradle in the House of the Gem. Perhaps they had died from other causes before their parents left them when the eruption started? Their parents could well be amongst the skeletons found on the shore.

Stabiae, 25 August, AD 79

As Herculaneum was being removed from the face of the earth, in Stabiae, Pomponianus and his servants were wide awake, watching the situation getting worse and worse as the night went on, and Pliny the Elder was still snoring away. As Pliny the Younger reported,

> eventually the courtyard outside began to fill with so much ash and pumice that, if he had stayed in his room, he would never have been able to get out. He was awakened and joined Pomponianus and his servants ... They wondered whether to stay indoors or go out into the open, because the buildings were now swaying back and forth and shaking with more violent tremors. Outside, there was the danger from the falling pumice, even if it was only light and porous. After weighing up the risks, they chose the open country and ... tied pillows over their heads with cloths for protection. [The pumice must have already been about a metre deep in Stabiae by then.]
>
> It was daylight everywhere else by this time, but they were still enveloped in a darkness that was blacker and denser than any night, and they were forced to light their torches and lamps.

Even as the eruption gained momentum at Stabiae, Pliny the Elder kept his composure better than his companions.

> My uncle went down to the shore to see if there was any chance of escape by sea, but the waves were still running far too high. He lay down to rest on a sheet and called for drinks of cold water. Then, suddenly, flames and a strong smell of sulphur, giving warning of yet more flames to come, forced the others to flee. He himself stood up, with the support of two slaves, and then suddenly

collapsed and died, because, I imagine, he was suffocated when the dense fumes choked him.

Pliny the Elder may have had a heart attack brought on by his exertions in the stifling atmosphere, or he may have been asphyxiated by hot ash and dust, or, indeed, may even have been poisoned by erupted toxic gases such as hydrogen sulphide. Whatever the cause of his death, by the early morning of 25 August, Vesuvius had claimed its most distinguished victim. His nephew ended his first letter to Tacitus with the discovery of his uncle's body . . .

> When daylight returned on the following day, his body was found intact and uninjured, still fully clothed and looking more like a man asleep than dead.

Pliny the Elder had been killed by the largest of all the nuées ardentes that Vesuvius erupted during those two days. It was, in fact, the sixth nuée that erupted in all, and there were several more to come. It spread 17km southwards to Stabiae and also surged 32km across the Bay of Naples to Misenum, where its leading edges almost reached, and could well have killed, Pliny the Younger and his mother.

Misenum, 25 August, AD 79

Pliny the Younger and his mother had stayed in Misenum throughout the afternoon of 24 August. Their own nightmare was about to begin.

> After my uncle left us, I studied . . . dined, and went to bed, but slept only fitfully. We had had earth tremors for several days, which were not especially alarming because they happen so often in Campania. But, that night, they were so violent that everything felt as if it were being shaken and turned over. My mother came hurrying to my room . . . and we sat together in the forecourt facing the sea nearby. I don't know whether to call it courage or folly on my part (I was only 17 at the time), but I called for a volume of Livy and went on reading as if I had nothing else to do. I even went on making the extracts that I had started.

No ash apparently fell on Misenum that night, because the naval base was well upwind of Vesuvius. But, when dawn broke, the daylight was only faint and the ground beneath Misenum was starting to shake violently.

> The buildings around were already tottering and we would have been in danger in our confined space if our house had collapsed. This made us decide to leave town. We were followed and hurried along by a panic-stricken crowd who chose to follow someone else's judgment rather than decide anything for themselves. We stopped once we were out of town [on the Monte di Procida hill above Misenum]. Then some extraordinary and alarming things happened. The car-

riages we had ordered began to lurch to and fro although the ground was flat, and we could not keep them still, even when we wedged their wheels with stones. Then we saw the sea sucked back, apparently by an earthquake, and many sea-creatures were left stranded on the dry sand.

The sea probably withdrew during the first stages of a tsunami, or volcanic sea-wave – a smaller-scale version of those at Krakatau in 1883. Such a wave would soon have crashed inland again. (During the eruption of Vesuvius in 1631, the level of the Bay of Naples dropped by 3m for ten minutes before a wave nearly 5m high broke over the shore.) But, Pliny the Younger's attention was distracted by an even more pressing danger: the huge (sixth) nuée ardente erupted by about 8 a.m. on 25 August. Unbeknown to him, this was the cloud that killed his uncle at Stabiae.

From the other direction, over the land, a dreadful black cloud was torn by gushing, twisting, flames [glowing, red-hot ash], and great tongues of fire like much-magnified lightning . . . The cloud sank down soon afterwards and covered the sea, hiding Capri and Cape Misenum from sight. My mother begged me – and even commanded me – to leave her and escape as best I could. She said that a young man might be able to escape, whereas she was old and slow, but she could die in peace provided that she knew that she had not caused my own death as well. But I told her that I would not save myself without her. I took her hand and made her hurry along with me. Ash was already falling by now, but not very thickly. Then I turned round and saw the thick black cloud advancing over the land behind us like a flood. 'Let us leave the road whilst we can still see,' I said, 'or we will be knocked down and trampled by the crowd.' We had hardly sat down to rest when the darkness fell upon us. But it was not the darkness of a moonless, or cloudy night, but just as if all the lamps had been put out in a completely closed room.

We could hear women shrieking, children crying, and men shouting. Some were calling for their parents, for their children, or for their wives, and trying to recognize them by their voices . . . Some people prayed for death because they were so frightened of dying. Many begged for the help of the gods, but even more imagined that there were no gods left and that the last eternal night had fallen on the world.

The people of Misenum were obviously so terrified that they had abandoned all hope, as if they had entered Hell. And they were 32km from the volcano. Their terror makes it all the harder to imagine the agony of the Pompeiians. Even at Misenum rumours made things no better.

There were also those who added to our real perils by inventing fictitious dangers. Some claimed that part of Misenum had collapsed, or that another part was on fire. It was untrue, but they could always find somebody to believe them.

A glimmer of light returned, but we took this to be a warning of approaching fire rather than daylight. But the fires stayed some distance away. The darkness came back and ash began to fall again, this time in heavier showers. We had to get up from time to time to shake it off or we would have been crushed and buried under its weight. I could boast that I never expressed any fear at this time, but I was only kept going by the consolation that the whole world was perishing with me.

After a while, the darkness paled into smoke or cloud, and the real daylight returned, but the sun was still shining as wanly as during an eclipse. We were amazed by what we saw because everything had changed and was buried deep in ash like snow. We went back to Misenum, attended to our physical needs as best we could, and spent an anxious night [25–26 August] switching between hope and fear. Fear was uppermost because the earth tremors were still continuing and the hysterics still kept on making their alarming forecasts . . . But, by then, my mother and I had no intention of leaving the house until we got news of my uncle.

So ends the first surviving detailed account of any volcanic eruption. Pliny the Younger, his mother, and indeed all the people in Misenum were very lucky. The sixth and largest of the terrible nuées ardentes stopped just short of the naval base. Neither was Misenum showered with hot pumice.

The horror was far worse to the east. It is odd that the exact fate of Naples is not recorded, but the sixth nuée ardente must have killed many people near the harbour and in the eastern suburbs that were closest to Vesuvius.

There is no doubt about what happened to Pompeii.

Dies Irae, Pompeii, 25 August, AD *79*

Dies irae dies illa
Solvet saeclum in favilla.
[The day of wrath, that day will dissolve the world in ashes]

Falling ash and pumice were burying the city. Ground-floor doors were blocked. More and more roofs were collapsing under the weight. The mistress of the splendid House of the Faun collected all her jewellery together and was then buried alive when the roof fell in on top of her. Fine, hot dust and ash swirled throughout the city, penetrating every room, however carefully it had been sealed, and entering every pair of lungs, however carefully victims tried to keep it at bay with moistened cloths. How many people suffocated? How many died of fright during that appalling night? How many took their last faint chance of making an escape? At least 2,000 people stayed on and survived this ordeal, only to succumb to something worse.

There had been total darkness in Pompeii since just after 1 p.m. on 24 August. The Pompeians found it harder and harder to keep their oil-lamps

lit. They had no means even of telling the time. They had no way of understanding what was happening to them and could have no inkling of when – if
ever – their ordeal would end. Some may have suspected that they were the
victims of a great volcanic eruption. Everybody must have been filled with
anguish and despair. Death must have seemed very close. The people in
Pompeii were enduring the longest night of their lives. And they were never
to see another dawn.

The erupting column was now soaring 33km above Vesuvius, several nuées
ardentes had rushed down the slopes of the volcano, and Herculaneum and
Oplontis had already been destroyed. Many rich villas on the flanks of Vesuvius had also been overwhelmed. They included the sumptuous house that
had belonged to Poppaea Sabina, the second wife of the Emperor Nero. She
had died in AD 65, after he kicked her in a fit of temper because she had complained when he returned late from a chariot-race meeting.

The first two nuées ardentes did not reach Pompeii. The third, at 6.30 a.m.
on 25 August, stopped at its northern walls. At the same time, bigger earthquakes began to shake the city, and perhaps spurred some of those still sheltering in Pompeii to flee. But the hapless fugitives now had to struggle through
2.4m of hot ash and pumice that choked the streets and buried the ground
floors of many buildings. Would it still not be better to hold on and shelter at
home until the worst was over?

At 7.30 a.m. on 25 August, AD 79, all the people still sheltering in Pompeii
met their destiny. The fourth nuée ardente swept down over the city, flattened
most of the upper storeys of the buildings, ripped off the remaining rooftops,
and added bricks and tiles to its fearsome armoury of red-hot ash, pumice and
gases. Each element in the cloud had a way of killing – and did – but most
victims were asphyxiated. They died in breathless agony, often clutching their
most treasured possessions in one hand while trying desperately to stop the
deadly mixture of gas, hot dust and ash, and mucus from clogging their
mouths and lungs. They only suffered for about two minutes.

Those struggling in the streets may have seen the glowing cloud rushing
through the pitch darkness towards them. They tried to run but were thrown
down and they perished. Three families had battled downhill to the Nocera
Gate when they were caught opposite the southern cemetery. A slave, bent
double under a sack of provisions, collapsed. A woman died with her handkerchief stuffed into her mouth. Behind her, an old man, perhaps her father,
stumbled and then expired as he struggled to raise himself onto his elbows.
Two young boys, holding hands, suffocated as they tried, in vain, to protect
themselves beneath a roof-tile. In the Forum, two priests were crushed when
part of the colonnade was thrown down upon them. Another priest was
asphyxiated in the main street as he tried to save (or make off with?) the
treasure of the Temple of Isis.

Those who stayed indoors were only granted the favour of dying at home.
Hundreds of people perished in barricaded rooms or cellars with their loved
ones, their jewellery or their life savings. In the Diomedes villa, a family of

eighteen and their servants died with ten gold pieces and enough bread and fruit to tide them over until the eruption should end. Nine men, led by a porter carrying a lamp and two slaves protecting their heads with pillows, suffocated as they tried, at last, to leave the House of Menander. They left behind 115 items of silverware hidden in a box in the bathroom. A surgeon with his bag of instruments and an athlete clutching his bottle of body-oil perished in the exercise courtyard, the Palaestra. In one house, a forgotten, chained-up dog expired as it arched its back in one last desperate effort to break loose. In another house, a hungry dog was eating its dead master when the nuée ardente arrived.

Many gladiators seem to have decided to weather out the storm in their barracks. Two had no choice: they died in their chains. One gladiator died lying alongside a noble lady, bedecked with an emerald necklace, who had evidently come to pay homage to her favourite sportsman, but most of the other sixty gladiators died as lonely a death as if they had perished in the arena.

Within two or three minutes, nobody – nothing – was left alive in Pompeii. The larger fifth and sixth nuées ardentes swept over the city to Stabiae. Pumice and ash, and then ash alone continued to fall in the darkness and soon completely buried the city.

Aftermath, 26 August, AD 79

The eruption of Vesuvius waned on the morning of 26 August. When daylight returned, over 8km^3 of fuming pumice and ash covered 300km^2 around Vesuvius in a grey blanket. In all that area, not a town, not a village, not a villa, not a farm, not a vineyard, not a tree, not a bush, and not a living soul was to be seen. The upper 700m of Vesuvius had vanished and a huge crater fumed in its place. The Roman Empire witnessed no other natural disaster on such a scale. (When their turn came, the Goths, Vandals and their friends worked on a different register.) The Emperor Titus appointed two eminent former Consuls to deal with the social and legal consequences of the calamity. But Titus died in AD 81 and was succeeded by his psychopathic brother, Domitian, which did not create a happy climate for public welfare.

Thus Herculaneum, Pompeii and their neighbours vanished off the face of the earth. From the archaeological point of view, the fate of these towns went far, far beyond the plight of the dying, for their whole way of life was buried, and often closely moulded by the fine ash that settled on top of them.

During the Middle Ages, Resina-Ercolano was built over Herculaneum, Torre Annunziata over Oplontis, and Castellammare over Stabiae. No new town grew up over buried Pompeii. But, although the abandoned spot was known as Civitas or La Città, nobody realized its real significance for a long time. In 1592 the Roman architect, Domenico Fontana, found a few old stones – and nearly found the amphitheatre, when he was cutting an old water conduit. In 1607 a stone inscribed 'Decurio Pompeiis' was discovered, which

A victim killed by flying masonry at Pompeii, 25 August AD 79.

ought to have inspired more digging. But in those days archaeology did not exist, and architects merely used old stones and old buildings as convenient quarries. During the next 150 years, odd excavations also raised statues that were sold like trinkets to decorate 'classical galleries' built by eminent aristocrats. Planned and rather more scientific excavations began under King Carlo III of Naples in 1738 at Herculaneum and in 1748 at Pompeii; others followed during the Napoleonic occupation.

Archaeological excavation really began when Giuseppe Fiorelli took charge of the site at Pompeii in 1861. It was Fiorelli who revealed the shapes of the dead. In AD 79, the fine, stiff, dry ash had encased the victims where they fell. Over the centuries, their clothing and flesh had decayed, leaving behind a hollow that was, in effect, a mould of the victims. Fiorelli hit upon the simple and brilliant idea of pouring liquid plaster of Paris into the hollows as soon as they were discovered. Once the plaster set, the encasing ash was carefully

Contemporary engraving of nuées ardentes descending Vesuvius in 1631.

scraped away to reveal the shape. The plaster registered the details of the last actions of the victims of the nuée ardente at 7.30 a.m. on 25 August, and even the very grimaces they had made in their death-throes. These graphic casts are far more lifelike than Egyptian mummies. It proved impossible to do the same at Herculaneum. Soon after the eruption, the town subsided by about 4m, taking the lower layers of ash into the damp below the water-table. The wet ash settled, and crushed the decaying bodies of the victims so that only their skeletons remained when they were found. But the dying panic of those on the shore could still be read in their entwined bones.

Although scientific excavations have been going on for over a century, perhaps a quarter of Pompeii, and maybe as much as two-thirds of Herculaneum have still to be revealed. Because Resina-Ercolano is built over Herculaneum, excavation is limited and often has to be done by tunnelling. Only 85m of the old shore has been excavated and many more victims probably await discovery there. Excavations are still going on at Pompeii too, where there are supplementary problems. There are now often more tourists in a day than ever thronged the streets of ancient Pompeii, with the resulting dangers of damage and litter. The city was bombed in 1944 and damaged by an earthquake in 1980. Theft and vandalism have gone on for years. Many houses are now locked for their own protection, and the keepers cannot always be bothered to open them for visitors. The result is that Pompeii now has none of the cosy charm of Herculaneum, which has kept the Roman atmosphere much better than its more famous rival.

Vesuvius has been quiet since 1944, when it greeted the advancing Allied armies with an eruption. Experts agree that its next outburst will probably be the greatest since the devastating eruption in 1631. About a million people live in the potential danger zone. They may have to be evacuated very quickly indeed if they are to avoid the fate of the Pompeiians.

Whatever happened to Pliny the Younger? After Titus died in AD 81, Pliny survived the murderous whims of the Emperor Domitian and became a famous writer and lawyer. He later became the friend and one of the ablest administrators of the Emperor Trajan. He was elected Consul in AD 100 and was Governor of the Province of Bithynia in Asia Minor in AD 111–12. He probably died in AD 113 at the age of fifty-one.

4

Monte Nuovo, 1538

Accounts of the eruption of Monte Nuovo provide the oldest surviving descriptions of the birth of an entirely new volcano. It was a small eruption, but happened after the land had been swelling up for several decades. Similar swellings have occurred in the district twice in the past forty years. There is thus a chance that another eruption might occur in what is now a densely populated area west of Naples.

The Underworld

The Ancient Romans believed that the entrance to the Underworld lay just west of Naples in the Phlegraean Fields. This 'Land of Fire' is, in fact, a cluster of old volcanoes, but most of them are either extinct or dormant. Only a few, like La Solfatara, near Pozzuoli, are still giving off sulphurous fumes and steam. Indeed, the 'Land of Fire' has lived up to its name only once during the past 3,000 years, when molten rock erupted in 1538 and formed a new volcano called Monte Nuovo. It was a modest little eruption that only lasted from 29 September until 6 October, and it had nothing like the effortless power of Vesuvius. But it has some significance at present because there have been signs recently that another reawakening may be on the way. Before Monte Nuovo erupted, the land had been jerking upwards for several decades, causing many damaging earthquakes. A similar rise, with similar earthquakes, has taken place twice since 1969. But – so far – there has been no volcanic eruption.

The eruption that occurred in 1538 is important in history because it was one of the first in modern times that was described in some detail by eyewitnesses. Few, if any, of the witnesses could ever have set eyes on an erupting volcano before, for Stromboli, and even Etna, were remote; and Vesuvius had not erupted molten rock for several centuries. They compared it to the most fearsome thing in their experience – the cannons of war. Many of these accounts, some found by Sir William Hamilton in Palermo, some turning up in archives in Naples over the centuries, were gathered together by Antonio Parascandola and published in Italian in 'Il Monte Nuovo ed il Lago Lucrino' in the *Bollettino della Società dei Naturalisti in Napoli* in 1946. Experts also analysed the recent changes in land levels in a special number of the *Bulletin of Volcanology* in 1984; and a special issue of the *Journal of Volcanology and Geothermal Research* was devoted to the Phlegraean Fields in 1991.

In 1538, Pozzuoli was the leading trading centre in the Phlegraean Fields, just as it had been ever since Roman times, when its amphitheatre had been

The Campi Phlegraei.

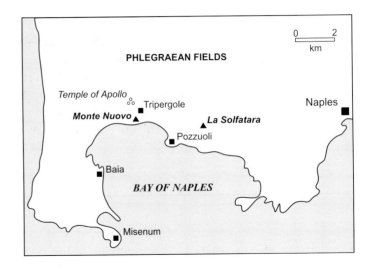

The location of Monte
Nuovo.

one of the largest in the Empire. It was also one of the earliest Christian
centres, and St Paul had stayed there for a week on his way to Rome. San
Gennaro (St Januarius) had been beheaded on 19 September, AD 305 during
one of the Emperor Diocletian's purges, and a commemorative chapel was
later built on the spot. San Gennaro became the patron saint of Naples and
Neapolitans still believe that his relics will protect the city from the worst
excesses of Vesuvius.

For over a thousand years after the collapse of the Roman Empire,
southern Italy passed from one foreign master to another. In 1538 the region
formed part of the vast dominions of Charles V, King of Spain and Holy
Roman Emperor, who delegated local power to a Viceroy. The Viceroy ruled
from Naples, which was then the most populous city in Christendom, with
250,000 inhabitants. From 1532 to 1553 the Spanish Viceroy was Pedro de
Toledo – one of the most able of them all. It was he who modernized Naples
and also made it one of the greatest capitals in all Europe. Pozzuoli was not
built on that scale, but it was still a thriving port and cathedral town, with
about 20,000 inhabitants. Every year at Whitsun, the ordinary folk of Pozzuoli
used to journey out along the old Via Domiziana to Tripergole, where the villagers treated them to bread-rolls and cherries.

Tripergole was a little spa with a long history, about 5km west of Pozzuoli.
The hot springs had been used for centuries, and a hospital had been set up
in 1307, followed soon afterwards by a pharmacy. Three inns catered for the
gentry and rich people with money to spend. A thirteenth-century castle dominated the scene from the Monticello del Pericolo – the Hill of Danger. As
things turned out, this was to prove a prophetic name.

Ironically, in 1538 it was not one of the many dormant volcanoes in the Phlegraean Fields that sprang back into life; instead an entirely new volcano was
born – right on top of Tripergole. The people had, in fact, been warned, but
they had not understood the warnings. Years of earthquakes had caused wide-

spread damage and fear, but nobody at that time could have expected a volcanic eruption into the bargain. When the eruption ended, Pozzuoli had been shattered, twenty-four people had died, thousands were homeless, and a volcanic cone completely buried Tripergole. In spite of all the poetic genius in this historic region, shock seems to have deprived the people of inspiration, for they could only give the new volcano the supremely banal name of Monte Nuovo.

Mobile Ground

Long before the eruption, the land had started to rise when masses of molten rock rose slowly from the depths, cracking and dislodging the earth's crust and making it swell upwards. Eventually, some of the molten rock burst out onto the land surface and formed the new volcano. Such swellings of the earth's crust are quite common on active volcanoes, but there are few places in the world where they have been so obvious for so long. The Phlegraean Fields have moved up and down for at least 2,000 years and Roman remains in the area have been greatly affected. The most famous of these Roman relics is the so-called Temple of Serapis in Pozzuoli (which is, in fact, a Roman market).

The Beheading of San Gennaro, by Mattia Preti.

The Roman market in Pozzuoli called the Temple of Serapis.

Its main claim to fame amongst earth scientists and archaeologists is that it has been in and out of the water ever since it was built about 100 BC. The fluctuations of the land have been registered on its columns. Just after it was built, the land sank and its pavement had to be replaced by another about 2m higher. When the Roman Empire fell, the market was abandoned and rubble buried the lower 3.6m of its columns. The land went on sinking, so that, by the tenth century, the building had sunk by as much as 5.8m. The flooded parts of its columns were then attacked by the mollusc, *Lithodomus lithophagus*, which bores into stone.

Earthquakes, 1400–1538

The ground started rising again in the fifteenth century. The floor of the market rose above the waters, revealing the once-submerged surface of the pillars pitted by the mollusc. When the rubble was cleared from the market, the smooth, still-intact faces of the lowest parts of columns that the rubble had protected were also laid bare. These columns, therefore, became a kind of register of the fluctuations in the level of the land.

The land did not bulge up regularly, like a balloon being blown up. Instead, it popped up from time to time as the molten rock surged up from below the earth's crust. And each jerk upwards produced an earthquake. Although the individual jerks were very small, they totalled about 5m or 8m during the first forty years of the sixteenth century. The upward bulging naturally also exposed new areas of dry land, which immediately became the property of the Spanish King, Fernando of Aragón, who ruled much of southern Italy at that time. He granted it to the authorities of Pozzuoli on 23 May 1511. This was not out of the kindness of his heart – it was because he could then tax the new owners.

The taxes did not stop the earthquakes. Cola Aniello Pacca recorded one memorable earthquake in 1534. On Easter Saturday morning, he said, the priest in the Cathedral in Naples was reading from the Gospels about the Resurrection. (He must have been reading from St Matthew 28:1–2: '. . . came Mary Magdalene and the other Mary to see the sepulchre. And, behold, there was a great earthquake'.) Sure enough, Pacca claimed, at that very moment, 'an enormous movement rocked the whole city'. Pacca also said that there was another big earthquake 'on the eighth day of November 1534', which just happened to be his birth date. Such timings may be suspect, but the increase in the violence and frequency of the earthquakes was real enough – especially during 1537 and 1538. The Neapolitan doctor Simone Porzio recalled that, in and around Pozzuoli, 'no house remained undamaged, and all the buildings seemed threatened with certain and imminent destruction'. The earthquakes reached a shuddering crescendo throughout 27 and 28 September 1538. The ground must have been really shaking in Tripergole, but nobody knows for sure, because no records of the crisis have survived from the village.

At 6 p.m. on 28 September, the land around Pozzuoli suddenly rose up by about 5m, making the sea retreat some 350m from the shore. The startled fish were stranded on the sands, at the mercy of the inhabitants of Pozzuoli. The sudden supply of free fresh fish must have seemed like a consolation from the Almighty for the damage to their homes . . .

Nowadays, earth scientists would flock to such an area with every instrument that they could lay hands on. The prospects of a research article and free fish would be irresistible. A similar upward swelling of the land would be taken as a clear warning that an eruption was very likely to follow. In 1538, these warnings could not be understood. The eruption came as a complete surprise.

The Eruption Begins, Sunday, 29 September 1538

The eruption started on the Feast of St Michael the Archangel, Sunday 29 September. The ground cracked open. However, it was not molten lava, but cold water that first gushed forth. Soon the waters became hot and started to bubble with sulphur dioxide gas. Then, as darkness fell, the pace of events increased. Molten rock began to glare from the gaping fissures in the ground; and the earth seemed to be bouncing up and down near Tripergole. The main fissure cracked open through the village. At 8 p.m. on 29 September, molten rock shot from the 'hideous abyss'. They heard the explosions in Naples. This was the real thing.

Hot ash and cinders soon began showering down on Tripergole, but everyone must have already abandoned the village – sick, infirm, 'rich spenders' alike – for none of the witnesses ever mentions deaths there. The eruption was an impressive sight from Pozzuoli. The Neapolitan doctor, Pietro Giacomo Toleto, described how the earth had exploded like thunder, and had spat out 'fire, stones and an ashy mud'. They soon formed a column 'that seemed as if it would reach the very vault of Heaven'. In fact, it probably rose no more than 2km or 3km. Some parts of the column 'were darker than darkness itself; others were as white as the finest cotton'. The whole billowing mass was made more terrible by the lightning and thunder playing around it. Some of the rocks thrown out 'were bigger than an ox' and clouds of cinders rose 'as high as a cross-bow shot can carry' before falling back to earth. At the same time, the sulphur dioxide and hydrogen sulphide expelled gave the fragments a fetid smell, 'as if they had been shot from a gun'.

The cone grew fast. Toleto guessed that it had reached a height of 1,800m in twelve hours, although sober surveyors later measured the cone at 130m. The really extraordinary element, however, was the muddy ash that spattered the countryside and reached Pozzuoli, and even Naples, where 'the scourge quite spoilt the beauty of the palaces'. Plants and trees were knocked down, or lost their leaves or branches. Birds and many little animals, coated with the muddy ash, 'either died, or just let themselves be taken prisoner by the hand of man'. Even in Naples the eruption sounded 'like heavy artillery fire when two opposing armies had just engaged hostilities'. The wind blew the finest ash as far away as Calabria. The puzzling mud was produced because the molten rock exploded through wet ground and formed steam as well as the more usual volumes of ash and cinders. In the air, the steam condensed on the ash to form the mud that stuck to birds, trees and fine façades alike.

The eruption reached its little climax during that first night of 29–30 September. The westerly wind showered more and more muddy ash over Pozzuoli, and its citizens were terrified. But the threat to Pozzuoli from the volcano was more apparent than real. It was just bad enough to encourage people to leave town, but not bad enough to force them to barricade themselves into their homes. But the shuddering earthquakes had built up their fears just as surely as they had knocked down their houses. The eruption was the last straw. Yet the citizens could not know that this was only a mild eruption – nothing at all like that notorious outburst of Vesuvius in AD 79. But the people of Pozzuoli did not stop to consult the letters of Pliny. Flight seemed the only salvation. They fled.

In 1587, the 80-year-old Antonio Russo recalled the exodus from Pozzuoli, although his imagination perhaps ran riot after fifty years. An earthquake, he said, had increased the panic on the morning of the Feast of St Jerome (30 September). Everyone rushed for safety. Some people even fled naked from the city. And, when Russo and his family reached the gates of Pozzuoli, they

Contemporary depiction of the eruption of Monte Nuovo, entitled 'The great and stupendous prodigy that appeared above Pozzuoli'.

saw 'Zizula, the wife of Master Geronimo Barbiero, leaving the city in a shift, hooded and sitting astride her horse like a man . . .' No wonder it seemed as if the world was on the verge of destruction. No wonder everybody was weeping and crying out *Misericordia*!

Marco Antonio delli Falconi also described the flight from Pozzuoli on that grim Monday morning in a letter to the Marchesa della Padula. He was a priest who had dabbled in philosophy and science, and he later became Bishop of Cariati in Calabria.

> The unfortunate inhabitants of Pozzuoli, terrified by such a horrible spectacle, abandoned their homes . . . fleeing from death, but with the colour of death painted on their faces; some with their children in their arms; some with sacks filled with their possessions; others with a laden donkey; all guiding their frightened families towards Naples. Yet others were carrying birds of all sorts that had fallen dead in great numbers when the eruption began, as well as the fish which they had found dead a-plenty upon the dried-up shore.

Many rushed mindlessly, hither and thither, about the countryside until exhaustion brought them to their senses. They had no one, of course, to guide or to advise them. Most of the fugitives poured breathless into Naples, where they terrified the Neapolitans and excited their Viceroy's curiosity.

Thus it was that, on Monday afternoon, 30 September, the Spanish Viceroy, Pedro de Toledo, rode out from Naples with a vast retinue to inspect the new marvel and to assess the situation in the Phlegraean Fields. The new volcano appeared unimpressed by its distinguished visitors. Ash and smoke blew so strongly into the faces of the viceregal party that they could get no farther than the commemorative chapel dedicated to San Gennaro, near La Solfatara. 'There,' wrote the Viceroy's biographer, Scipione Miccio in 1600, 'they looked down upon the terrifying spectacle and the miserable city [Pozzuoli] which was so completely covered with ash that the remains of the houses could scarcely be seen.' The Viceroy and his party suffered the spectacle only for a while. Then they returned to Naples, splattered with even more ash than their palaces. Those who saw deep meanings in the works of nature claimed that all these projectiles, thrown from west to east, foretold that the Emperor Charles V would soon be attacking the Turks. The Emperor, in fact, was on a losing streak. Although the news had not yet reached Naples, the Turks under that shameless renegade, Barbarossa, had already routed the imperial fleet on 27 September, at Préveza in Greece.

Marco Antonio delli Falconi was more persistent and inquisitive than the Viceroy, and he set off from Pozzuoli on 30 September to inspect the eruption at closer quarters. On the way, he met 'that honourable and in-comparable gentleman, Fabritio Maramaldo', and the pair soon discovered that

> The sea towards Baia had retired a great distance, and the coast seemed almost entirely dry because of the ashes and broken pumice stones thrown up by the eruption. I saw two springs . . . one of hot, salty, water and another of cold, fresh water on the shore. [The volcano was also making a noise like heavy gunfire.] It seemed to me as if [the mythical giants] Typhoeus and Enceladus had just waged war again with Jupiter . . . and I imagined that I could see those torrents of burning smoke that Pindar described in an eruption of Etna.

Here was a well-read Renaissance priest. The Ancient Greeks and Romans believed that these giants had been entrapped beneath volcanoes, and that their struggles to escape caused earthquakes and eruptions. In fact, however, Monte Nuovo was to erupt no lava-flows, such as the poet, Pindar, had described on Etna.

The Mid-week Lull

After two hectic days of explosive effort, the new volcano calmed down on Tuesday, 1 October. Marco Antonio delli Falconi sailed across the bay, past the volcano to the island of Ischia. At the same time, a solemn procession brought the head of San Gennaro from Naples to his chapel above Pozzuoli. Many believed that the Saint had appeased the new eruption, just as he had calmed the anger of Vesuvius in the past. Whether the presence of the head had any influence on the course of events is uncertain, but, in any case, no more effective means of stopping eruptions has yet been devised.

On Wednesday, 2 October, the eruptions stopped altogether. Monte Nuovo emerged from its pall of ash and black fumes and was exposed to the wonderment of the onlookers. Now that it seemed safe, some people felt brave enough to approach the new mountain. Pietro Giacomo Toleto was amongst those who climbed to the summit and gazed down – in some awe – at the fuming mouth that was nearly 500m in circumference. The volcano appeared to have already lapsed into the sleepy state of La Solfatara.

But Monte Nuovo still had one or two nasty spasms to come. Marco Antonio delli Falconi remarked that the eruption kept starting up again, 'like the ague or the gout'. He saw one of these spasms almost too closely for his own comfort at 4 p.m. on Thursday, 3 October, when he was sailing back from Ischia. The boat was just off Miseno, about 7km from the volcano. 'I saw many billowing columns of smoke shoot up in a very short time, with the loudest noise I ever heard . . . The ashes, stones and smoke approached our boat and looked as if they would cover all the earth and the sea.' (This must have been a small nuée ardente, similar to those that Vesuvius had expelled in AD 79.) Luckily for the passengers, the outburst stopped as quickly as it had started. The hot cloud lost its impetus just before it could reach the boat and sink it. Delli Falconi lived to write his letter.

Meanwhile, Francesco Marchesino was waiting in Naples for a chance to see what was afoot at the volcano. Friday, 4 October was calm enough for him to sail – 'not without fear' – for Pozzuoli. When he left Naples, 2cm of ash was still sticking to the buildings. Nearer Pozzuoli, the ash covered the crops and gardens, and had badly damaged all the trees. Many hares, rabbits and other small animals had died, perhaps from carbon dioxide poisoning or from starvation. Floating pumice, 45cm deep, choked the sea-shores all the way from Pozzuoli to Baia. Pozzuoli presented a baleful sight when the boat finally struggled into the harbour. Yellowish ash, 30cm deep, covered the earthquake-shattered ruins. Half of the cathedral had collapsed; and the other half was tottering. The church archives had been destroyed. Marchesino claimed that 'there were not ten houses still intact; most were crushed or ruined; in some places, hardly one stone remained standing above another'. Everybody had fled. The ash-carpeted streets were silent. 'The city was without a single citizen.' Marchesino felt that the very buildings were crying out in distress. He was so overcome that 'Latin authors' sprang to mind. The buildings seemed to be telling him: 'Now I am black but once I was beautiful'; and 'There is no health in any part of me, nor is there peace for my bones.'

The chastened Marchesino then sailed on, through the pumice floating on the bay, and landed at the foot of the volcano itself. The Monticello del Pericolo was now nothing but a half-buried hump on the side of Monte Nuovo.

Not, of course, knowing how volcanoes worked, Marchesino was amazed to discover the gaping crater when he reached the summit. The mountain, he declared, 'was not full inside, but empty!'

Tripergole was nowhere to be seen. Every building in the village lay buried for ever beneath the volcano – except old Roman Baths called the Temple of Apollo. His curiosity satisfied, Marchesino returned to Naples, described his experiences the following day in a letter to an unknown churchman in Rome, and stepped out of history as effectively as Tripergole.

The Last Eruption, 6 October 1538

Monte Nuovo had one final – and lethal – fling just when many people were taking a thrilling Sunday afternoon stroll up the southern flanks of the new cone. Marco Antonio delli Falconi described what happened at about four o'clock on 6 October:

> Some had ascended half the mountain, and others rather more . . . [when] there was such a sudden and fearsome eruption, with such a mass of thick smoke, that many of these people were suffocated, and some were never found either dead or alive. They say that those who were found dead – and those that were never found at all – numbered about twenty-four.

Pietro Giacomo Toleto added that 'some were suffocated by the fumes, some were knocked down by the stones, and some were burnt by the flames'.

Then the mountain calmed down almost completely, although it gave off steam and fumes for several centuries and frequent earthquakes rocked Pozzuoli on and off for over fifty years. What amazed everybody, though, was the speed with which 'such a considerable mountain could have been formed in such a short time'.

At first, the citizens of Pozzuoli were determined to abandon their city for ever. But tax advantages persuaded them otherwise. Two papal decrees exempted the clergy from the *decimo* tax for twenty years. More importantly, Pedro de Toledo took a hand. As his biographer, Scipione Miccio wrote,

> The Viceroy could not permit the desolation of such an old-established and useful city. He decreed that everyone should be repatriated and allowed exemption from taxes for many years. To demonstrate his good faith, he built a palace with a fine strong tower, and public fountains, as well as a terrace a mile long with many gardens and fountains. He reconstructed the road to Naples and widened the tunnel so that it could be traversed without lights. He built the church of San Francesco at his own expense. He also had the satisfaction of completing his own palace and of seeing that many Neapolitan gentlemen had also built mansions. He also restored the hot baths as successfully as possible, and had the city walls rebuilt. And to stimulate interest in the city, he decided

Monte Nuovo from Pozzuoli.

to spend half the year in Pozzuoli, although ill-health subsequently enabled him to stay there only in the spring.

Monte Nuovo in Campi Phlegraei, 1776 and 1779

It was Sir William Hamilton who provided the first good description of Monte Nuovo in his famous book, 'Campi Phlegraei, Observations on the Volcanoes of the Two Sicilies', published in 1776 and 1779, which is one of the first great studies of volcanoes. Sir William was British Ambassador, and friend to the young King Ferdinando IV of Naples, with whom he shared a passion for hunting. He was also one of the first to appreciate and excavate the newly discovered ruins of Pompeii; and his collection of antiquities, bequeathed to the British Museum, formed the basis of its treasures. His worthy scientific reputation, however, has been rather overshadowed. He became one of history's rarities – a famous husband. Yes, his second wife was Emma Hart, and he is, therefore, better known as the complaisant third leg of a *ménage à trois* with her and Admiral Nelson.

Sir William's book was illustrated by beautiful gouaches that he commissioned from Pietro Fabris. In 1779 Monte Nuovo stood out as a graceful cone, covered by low evergreen shrubs. Its bare, steep-sided crater was still giving off steam and gas. A spring, called the Baths of Nero, hot enough to cook eggs and fish, issued from the seaward base of the cone. Even better, the hot vapours concentrated in an underground passage were said to relieve the dire effects of what Sir William delicately called 'that distemper which is supposed to have made its appearance at Naples, before it spread its contagion over the other parts of Europe'. His readers would have known, perhaps to their cost if they had been on the Grand Tour, that syphilis had begun its rampant journey half a century before Monte Nuovo erupted. Sir William also noted that Monte Nuovo was a prime source of pozzuolana, those fine volcanic cinders that have been used as a cement ever since Roman times, and latterly as a very resistant road metal.

The harbour at Pozzuoli.

Pozzuoli Threatened Again

At present, Monte Nuovo forms a squat cone, covered with trees and shrubs. It is clearly visible from Pozzuoli and stands as a warning to that troubled city. But, nowadays, many of its inhabitants have no idea where it is, let alone what it signifies.

They would do well to treat Monte Nuovo with a little more respect – not for what it will do, for it is almost certainly as extinct as the dodo – but for the threat that it represents. It so happens that ground movements like those which preceded the eruption of Monte Nuovo in 1538 have started again. From 1969 to 1972 and again from August 1982 until December 1984, the area around Pozzuoli gradually bulged upwards by an overall net amount of 2.5m. And the apex of the swelling was at the harbour in the heart of the city. There were many shallow earthquakes during each swelling, culminating on 1 April 1984 with a swarm of 500 tremors. These earthquakes and the swelling were once again caused by molten rock rising from below the earth's crust. Luckily, none of it has so far erupted onto the land surface and formed a volcano. The earthquakes, however, caused a lot of damage and many buildings became unsafe to live in or to work in. There was understandable panic in the city. In early October 1984, some 40,000 people were evacuated for a time from the town centre. But about 400,000 people were living in the surrounding area and ran the risk of being made homeless. When the movements

stopped, the quaysides of Pozzuoli had been carried so high above sea-level
that they could not be used by local boats. New, lower, quays had to be built
in the harbour. The molten rock still remains only about 4km below the land
surface – well able to erupt swiftly if subterranean conditions change. If the
molten rock were to begin rising again, and make the land start bulging
upward, then a volcanic eruption would be highly likely. The events of 1538,
which took place less than 5km away, have more than an abstract, technical
interest for Pozzuoli. There is a distinct prospect that another Monte Nuovo
could form – this time, perhaps, in the middle of Pozzuoli itself.

5

Etna, 1669

Etna is the largest active volcano in Europe and it has the longest recorded history, although its eruptions are nothing like as dangerous as those of Vesuvius. Etna is nearly always erupting something – even if it is only steam – and it was the main source of volcanic speculation amongst the ancient Greeks and Romans. Many outbursts of Etna take place on its lower slopes, well below the summit. Such was the spectacular eruption of lava in 1669.

A Goodly Mountain to Look Upon

Etna is by far the largest active volcano on land in Europe: 3,350m high, 1,250km^2 in area and over 500km^3 in volume. Its massive cone presides over all eastern Sicily, and, as an English merchant of Messina remarked in 1669, 'it is a very goodly mountain to look upon . . . standing alone by itself'. Etna is so vast that over 200 smaller volcanic cones, many nevertheless reaching 200m high, are scattered over its spacious, gentle slopes. It forms a dramatic back-cloth to the Greek theatre in Taormina and a brooding reminder of a threat on the northern skyline of Catania. 'When Etna sneezes, Catania shivers.' But, as volcanoes go, Etna is benign. It has none of the violent temper of its smaller Italian rival, Vesuvius. Etna is no mass murderer; it can scarcely have caused more than a few dozen deaths in the past 2,500 years during which history has been recorded – albeit imperfectly – in the Mediterranean region.

Etna entered recorded history when the Greeks founded Katanê ('below Etna' – Catania) in 729 BC, and it has been an inspiration to poets, scientists and travellers ever since. It is a boon to modern scientists too, for it erupts often, but rarely dangerously, and has a happy knack of producing something interesting for their research at regular intervals. Thus Etna has probably the largest and most varied collection of biographical studies of any volcano in the world.

Many people live on the lower flanks of Etna, where the centuries-old lavas have weathered to form soils rich in plant nutrients. The summit snows melt and provide indispensable water. The Sicilian sunshine does the rest. The land has 'the prodigious fertility of the Golden Age'. Vineyards, orchards and plots of cereals surround the many large villages. But it must also be said that most of the destructive eruptions come from the flanks of Etna rather than from its summit, and many of them send lava towards the most densely peopled area near Catania. But, even then, the volcano is so vast that it is unlikely that any one property will be destroyed during the lifetime of its occupants. The potential victims believe that this is a chance well worth taking. Indeed, the

Etna from the Greek theatre at Taormina.

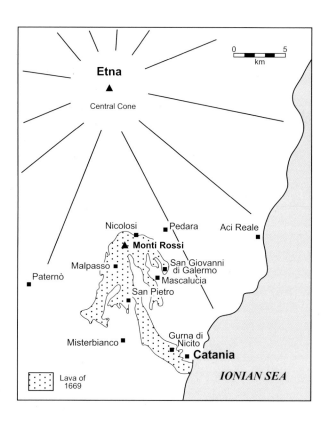

The eruption on Etna in 1669.

people living on Etna have an ambivalent attitude to its behaviour. They revere rather than fear the volcano, almost as if it represents the power of some Mediterranean earth-goddess. As one man remarked during the eruption in 1992, 'Etna is like a mother to us, she feeds us and protects us, even though she [sometimes acts] like a cruel stepmother.' Before a lava-flow had destroyed his home, he had left an offering of wine and bread on the kitchen table for the lava to swallow – and he had written some criticisms of the government on the wall . . . The victims of an eruption always seem to react positively, rebuilding roads, houses and even whole villages as soon as it stops, for, throughout historic time, most of the inhabitants have believed that they were living in one of the most attractive places on earth.

This mixture of attitudes to Etna formed an underlying current to reactions to the great eruption in 1669. It is also, perhaps, reflected in the name of the volcano. The Phoenician *Attana*, the Greek *Aitnaia*, the Latin *Aetna*, the Arabic *Gebel Huttamat*, as well as the modern name, Etna, in many European languages, all have a common root in 'furnace', or 'glowing, fire mountain'. But, for centuries, the local people called it by the more neutral hybrid *Mongibello* – from the Latin, *mons* and the Arabic, *gebel*, both meaning mountain – perhaps to avoid branding the volcano with a fiery, accusing, name, but at the same time stressing that it was *the* mountain in their lives.

The eruption in 1669 was a particularly persuasive reminder of the dangers that Etna could present. This memorable eruption entered the annals of Etna because it took place unusually low down on the flanks of the volcano, and because the lavas gushed out particularly quickly. Catania, with a population of 20,000, and the second most important city in Sicily, was partly destroyed. At the time, Sicily belonged to the Spanish Crown and was ruled by a Viceroy. In 1669 the Viceroy was Francisco Fernandez de la Cueva, Duque de Albuquerque, who ruled Sicily on behalf of the eight-year-old, mentally and physically handicapped King Carlos II. Luckily there was more local vigour in and around Catania. Many eye-witnesses not only described the eruption, but also tried to combat the advancing lavas. Their invaluable observations, which form the basis of this account, were collected together almost a hundred years later by Canon Giuseppe Recupero of Catania, who had made the study of Etna his life's work. It was he who acted as guide to Sir William Hamilton on his visit to Etna in 1769. There are also two eye-witness accounts of the eruption in English: one by the Earl of Winchilsea; and the other by 'some inquisitive English Merchants' who were living in Messina.

Canon Guiseppe Recupero of Catania.

Some Eruptions in Antiquity

Few ancient authors studied Etna, or any other volcano, as diligently as the Greek philosopher, Empedocles (*c.* 490–430 BC). He believed that the earth's interior was molten, and that volcanoes formed when the liquid rock rose to the earth's surface. To test this theory, he left his home at Akragas (Agrigento) in western Sicily and went to live on the summit of the volcano. Legend has it that he was so fascinated by the seething commotion there that he fell into the crater and perished – leaving behind a single sandal on the brink. But Aristotle, the killjoy, asserted that Empedocles died peacefully in Greece at the age of 60, without revealing the results of his research. Lucretius, on the other hand, who looked on from a safer distance some 300 years later, believed that Etna was hollow, like all volcanoes. Violent winds, he thought, swirled around in the underground caverns until they grew so hot that they sparked off fires in the encasing rocks. The hot, smoking, fragments were then thrown from the throat of the mountain. In those days trapped Titans offered another favourite explanation for both earthquakes and eruptions. In his *Metamorphosis*, Ovid (43 BC–AD 17) claimed that the Titan, whom he called Typhoeus, not surprisingly resented being imprisoned under Etna, and that he made the earth tremble and spat out ashes and flames as he struggled to get free. According to Ovid, human beings were not alone in suffering distress as a result. Pluto, the God of the Underworld, was very worried that the Titan's struggles would split the earth open, let daylight into his kingdom, and terrify the shades of the dead who stayed there. Pluto, no doubt, thought that the shades had enough trouble in the Underworld as it was . . .

The Greek poet Pindar (*c.* 518–438 BC) was one of the first to describe an actual eruption of Etna, in 475 BC (or 479 BC), in the first *Pythian Ode*. More or less the same thing was to happen in 1669:

> Snowy Etna, the nurse of perennial snows, from whose innermost caverns burst forth the purest fountains of unapproachable fire. It pours out a lurid, eddying stream of smoke by day, but it sweeps along like a ruddy flame in the gloom of night; and, all the while, it whirls the burning rocks with a noisy uproar down to the deep sea far below. The monster flings aloft the most fearsome fountains of fire, a marvel wondrous to behold or even to hear.

This, perhaps, was the fabled eruption when the 'Fratelli Pii' (the Pious Brothers) took their aged parents onto their shoulders and carried them safely away from the advancing lava-flows. These flows devastated parts of the south-western flanks of Etna and destroyed much of the Greek town of Katanê (Catania). Hieron I, tyrant of the rival Greek city of Syracuse, took advantage of the situation and forced the demoralized people of Katanê to settle in Leon-tini to the west. But they came back and reoccupied the site in 461 BC after Hieron had died. This was the first of many such reconstructions of Catania; lava-flows from Etna have destroyed the city again and again; and, every time,

Molten lava erupting on Etna.

the people have rebuilt it. There must be layer upon layer of archaeological treasures sealed beneath those solid black lavas.

After the Roman conquest of Sicily between 264 and 210 BC, the Latin poets also found inspiration in Etna. Lucretius (96–55 BC) referred to the eruption in 122 BC in *On the Nature of Things*:

> It was no common devastation that accompanied the fiery storm that arose and overwhelmed the fields of Sicily. The people around were spellbound, and, when they saw the whole sky smoking and sparkling, their hearts were filled with panic, dreading what new design Nature might have in store for them.

It seems that the ash clouds were so thick that widespread darkness lasted for three days and fearsome lightning flashed about the summit; people could not recognize each other in the streets. Molten lava flowed down to the Ionian Sea. A great crater, the Caldera del Piano, 1,200m across, formed at the crest of the volcano, which 2,000 years of eruptions have now filled up with lava. Hot ash rained down on the southeastern slopes of Etna, destroying crops, farms and many dwellings. At Catania, 25km from the summit, roofs were set alight, or collapsed under the weight of the ash. The Roman Senate later took pity on Catania and granted the city exemption from taxes for ten years. Even today, that layer of ash still lies 50cm thick some 6km from the crater. Some scientists believe that this has been Etna's most powerful outburst for the past 2,500 years at least. Other scientists, however, think that the eruption in 44 BC may have been just as violent.

THE IDES OF MARCH, 44 BC

Pliny the Elder recorded that, in 44 BC, Etna belched out hot ash in 'billows of flame' that spread between 70 and 150km from the summit, reaching Reghium (Reggio di Calabria), beyond the Straits of Messina. Appian reported, too, that lava-flows also entered the sea. Soon afterwards, Strabo (*c.* 64 BC–AD 25), in his *Geography*, interviewed some men who had recently climbed to the crest of the volcano. They explained that the eruptions were always changing the shape of the summit: 'sometimes the fire concentrates in one crater, but at other times it is distributed into several craters. Sometimes, too, the mountain sends forth lava, but, at others, flames and fiery smoke – and even occasionally expels red-hot masses of rock'.

In Book III of the *Aeneid*, Virgil (70 BC–19 BC) gave the eruption in 44 BC a less prosaic description:

> . . . Etna thunders with terrifying crashes. Sometimes it hurls a dark cloud of whirling black smoke and glowing ashes into the sky, and shoots out tongues of flame that lick the stars. Sometimes it gives out rocks torn from the very entrails of the mountain, and seething molten rock surges, roaring, from its lowest depths high into the air. The story has it that the body of Enceladus, charred by a thunderbolt, is weighed down beneath the mighty pile of Etna, which breathes out flames from its bursting furnaces. Often, as he turns from one weary side to another, all Sicily groans and trembles, and the heavens are veiled in smoke.

The ancient writers may have had no idea about what caused volcanic eruptions, but they could make up a good tale. Meanwhile, in the harsh real world of 44 BC, things were not going too well. On 15 March, Cassius, Brutus and their friends assassinated Julius Caesar in the Senate in Rome. The eruption of Etna at once took a hand in the aftermath. Some of its real effects have been unravelled by Phyllis Forsyth from the tangle of myths, portents and prodigies that the Ancient authors recorded after such an important event. Etna seems to have erupted a vast aerosol of volcanic ash and sulphur dioxide that spread over a wide area for several years. Its effects were felt far beyond the volcano – in Italy, in the Balkans and in Egypt – and even, perhaps, on the Greenland ice-cap. The eruption in 44 BC was linked with weird features in the sky, unusual cold in the air, and famines in the Roman Empire. However, it is perhaps just as well that there is no evidence to sustain Horatio's claim in Act I of *Hamlet* that 'a little ere the mightiest Julius fell, the graves stood tenantless and the sheeted dead did squeak and gibber in the Roman streets'.

Nevertheless, the Roman sky certainly went dark after Julius Caesar was assassinated. Astronomers know that it was not caused by an eclipse of the sun, and a thunderstorm – especially in March – could hardly have lasted so long. In the *Georgics*, Virgil himself directly linked the darkness to the eruption of Etna. The sun shone weakly for many months, no doubt because of the aerosol in the upper atmosphere. In his *Natural History*, Pliny the Elder noted that there had been almost a whole year of continuous gloom after Caesar's murder. In his *Life of Caesar*, Plutarch (*c.* AD 45–*c.* AD 125) described how

> the sun's rays were veiled. Throughout that year [44 BC], its orb rose pale and without radiance, while the heat that came from it was slight and ineffectual . . . and fruit remained [on the trees] imperfect and half-ripe, and withered away and shrivelled up due to the coldness of the atmosphere.

Tibullus (50 BC–*c.* 18 BC) put it even more poetically in the *Elegies*: 'the light departed from the Sun himself, and the cloudy year saw him yoke dim horses to his chariot'.

But there were more down-to-earth consequences than for the Sun God, Hyperion, and his sun chariot. When Julius Caesar's nineteen-year-old great-nephew and adopted son, Octavian, made his grand entry into Rome after the assassination, the sun was surrounded by a rainbow-like halo, probably caused by volcanic dust from Etna that was still suspended in the atmosphere. That morning in Rome, the crowd took the halo to be a divine and happy omen for Octavian and a curse upon the assassins. But, to succeed, he had to win a prolonged civil war in which the dust veil from Etna may also have played a small role.

The dust reduced not only the light but also the heat from the sun, so that the years just after the eruption seem to have been unusually cold. Weak sunshine, cold, and unripened crops naturally produced a famine that seems to have affected at least Italy, Greece and Egypt during the next two years. There were widespread crop failures in Italy from autumn 44 BC. Mark Antony, fleeing from Brutus after the battle of Mutina (Modena), experienced the effects of the famine, and was 'forced to eat wild fruits, roots and even bark and animals never tasted before by men'. There was a severe famine in Cleopatra's Egypt in 43 BC and 42 BC because the River Nile did not flood as usual and leave behind its fertile layers of silt when it sank back again. The dust veil from Etna might have altered the circulation patterns in the atmosphere and caused a drought in East Africa where the Nile rises, thereby preventing the usual summer floods that would bring fertility to the Nile valley in Egypt. In any case, even if the Nile did flood, the sun's rays might still have been so weak that the grain could not ripen.

It was intensely cold in October 42 BC at Philippi in northern Greece, where the army of Octavian and his brother-in-law, Mark Antony, beat the army led by the assassins Cassius and Brutus. Suetonius, in *Augustus*, recounts how Octavian always suffered badly from extremes of temperature; and, before the battle, his companions thought he was even going to die. But Octavian survived this possible legacy of Etna's dust veil, eliminated his old ally Mark Antony at Actium, in western Greece, in 31 BC, and became Augustus, the first Roman Emperor, in 27 BC.

Nicolosi, Monday, 11 March 1669

In 1669, the village of Nicolosi seemed to be quite a safe place to live, 800m above sea-level, 2,000m and 14km below the summit of Etna. It lay in the pleasant woodland belt, with attractive views over the richer vineyards and orchards stretching down towards Catania. The bleak, snowy summit zone of naked volcanic rock seemed very far away. On the other hand, the dozens of volcanic cones scattered around Nicolosi showed that Etna had often erupted on its flanks in the past, and thus could well start again at any time. In fact, these eruptions from the flanks of the volcano have usually destroyed far more property than the outbursts from the summit, which have often been more powerful, but have occurred too far from centres of population. This was about to happen again. As usual, the witnesses differ slightly about the timing of some events, but the broad sequence is clear enough.

During the first two months of 1669, the summit crater of Etna gave off much more gas and steam than usual, but the real warnings of an impending eruption began on 25 February, when earthquakes began and quickly increased in strength. In early March, all the southern slopes of Etna suffered much 'thunder and lightning and frequent concussions of the Earth'. Nicolosi bore the brunt of these earthquakes. Father Vincenzo Macrì, priest at the church of Santo Spirito, described how, an hour before nightfall on 8 March, the Holy Sacrament had been interrupted by 'a terrible whirlwind that seemed to want to smash the structure of the building'. Four hours later, the earthquakes resumed. 'We saw the earth, the trees, and buildings move, like blocks of wood floating on water.' Next day, as the earthquakes grew stronger and more frequent, people were afraid to enter their houses; and the priest said mass at great speed so as not to tempt fate. The shaking continued so violently that, by Sunday 10 March, buildings in Nicolosi had begun to collapse, and Father Macrì described how, after dark,

> the terrified population began to cry out *Misericordia!* – the Lord have mercy upon us . . . They were forced not only to abandon their houses, valuables and their homeland, but also their children or their parents . . . they fled terrified into the darkness . . . [and only then] began to search for their relatives . . . Those in the most terrible plight were the poor pregnant women, and the fathers and mothers carrying their children and babies through the darkness of that terrible night.

Those of a more practical turn of mind built cane huts in which to shelter outside, beyond the danger of falling masonry, 'beholding, with grief and astonishment, the ruine of their habitations'.

'Alora, si aprì la terra . . .' On 11 March, Etna split open. With a sinister ripping sound and a terrible quaking of the earth, a glowing, gaping wound cracked open in a jagged line stretching from the Piano di San Leo, just above Nicolosi, to Monte Frumento, 2km from the summit. The fissure was 2m wide and 12km long. Nobody dared peer into it to guess how deep it might be, but the livid molten lava gave clues enough.

About two hours before sunset on 11 March, gas began to explode from several fiery mouths at the lower end of the glowing crack. As night fell, another and much larger mouth burst open with a menacing roar, threateningly close to Nicolosi itself. As an anonymous eye-witness related,

> It threw up its flames with much fury and violence about a hundred yards [90m] in height, its noise not roaring only inwards from the belly of the mountain [Etna] as before, but violently cracking like peales of ordnance or thunder, throwing out vast stones, some of them 300 pound weight [136kg], which being (as it were) shot through the air, fell several miles distant from the place, whilst the whole air was filled with smoak, burning cinders, and ashes, which fell like a fiery rain upon the country.

The mouth was to go on erupting for four months, and form the Monti Rossi (the Red Mountains) that eventually reached a height of 250m. During the

Monti Rossi.

eruption itself, they were known by the more graphic name of the Monti della Ruina (the Mountains of Ruin). Father Macrì described how the glowing fragments were thrown 'into the second region of the air' with a 'most terrible and vigorous din'. 'This cannonade' was to last until 11 July.

Soon after darkness fell on 11 March, molten lava also began to surge out of the lower stretches of the fissure. It was 'a vast torrent of melted and burning matter, which, like an inundation, drowned [the country] as in a flood of fire'. The lava first emerged as hot as 1,200°C, at a rate of almost 100m³ per second (four times as fast as the average rate on Etna), and at a speed that might, at first, have surpassed 50km an hour. In no time at all, it formed a bright vermilion stream, 'the colour of melted glass', rushing on its way to Catania.

The 'Superb Stream'

The 'superb stream' of lava branched round and flowed under the old volcano of Monpilieri. The villages of Monpilieri and Falicchi were 'wholly destroyed and lost, not so much as any sign of them remaining'. And with them also vanished the esteemed image of the *Lady of the Annunciation*, 'the wonder of Sicily'. The lava then swamped the hamlet of La Guardia and advanced southwards upon Malpasso on 12 March. Its 8,000 inhabitants had time to leave their homes and flee with whatever they could carry away. They set a pattern that was to be repeated a dozen times or more during the days that followed. The molten lava issued very quickly from the crack, 'its flame like that of brimstone, and its motion like that of quicksilver', but the air and ground soon cooled the flow down and wrapped it in a solidified black crust that greatly reduced its speed. The molten lava flowed so fast that crops and fixed property could not be saved, but slowly enough for people and animals to be able to run away and save their lives. Lava-flows are much more considerate – and slower – than nuées ardentes.

The people of Catania, however, realized their peril and many 'ran with cries and lamentations about the city and country, expecting nothing but to be swallowed up, or consumed by fire, having no other apprehensions but of death and a general conflagration'. The more reflective and religious citizens of Catania adopted their age-old remedy. Everybody in Sicily knew that divine intervention had stopped lava-flows in the past. Many now took to prayer, imploring Sant' Agata to protect them. The saint had been martyred in Catania in AD 251, and, when Etna had erupted on 1 February, AD 252, her veil had been presented to the advancing flow. And the lava-flow had halted on 9 February. The story had it that the veil had been equally effective when called upon on many times afterwards, including, for example, in 1408 and 1444. Another anonymous Italian eye-witness recorded the scene on the morning of 13 March 1669:

The whole town [of Catania] went out in procession, barefoot, and dressed in the habit of penitents, carrying the most holy veil of our Saint Agata. This was the veil that, 1400 years ago, the peasants had brought from the sepulchre of the saint, and had carried up against the fire, which had duly stopped... An altar was built, and Mass was said, and... the benediction was given with the holy veil. At that spot, the fire obviously stopped, although it went on advancing in other directions. That evening they took the holy veil to Misterbianco, where everyone spent the night in the church, at prayer, in self affliction, and in other forms of penitence... nobody had eaten during the day ... And all the way along, there had been nothing but tears and people in flight.

However, the snout of the unstoppable flow pressed forward; and molten rock burst out from within the tongue from time to time. The lava-flow travelled 4km in less than two days and swamped the vineyards, orchards and small-holdings, as well as the buildings of Monpilieri and the lower parts of Mas-calucia on 13 March and San Pietro and Camporotundo on 14 March. By now, the flow was advancing at an average rate of only about 100m an hour. Thus forewarned, the villagers at least had time to pack a bag and a cart with their (few) movable possessions before they had to flee.

Meanwhile, in Catania, supplementary problems had arisen. As an anony-mous eye-witness recounted,

Whilst the people were busied in their devotions and astonished by their fears, news was brought to the magistrates of the city that a considerable number of thieves and robbers had taken the opportunity of this general distraction to make a prey of the already distressed people, and that they had murdered several of them for their goods; and that it was to be feared that the city of Catania itself might run some danger from the great numbers of them which were about the country, and from thence took their opportunities to get into the town.

It was a time for rough justice. The authorities reacted in customary fashion. The Commander of the Castle sent out several parties with orders to

seize on all suspected persons, and such as were not able to give a good account of themselves; and, for such as were taken in the fact of robbing, to execute them by martial law, without further tryal, [the Commander] accordingly caused three pair of gallows to be set up for their speedy execution.

Several robbers did, indeed, kill a number of Catanians, and some of those brought to summary justice were hanged 'to encourage the others'. They proved to be the only human fatalities of this eruption. As always, the felon-ious behaviour of the few handicapped the law-abiding masses. Many genuine refugees found it hard to find lodgings in Catania, because the citizens had locked their doors for fear of these robbers from the wilds of Etna. The helpless refugees, 'with great lamentations', spurred the magistrates and the clergy to take pity upon them, and the more enlightened Catanians, including the Bishop, Monsignor Cambuchi, and 'all persons of quality and estate', took them into their homes. Indeed, the people of nearby Messina and other cities sent them supplies as soon as they got news of their plight. The Catanians, however, were soon to face a far more potent threat than refugees or suspected robbers.

So much lava was gushing from the great fissure that it rarely formed a single uniform stream, but kept on branching and meeting up again. Within a week of the start of the eruption, new, and stronger, surges of molten rock broke out from the flow and covered areas that had previously been spared in Malpasso, Mascalucia and Camporotondo, for instance. On Saturday, 16 March, the main tongue of lava flowed over San Giovanni di Galermo and Torre di Grifo, 6km from its source. Another stream branched westward and overwhelmed Valcorrente on the following day. The flow was lengthening, widening and thickening all the time.

In all these villages, the advancing lavas pushed down the buildings or sealed them in a black embrace. Sometimes, the lava arched up over large obstacles and formed caverns that were hidden for ever. But, in 1704, workmen dug their way through 10m of solid lava that had arched above the entrance to the old parish church of Monpilieri. They found the altar bells and three once-revered statues intact in their cavernous tomb . . .

As the lava-flow neared Catania, apprehension increased in the city. On Monday 18 March,

> the Senate, with Monsegnior Cambuchi . . . followed by all the clergy, secular and regular, and an infinite number of people, went in a solemn procession . . . to Monte St Sofia, carrying out with the greatest devotion their choicest relicks, and, upon an altar erected in view of the mountain, exposed them where they celebrated mass, and used the exorcisms accustomed upon such extraordinary occasions.

But the volcano kept up its activity. The hot ash burnt the grass and 'obliged the people to drive away their cattel to a farther distance, which would otherwise have perished for want of food'.

On 25 March, strong earthquakes shook the summit of the volcano, which had hitherto been a silent spectator of the events on its lower flanks. The earthquakes heralded the eruption of a huge, billowing flurry of glowing ash that spread out and darkened the sky all day over the whole of Etna. At the same time, the core of the crowning cone collapsed with a great rumbling noise into the abyss, doubling the size of the crater. 'The birds and fowl . . . either through want of food or illness of the ayre, which was corrupted with noisome smells arising from these burnings, were observed to lye dead in all places.'

On 29 March the main tongue of lava divided into two as it reached Misterbianco, 9km from its source. One branch surrounded the west of the town and the other wrapped around the east. That evening, the branches of the flow thickened and joined up in the midst of the town, destroying practically every building except the parish church and a few houses nearby. Another surge of molten lava then covered the hamlet of Porcaria where the stream was so hot that it set a field of green oats on fire. More frighteningly, the lava tongues were now so thick that they easily covered hillocks and large buildings. Often, the sites of the swamped villages were little more than 'confused heaps of ragged stone, yielding a noisome fume'. The lavas had shown that they could even move hills. Near the village of Albanelli, covered on 1 April, the flow pushed aside a clay hillock that had been sown with wheat. It was finally deposited on a vineyard belonging to one Francesco Ansalone, whose views on the gift were not recorded. Much the same thing happened to a vineyard planted on a hill: it was picked up bodily and carried along for 800m, without disturbing the budding vines. It is true that these vines belonged to the Jesuits.

The Lava at Catania, April–May 1669

In early April the sinister flow was standing within 2km of the walls of Catania like an enemy about to invade the city. It almost taunted the Catanians by increasing their agony and ever decreasing their hopes of preserving their homes. Soon it began to press forward again. It first covered the Morsello Hermitage, then 'the delightful garden that Monsignor Branciforte had created', and finally completely covered the lovely lake called the Gurna di Nicito in the vast valley lying beyond the western walls of the city, 'where pleasant shooting parties had often been held'. The flow overran smallholdings and vineyards with impunity, and had destroyed 63,000 vines in four days.

But the Catanians were still living in hope. They were sure that the lavas would take at least two or three weeks to fill the valley out to the west; and equally sure that by then the eruption would have stopped before the flow could invade the city. Privately, too, the citizens were (almost) convinced that their favourite saints would save their property from destruction. But, probably on 12 April, they were chastened to see the flow suddenly fill the whole valley within six hours, and stop within a stone's throw of the walls . . . On 14 April the lavas thickened and wrapped around the 20m-high western wall of the city, and may have oozed through a couple of the gates. But, in fact, most of the lava turned to flow between the southern wall and the sea. The frantic citizens hastily blocked the exposed city gates and placed a barrier of loose stones on top of the walls. At the southern edge of the city, the lava was soon threatening the Ursino Castle, where the Spanish Viceroy always stayed on his visits to Catania.

The advancing lava-flow halted for Easter week. The main snout hesitated for a while. Then, soon after Easter Sunday, 21 April, like a bull distracted and led away by a matador's cape, the glowing southern tongue began to move forward again. It reached the sea two hours after sunset on Tuesday, 23 April. The combat between fire and water fascinated all who saw it, Catanians and visitors alike.

The 'fire', as the people called it, was indeed beginning to attract visitors, who took up vantage points on the towers and walls of Catania to watch the 'superb and terrifying spectacle'. Some only came to frighten themselves in reasonable safety. Others came from afar, like those 'inquisitive English merchants living in Messina', as they called themselves. They were so struck by what they saw that they sent an account of the eruption to the recently formed Royal Society in London. The Earl of Winchilsea, who had a better class of contact altogether, wrote to King Charles II in person. The Earl stayed with the Bishop of Catania on his way home after being HM Ambassador to Sultan Mehmet IV in Constantinople. It is not known whether His Majesty had time to read the letter, because he was forging an alliance with Nell Gwyn at the time.

The Earl was enthralled by the lava-flow, especially at night. It was 'a river of . . . a terrible fiery red colour, the stones of a paler red [seemed] to swim thereon . . . all the country [was] covered with fire, ascending with great flames, in many places smoking like a violent furnace of iron melted'. The flow was usually less fearsome by day because it then became what the English merchants described as 'a dark, dusky blew'. The lava was hot and smoking, although its surface was often solid and cool enough for the brave to walk upon. But every cleft in the crust revealed the molten interior, which would burst out in vermilion rivulets from time to time.

Where the southern branch of the flow entered the sea, the Earl of Winchilsea was impressed to observe, on Saturday, 27 April,

> this matter, like ragged rocks burning in four fathom water [7m] . . . some parts liquid and moving, and throwing off . . . the stones about it, which, like a crust of a vast bigness, and red hot, fell into the sea every moment . . . causing a great and horrible noise, smoak and hissing . . . in the middle of this fire, which burn'd in the sea, it hath formed a passage like to a river, with its banks on each side very steep and craggy; and, in this channel moves the greatest quantity of this fire, which is the most liquid, with stones and cinders all red hot . . . Where it meets with rocks or houses . . . they melt and go away with the fire.

Meanwhile, the lavas were redoubling their onslaught on Catania. They had covered the Torre di Gullo jetty on 25 April and had banked themselves up against the Tindaro Bastion on the city walls. In the afternoon of 30 April the lavas pushed down the walls and entered the higher, north-western part of the city through the 50m-wide breach. The ghastly spectacle stupefied the Catanians. They prayed and implored Sant' Agata to protect them. They paraded her veil once more in a passionate procession. But, now, the veil failed them.

The snout of the flow shuffled on through the northwestern streets of the city, where the Benedictine monastery became an early victim of the invasion. The English merchants bemoaned the fate of this 'very stately convent'. Soon, the lavas had filled all its gardens, stretching out to the city walls. As it banked up against the buildings, the flow thickened until the English merchants estimated that it was 'almost as high as the higher shops in the Old London Exchange . . . 'Tis certain that had this torrent fallen on some other part of the town, it would have made havock amongst the ordinary buildings.'

Now that the lavas had invaded the city at one of its highest points, it seemed that most of Catania was at their mercy. The way was open to the city centre. But prayer, or the threat of doom, stiffened the resolve of the citizens. They began to try their best to impede the flow, but they could do little to stop it, however slowly it advanced. The English merchants commented that it was

> a strange sight to see so great a river come so tamely forward [inside the city], for, as it approached into any house [the citizens] not only, at good leisure, removed their goods, but the very tiles, and beams, and what else was moveable.

All the explosives, the artillery, and even the brass cannons were removed from the Ursino Castle, and church bells were taken down from their steeples. The people were busy barricading the ends of streets and passages wherever they thought that the lavas might break in. They even pulled down houses that had been abandoned and made ramparts out of the loose rubble. As it was, the lavas destroyed 300 houses, some palaces and a few churches, besides much of the Benedictine monastery, before this particular branch of the flow came to a halt about 8 May. The snout was banked up against San Nicolò, the grandest church in all Sicily, which was still incomplete after a century of construction work.

A Short Diversion, Monday, 6 May 1669

By early May, most Catanians were probably convinced that their city was lost. But a few others were determined to continue the struggle. Dr Saverio Musumeci and Giacinto Platania, both citizens of the neighbouring town of Aci Reale, believed that the flow could be halted and dammed up by building a great rock wall athwart its path. Alternatively, they thought that the flow could be turned aside if strong iron hooks were used to break up the crust and pull it aside from its course. The anxious Catanians took a dim view of these bright ideas: any lava-flow that could throw down city walls was not going to have much trouble with iron hooks and walls of rubble.

Indeed, the Earl of Winchilsea had declared to his sovereign, Charles II,

> I assure Your Majesty, no pen can express how terrible it is, nor can all the art and industry of the world quench, or divert, that which is burning in the country. In 40 days' time it hath destroyed the habitations of 27,000 persons

... Of 20,000 persons which inhabited Catania, 3,000 did only remain ... and preparation [was being made] to abandon the city. That night which I lay there, it rained ashes all over the city.

Diego Pappalardo, the priest of the already abandoned village of Pedara near Nicolosi, was altogether more resourceful. He determined to try to control the flow. The best method seemed to be to force the molten stream to run again and again over the same ground. Thus the flow gets thicker and thicker, but lengthens very little, and therefore damages a much smaller area. But it is very hard to make lava do this, even with modern equipment. Diego Pappalardo had to use the humbler technique of turning the flow sideways near its source. This method, however, has the major disadvantage of diverting lava onto someone else's property. Nevertheless, he recruited fifty men – some say a hundred – whom he had specially selected for their courage and dexterity. On Monday, 6 May, he led them up, west of the flow, near the old site of Malpasso – far enough from their source for the molten lavas to have developed a solid side-wall, but close enough for it not to have grown too thick. His men were armed with heavy hammers, iron crowbars and hooks; near the flow, they protected themselves with damp animal skins to keep off the heat. Diego Pappalardo aimed to break open a hole in the thin side-wall of the flow and divert the molten material sideways, thereby starving the snout and bring it to a halt before it could spread farther over Catania. It was a very risky undertaking indeed. The heat was unbearable, and if the men made too big a hole in the side-wall they would be drowned in molten lava at a temperature of over 1,000°C. They lined up and took turns to run in and hack at the lava-wall. But each man could hit it only once or twice before the heat forced him to retreat. Then the next man ran forward, and so on. Eventually they managed to knock a hole in the side-wall and the molten lava began to flow out safely westwards. But, for a couple of days, the branching stream remained small, until Diego Pappalardo directed his men to block the main molten channel as best they could with boulders. Only then did most of the molten lava opt for the new westward path ... Success!

But the new stream was making straight for Paternò. As soon as the bad news reached that town, a posse of its citizens came angrily up to the diversion and brandished their most threatening weapons at Pappalardo and his men, driving them away from the flow before they could do any more mischief. Paternò was saved. The new stream quickly congealed and the molten lava resumed its previous course and again swelled the snout of the flow then invading western Catania. Thus civil strife got the better of science.

Catania in Despair, May–June 1669

On 11 May, the eruption was two months old. It had already produced lavas that were twice as thick, had flowed twice as far and had gushed out for twice

Contemporary depiction of the eruption of 1669, in Catania Cathedral.

as long – and four times as fast – as the average eruption on the flanks of Etna. The volcano was obviously making an exceptional effort and showed no sign of stopping. The Catanians would have been in despair had they known that the eruption still had two months to run. But they would have been partly consoled if they had also known what modern studies of such fluid lavas have revealed – that flows commonly reach three-quarters of their ultimate length after about a quarter of the period of the eruption has elapsed. This, in fact, is what happened in 1669, where the flow made rapid progress for the first month and advanced much more slowly thereafter. The trouble, however, was that the lava was now advancing largely over the city itself, where a kilometre more or less of destruction would be of major concern to the Catanians.

And the terrifying mouths were still exploding close to the source of the lava-flow near Nicolosi. The explosions shattered the lava there into brilliantly glowing fragments that cooled as they fell back to earth as ash or cinders and built up the twin cone later called the Monti Rossi. At night, especially, these incessant explosions produced a superb spectacle, better than any firework display. Close at hand, however, swirling ash tended to spoil the show. The English merchants were both impressed and inconvenienced by the 'terrible sight':

We would have gone up to the mouth itself, but durst not come nearer than a furlong off [200m], for fear of being overwhelmed by a sudden turn of the wind, which carried up into the air some of that vast pillar of Ashes, which . . . exceeded twice the bigness of [Old St] Paul's Steeple in London.

Notwithstanding their caution, ash swirled around the merchants, who declared that 'neither Sun nor Starr were seen in all that part' since the eruption had started. The grass had long since been blanketed with ash, which was 2m deep near Nicolosi, and over 50cm deep at Pedara and Trecastagni, which had now been abandoned for weeks. The farm animals were starving. Trees, vines and crops were burnt. Diseases were beginning to spread. 'Now, for our sins,' the pious lamented, 'the scourge of God has come upon us.' There was also the danger of being gassed. 'There issued great store of a strong sulfureous smoak, wherewith some of our company were at first almost stifled through inadvertency.' The eruption was making 'a continual noise, like the beating of great waves of the Sea against Rocks, or like thunder a farr off'. The merchants had heard the roaring at home in Messina, and it could also be heard across the Straits, 100km from Etna, in Calabria. Fine ash had been blown across the Ionian Sea as far as Zante [Zákinthos]. This wind-blown ash was a constant irritation in Catania – and the Earl of Winchilsea lamented that it had troubled his eyes as he sailed home.

Near Monti Rossi, however, the most impressive sight of all was still the red-hot stream of molten lava issuing from the lower end of the great crack. As Pindar had written centuries before, it was 'unapproachable' until the inevitable cooling encased it in a dark crust. The central channel in the flow glowed at night all the way to Catania. It was so bright in the darkness 'that books and writings printed in the smallest characters could be read with ease throughout the city'. The 'fiery torrent' was the subject of a fresco painted on the walls of the sacristy in Catania cathedral. It was also the subject of more disturbing visions amongst the threatened citizens. As Professor Ferrara later explained, 'terror made such a great impression on their minds that their imagination was not a little troubled. Many of those who had to spend the night near the fiery torrent believed that they had seen satyrs and figures with most horrible forms.' It was not surprising, then, that the Viceroy, the Duque de Albuquerque, felt obliged to exempt Catania from taxes for ten years.

Throughout May, small flows broke over the city walls from time to time, but they usually did little damage because either their supply of molten lava ran out too soon, or the citizens confined them by thick barrages. However, three of these flows were impertinent enough to taunt the sovereign power of Spain by filling the moat and then invading Ursino Castle. On 13 May, lava broke over the southern walls of the fortress, and on 8 June one stream invaded it from the west and another from the east. Lava filled the Castle up to the first floor and formed a rugged black apron, one kilometre broad, which now separated it completely from the sea. But a hastily built rampart of rubble, a sudden end to the supply of molten lava, and 'widespread public prayers' combined to save the rest of the Castle. On 11 June, yet another flow threatened to overwhelm 'the finest part of Catania'; once again, a wall of loose masonry proved enough to halt it.

At sunset on Wednesday, 26 June, the great lava-flow had its last fling. Molten lavas broke from their strait-jacket of cooled crust near Giulio

Tedeschi's vineyard on the slopes outside the city. Luckily the flow missed Catania and sped due southwards and straight into the sea. Nobody had seen anything like it. Its rushing impetus, its sheer vitality and size, its glowing brilliance, and the very noise it made, had had no parallel. The citizens of Catania gathered on what remained of the city walls to gaze upon it, mesmerized. Four hours later, its ardour was spent and the stream slowed to a halt, blackening into a ragged arm as it cooled. At last, on Thursday, 11 July, molten lava stopped pouring from the great wound in the side of Etna above Nicolosi. The most famous eruption on Etna in modern times had come to an end.

The Legacy

Few eruptions in the recorded history of Etna had ever burst out so low, lasted so long, or expelled so much lava. The lava-flow stretched across the opulent lower slopes of Etna all the way from Nicolosi to Catania in a black rugged tract 25m thick and covering an area of 37.5km^2. Very nearly 1km^3 of lava had erupted. Ash and cinders had also built up the Monti Rossi to a height of 250m, amongst the largest cones on Etna. Over a dozen villages had been destroyed or badly damaged; many of them had housed well over 3,000 people. Fine ash had blanketed an area 3km across so that it still looked like a 'bare tract of the Arabian desert' even a century afterwards. The flow had damaged much of the western part of Catania and, when the eruption ended, only 3,000 of its 20,000 citizens still remained in the city. In the whole area affected by the flow some 27,000 people had been made homeless. But nobody had been killed.

With the remarkable resilience of those who live around volcanoes, the people returned to Catania as soon as the eruption calmed down and began to rebuild their homes, often on top of the new lavas. Some of the destroyed villages, such as Nicolosi, Malpasso and Misterbianco, were rebuilt above or near their old sites; but others, such as Monpilieri, were not.

The core of the great lava-flow stayed hot for more than eight years. The Catanians used to impress visitors by driving crowbars into the crust to make gas and flames escape from the depths. However, the flanks of Etna saw little activity for almost a century afterwards, as if the volcano had been exhausted by its unusual effort in 1669.

Rebuilding made good progress during the next twenty years. Then, on 9 and 11 January 1693, a great earthquake devastated much of eastern Sicily. Its effects made the eruption of 1669 seem puny. In a few terrifying minutes it killed between 60,000 and 100,000 people – including 16,050 in Catania alone. The vast destruction meant that an enormous rebuilding programme had to be undertaken. From the field of ruins rose some of the finest baroque buildings in the world. But that is another story . . .

6

Öraefajökull, 1727

Öraefajökull is quite rare amongst Icelandic volcanoes because it erupts violently. Melting part of the ice-cap on its summit, this causes 'glacier-bursts', which rush down the volcano as enormous, and dangerous, floods. Such was a local priest's description of the 'glacier-burst' in 1727.

A Change of Name, 1362

Öraefajökull is the highest mountain in Iceland, and one of Europe's largest volcanoes. It rises to 2,119m, almost directly from near sea-level, and much of its summit is hidden beneath a glacial ice-cap, or jökull, covering 14km^2. The featureless plains of southeastern Iceland at its feet are so isolated that it is claimed that no mice have ever found their way there. This, though, is one of the most sheltered parts of the country, even warm by Icelandic standards, with good pastureland and birch woods. But the area is called Öraefi, 'wasteland'; and the name of its dominating volcano means 'wasteland glacier'. These paradoxical names came about in 1362, when the volcano erupted violently and the whole neighbourhood became no more than a wasteland. Before its great eruption, the volcano had the less emotive name of Knappafell, 'the knobbly mountain', and its coastal fringe was called Litlahérad. Thus the new place names immortalized the disaster.

Rather unusual things happen when a volcano erupts under an ice-cap that lies in a large crater. The hot gases, steam and molten rock, expelled at temperatures of well over 750°C, melt the lower parts of the ice. The meltwater accumulates under the ice, fills the crater, and then suddenly gushes out from beneath the ice-cap and rushes downhill at great speed like a river in flood. For perhaps a day or more, the rate of discharge can be higher than that measured at the mouth of the River Amazon – about 100,000m^3 per second! The meltwater carries along vast quantities of ice and rock fragments that are eventually laid down on huge deltas or plains at the foot of the volcano. *Jökulhlaup*, or 'glacier-burst', is the graphic Icelandic term used to describe these powerful events. Generally speaking, they lie somewhere between flooding streams carrying unusual amounts of mud and rocks, and mudflows carrying unusual amounts of water. It was such a glacier burst that devastated the coastal areas south and southwest of Öraefajökull in 1362.

If the eruption goes on long enough, the hot materials will melt all the ice lying directly above the volcanic chimney. The hot fragments can then be

Öraefajökull, Skaftafell National Park, Iceland.

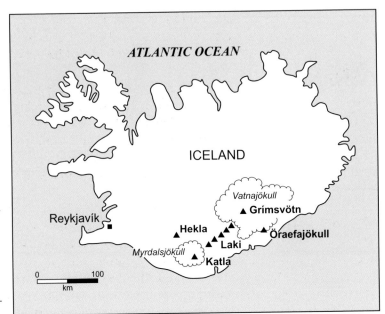

Some volcanic
features of south-
eastern Iceland.

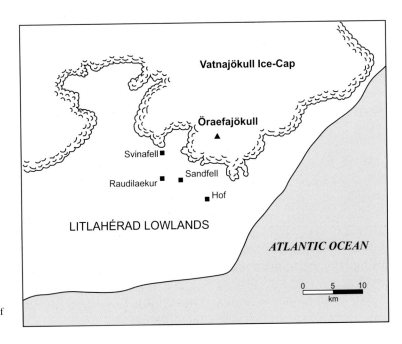

The location of
Öraefajökull.

thrown straight into the open air and scattered over a wide area, as in a normal eruption. This is what happened in 1362, when an area stretching at least 100km northeast of the volcano was covered by a thick blanket of ash and pumice.

Some of the effects of this eruption were pieced together from the fragmentary records by the Icelandic volcanologist, S. Thórarinsson. Iceland is lucky in having a recorded history that stretches back to the initial Viking settlement in AD 874. These records include the famous sagas, monastic accounts and cartularies, which are inventories of church property. Many, of course, are incomplete, and some of the accompanying commentaries are fanciful in the extreme.

About 1340, a cartulary indicates that Litlahérad had a population of some 200 people. There were four main churches, and thirty, maybe as many as forty, farms. Many of these were subdivided and were virtually small hamlets. Sheep, cattle and horses thrived on the pasturelands. Very few amongst this small coastal community lived through the devastation in 1362.

The oldest surviving record of the event is in the Annals of Skálholt, written at the Monastery of Mödruvellir in northern Iceland in the late fourteenth century.

> A volcanic eruption . . . kept burning from the flitting days [early June] until the autumn with such monstrous fury that it laid waste the whole of Litlahérad, as well as Hornafjördur and Lónshverfi districts [75–100km to the northeast]. At the same time, there was a glacier-burst from Knappafell into the sea, carrying such quantities of rocks, gravel and mud that they formed . . . a plain where there had previously been 30 fathoms [55m] of water. Two parishes, Hof and Raudilaekur, were entirely wiped out. On even ground [people] sank up to midleg into the sand, and the wind swept it up into drifts so that buildings were almost obliterated. So much ash was carried over the northern areas of Iceland that footprints showed up in it. So much pumice could be seen floating off the west coast that ships could hardly make their way through it.

Other records later commented that all Litlahérad was devastated. In the course of a single morning, the glacier-burst tore nearly every farm from its foundations and swept them into the sea. The wooden church at Raudilaekur was one of the few buildings – perhaps the only one – to remain upright. The darkness was so intense that the roads could not be distinguished even at noon. The glacier-burst cut the routes to the west; and the main river to the east completely changed its course. Hot ash and pumice rained down on the shore. Those who survived the initial glacier-burst faced a hazardous journey of almost 100km before they could reach safety. Few, if any, completed the exodus. Several hundred people may have died altogether, and most of these probably drowned. It was said that the priest and deacon of Raudilaekur church were the sole survivors of the catastrophe, but other tales claimed that only an old woman and a mare were spared.

Öraefajökull, with the remains of a glacier-burst in the foreground.

Öraefi was to remain a wasteland for almost a century. In later years, people settled again in some of the hamlets, but others were abandoned for ever. Eventually, the details of the catastrophe were forgotten, and only the place-name remained. But a folk memory lived on in a legend recorded during the first decade of the eighteenth century. It goes something like this:

Once upon a time, Hallur, the shepherd at the hamlet of Svinafell, had collected the ewes together, and the maids had started milking them, when they heard a loud noise come from Öraefajökull. They were astonished. Soon afterwards, there was another noise. Hallur said that they would be well advised not to wait for a third one. He immediately took refuge in Flosi's Cave, in the mountainside east of Svinafell. [It seems that the maids, unwisely, did not follow him, perhaps because they preferred to take their chance with the booming mountain.] Whilst Hallur was sheltering in the cave, the third noise duly came. It was the sound of the glacier-burst. It swept down every gully on the mountainside, and carried with it so much water and rock that they destroyed all the people and animals in the district except Hallur himself and a single horse with a blaze on its face.

Amongst a number of lessons that may be drawn from this story, the first is that it is best to climb up away from plains when a glacier-burst threatens; and another lesson is that, in such an eventuality, milkmaids should not hesitate to follow shepherds into caves.

A Sermon Interrupted: Sunday, 7 August 1727

Those who live on materials erupted from a volcano run the risk of being over-whelmed, if not killed, by a similar eruption in the future. And so it was that some of those living on the sands laid down by the *jökulhlaup* in 1362 suffered the consequences of another glacier-burst from Öraefajökull in 1727.

The Reverend Jón Thorláksson, Rector of Sandfell in Öraefi, described this rather small glacier-burst in 1727. Young and resourceful, the minister was about 26 at the time, and he lived to record his experiences in his eightieth year, after God had led him 'through fire and water [and] through much trouble and adversity'.

Events began when earth tremors disturbed divine service at Sandfell on Sunday, 7 August 1727. 'As I stood before the altar, I was conscious of a gentle concussion under my feet, which I did not [heed] at first; but during the delivery of the sermon, the rocking continued to increase so as to alarm the whole congregation'. Suddenly, a very old man got up and left the church. The zealous Reverend Thorláksson was at last forced to interrupt his discourse. When the old man threw himself down and started listening to the ground, the onlookers laughed at him. Soon, however, the old man returned to the church with his diagnosis. 'Be on your guard, sir. The earth is on fire!' At that very moment, a further tremor seemed to make the church contract. Jón Thor-láksson read the fear on the faces of his congregation. He saw that they were keener to save their lives than their souls. He abandoned the service. As he hurried back home to Hof, 5km away, he noticed that one of the summits of

The village of Hof.

Öraefajökull was heaving up and down, probably because the tremors, or perhaps the first eruptions, were disturbing the ice-cap.

> The following day, we not only felt frequent and frightful earthquakes, but we heard dreadful reports that were in no respect inferior to thunder. Everything that was standing in the houses was thrown down by these shocks; and there was every reason to apprehend that mountains, as well as houses, would be overturned in the catastrophe.

Eruptions might overturn houses but not mountains. In the event not even the houses fell over – but 'what augmented the terror of the people was that nobody could divine where the disaster would originate, or where it would end'. They had not long to wait.

The Jökulhlaup, Monday, 8 August

Jón Thorláksson recalled that

> Just after 9 a.m., three particularly loud reports were heard, which were almost instantaneously followed by several floods of water that gushed out . . . and completely carried away the horses and other animals that it overtook . . . When these floods were over, the glacier itself slid forward over the plains, just like melted metal poured out of a crucible. [The ice piled up in a great thickness and the floodwaters kept on rushing out from it, destroying all the remaining pastures in the process.] It was a pitiable sight to behold the agony of the females and [to see] my neighbours destitute of both counsel and courage.

When the great current changed course and began to threaten his own home, the minister apparently kept cool (he, of course, was telling the story). Like Hallur in the legend, he had time to decamp to a high rock on the mountainside: 'I caused a tent to be pitched, and all the church utensils to be conveyed thither, together with our food, clothes, and other things that were the most necessary'. The Reverend Thorláksson reasoned, rightly, that if another eruption were to break out, 'this height would escape the longest, if it were the will of God, to whom we committed ourselves'.

Then things changed for the worse. A bigger eruption at last melted the rest of the ice covering the volcanic chimney. The volcano could now throw hot ash far and wide.

> The glacier itself burst and many icebergs were run down as far as the sea [perhaps all of 10km away], but the thickest [ice] remained on the plain a short distance from the foot of the mountain. The atmosphere was so completely filled with fire and ashes, that day could scarcely be distinguished from night . . . which, in turn, was only lighted up by the glow from the fire that had broken

through five or six fissures in the mountain . . . The parish of Öraefi was tormented for three whole days by fire, water, and falling ashes.

Yet, [the minister confessed], it is not easy to describe the disaster as it was in reality . . . the ground was entirely covered with pitch black pumice sand. It was impossible to go out in the open air with safety on account of the red-hot stones that fell from the atmosphere. Many of those who did venture out covered their heads with buckets and other utensils.

Hot Water, 11 August

The atmosphere cleared up a little on 11 August, although the eruptions were still going on. The minister and three companions rode out to see what had happened at Sandfell, which was more exposed to the eruption than Hof. As they followed the new defile formed between the mountain on their right and the masses of ice newly dumped onto the plain on their left, the hot water that was still rushing down the defile made their horses almost unmanageable. The Reverend Thorláksson realized that they were in a most dangerous spot if the flood should increase. Almost at once, he saw a huge deluge of hot water descending upon them. But he had the presence of mind to react correctly: 'contriving, of a sudden, to get on the ice, I called to my companions to make the utmost expedition to follow me'. Finally they reached Sandfell only to find that the farm and the cottages were no more. The people stood crying in the church – where they had mocked the old man's forecast only four days before.

When the glacier had burst, a boy and a couple of women had scrambled onto a sheep-cote at Sandfell. But the swirling waters had uprooted it almost at once, and the three were carried out of sight, still clinging desperately to the roof. 'One of the women was found afterwards in the mud of the *jökulh-laup*, but she was burnt, and . . . partly cooked. Her body was so damaged and tender [that] she could hardly bear it to be touched.'

Everything was in a terrible state. The sheep were all lost, and some of the carcasses were washed up from the sea three parishes away. The cows often survived quite well, but so much hay had been destroyed that only a fifth of them could be fed. The horses seem to have been particularly vulnerable to the effects of the glacier-burst. Many were swept into the sea and drowned; others that managed to stay on land ended up 'completely mangled'.

Summer 1728

Öraefajökull continued to erupt until the following spring and gave off smoke until the end of the summer of 1728. In April 1728, the ash that it had expelled was still too hot to touch. Some stones were black and riddled with holes. Others were 'so loose in their contexture that one could blow through them'.

One of the ice tongues of Öraefajökull.

With the return of the better weather, Jón Thorláksson determined to assess
the extent of the damage:

> On the first day of summer, 1728, I went with a person of quality to examine
> the rifts in the mountain. It was possible to creep along them. I found a great
> quantity of saltpetre there, and I could have collected it, but I chose not to stay
> long in the excessive heat.

The rifts that had cracked the mountain were very deep. They dislodged a
boulder into one of the great cracks, but never heard it hit the bottom.

Jón Thorláksson's account ended at this point, and he, no doubt,
embarked upon the more monotonous life of 'trouble and adversity' that
was the lot of a country minister in Iceland at the time, until his eightieth
year, when he composed the story of the great event that occurred during
his early ministry.

The ice that had been dumped onto the plains – the dead ice – remained for years as a sinister landscape of chaotic lumps before it finally melted away. As late as September 1756, two travellers described the 'terrible area covered by ice blocks, and rocks, pumice, and ash' that stretched, 3km wide and 13km long, between Hof and Sandfell. The area is still called Svartijökull, or 'black glacier'.

The destruction in 1727 was nothing like as extensive as that in 1362, and the area recovered again fairly quickly. At present, the population of the district is about the same as it was before the eruption of 1362. When Öraefajökull erupts again, the people will be in serious danger.

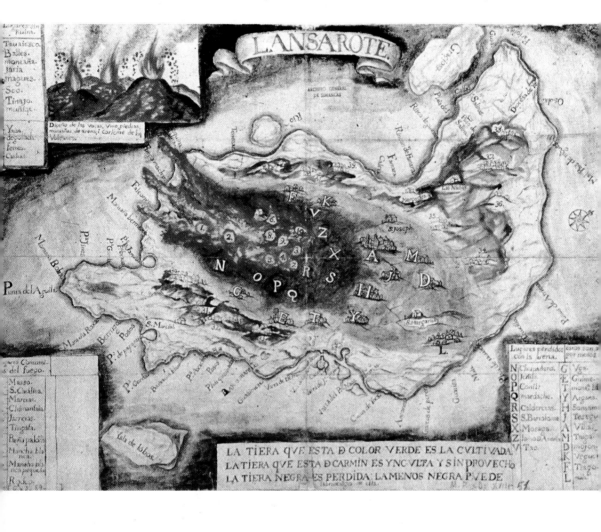

LANSAROTE.

LA TIERA QVE ESTA D COLOR VERDE ES LA CVLTIVADA
LA TIERA QVE ESTA D CARMIN ES YNCVLTA Y SIN PROVECHO
LA TIERA NEGRA ES PERDIDA LA MENOS NEGRA PVEDE

7

Lanzarote,
1730–1736

The eruption on Lanzarote was the longest ever recorded in the Canary Islands and gave an entirely new landscape to much of the western part of the island. The diary of a parish priest and newly discovered letters in the Spanish National Archives show one of the earliest surviving attempts to manage a volcanic crisis. Some rather unexpected changes in the economy of Lanzarote ensued.

Fortunate Islands

The Canary Islands are the 'Fortunate Islands'. They enjoy a climate of eternal spring that has been the foundation of their prosperous tourist industry. One drawback, however, is their volcanic eruptions. Luckily, they do not happen often; and they do not last long. The only exception was the great outburst in Lanzarote that occurred between 1 September 1730 and 16 April 1736. It lasted twenty times longer than any eruption recorded in the Canary Islands since the Spaniards first settled there under the French nobleman, Jean de Betancourt, in 1402. These were the eruptions that gave the spectacle to the landscape of Lanzarote, and five and a half years of anguish to its people.

*

It was in Lanzarote that the authorities made one of the first attempts to cope with volcanic activity and to control the civil crisis that it provoked. The administrators had few precedents to go on; and knowledge of how volcanoes behaved was slight indeed. They had to feel their way forward in the dark. They made mistakes, but it would be unfair to condemn those who tried to manage the emergency, given the meagre facts and techniques available to them. Indeed, since then, both earth scientists and administrators have made far more serious errors – with much more background knowledge at their disposal.

In the eighteenth century, the Spanish administrators in the Canary Islands did not think very highly of Lanzarote. They treated it, and its neighbour, Fuerteventura, almost as a colonial outpost, useful only as a strategic base and as a supplier of grain. Since Spain was often at war, and the Barbary pirates were rarely inactive, Lanzarote was well placed, just off the Barbary coast of Africa. It also had a couple of good harbours, notably at Arrecife, sheltering the fishing-boats and grain-exporting ships that were to play an important role during the eruption. The ports also protected the naval vessels defending Tenerife and Gran Canaria, where the chief Spanish administrators lived.

Oil painting of the devastation on Lanzarote.

The eruption on Lanzarote, 1730–1736.

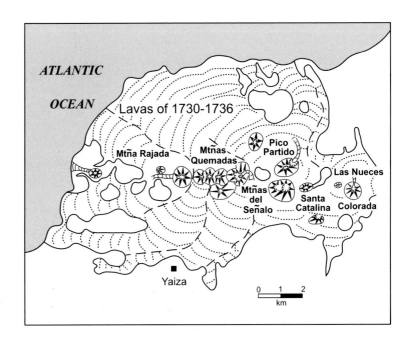

North-western Lanzarote, 1730–1736.

The agricultural yields of Lanzarote were high enough to produce an export surplus. The old volcanic rocks had weathered into buff-coloured clays that could be ploughed to grow wheat, barley and rye on the broad lowland swathes in the centre of the island. These cereals were the main source of revenue in Lanzarote. The low hills provided pastures for sheep and cattle. Aridity was the main agricultural handicap, for rainfall averaged less than 200mm a year. The climate of Lanzarote is rather like that of the nearby Sahara without the heat, for the temperatures rarely exceed 30°C. Water conservation has to be efficient and the many wells and water cisterns are vital features of the rural scene. Even now, teams of dromedaries seem perfectly at home ploughing the fields.

When the eruption started in 1730, Lanzarote had a population of 4,967, living in about sixty villages and hamlets distributed quite evenly over its 800km². The main settlements were Haría in the north, Yaiza in the west, and in what was then the capital, Teguise, in the centre. In 1730, the eruption began between Yaiza and Teguise and it was to become one of the longest in Europe during historic time. By 1736, a whole new landscape had been created in northwestern Lanzarote, much of the population had fled, and the chief administrators of the Canary Islands had seriously quarrelled with their subordinates in Lanzarote. And yet, no human lives were lost, and thirty years after 'the reign of the volcanic terror' ended, Lanzarote was far richer and twice as populous as it had ever been before.

Juan-Carlos Carracedo has written a fine study of the eruption in *Lanzarote, La Erupción Volcánica de 1730*. Its impact can be measured from two very different contemporary accounts that cover its early months. The first of these is the diary of Father Curbelo, the parish priest of Yaiza. It deals with the first fifteen months of the events. The original document no longer survives, but luckily, the German geologist, Leopold von Buch, summarized and translated it in 1825. The second account has recently been brought to light in the Spanish National Archives at Simancas. It is the correspondence between the *Regente* of the Real Audiencia (the Royal Court of Justice) in Gran Canaria, and his subordinate, the *Alcalde Mayor* (chief administrator) in Lanzarote. Unfortunately, this exchange of letters about the eruption lasted only until April 1731. The *Alcalde*, and the committee appointed on Lanzarote to manage the crisis, proved either unable or unwilling to follow the recommendations of the *Regente*. He lost patience with them, appealed to the Crown and sent a copy of the whole correspondence to Madrid. This is why it has been preserved in the royal archives at Simancas.

On the First of September 1730

The people of Yaiza had a grandstand view. The eruption began northeast of Yaiza near the village of Timanfaya. The parish priest, Father Andrés Lorenzo Curbelo, recorded its beginnings:

On the first of September 1730, between nine and ten in the evening, the earth suddenly opened up near the village of Timanfaya, two leagues [in fact, 8km] from Yaiza. During the first night, an enormous mountain [Los Cuervos] rose up from the bosom of the earth and it gave out flames for nineteen days. A few days later, a new abyss opened up . . . and a torrent of lava quickly reached the villages of Timanfaya, Rodeo, and part of Mancha Blanca . . . The lava flowed northwards over the villages, at first as fast as running water, then it slowed down until it was flowing no faster than honey. A large rock arose from the bosom of the earth on 7 September with a noise like thunder and it diverted the lava from the north towards the northwest. In a trice, the great volume of lava destroyed the villages of Maretas and Santa Catalina lying in the valley. On 11 September, the eruption began again with renewed violence. The lava began to flow again, setting Mazo on fire, and overwhelmed it before continuing on its way to the sea. There, large quantities of dead fish soon floated to the surface of the sea, or came to die on the shore. The lavas kept flowing for six days altogether, forming huge cataracts and making a terrifying din.

Then everything calmed down for a while as if the erupton had stopped altogether. This was the very first eruption on Lanzarote since the Spanish settlement, but, for some unknown reason, the *Alcalde Mayor*, Melchor de Arvelos, did not report it to his superiors. However, rumours of the outburst soon reached Juan Francisco de la Cueva, the *Regente* of the Royal Court of Justice in Gran Canaria. He was worried enough to write to the *Alcalde Mayor* on 13 September, urging him to take steps to protect the precious grain stocked in the barns and to make sure that enough grain was supplied to the people. The *Alcalde Mayor* was stirred into action. He asked two citizens to join him in a provisional *junta* (committee) to manage the crisis. So far, however, the eruption seemed to be just like those witnessed twenty-five years before in Tenerife; if so, it would soon stop. And, of course, it did. On 19 September, Los Cuervos calmed down and thereafter gave off nothing more than sulphurous fumes.

The next three weeks of tranquillity were deceptive. On 10 October, more powerful eruptions began from two or three holes on a new site, 1.5km north of Los Cuervos. Father Curbelo noted that they

gave off great quantities of sand [ash] and cinders that spread all around, as well as thick masses of smoke that belched forth from these orifices and covered the whole island. More than once, the people of Yaiza and neighbouring villages were obliged to flee for a while from the ash, cinders and the drops of water that rained down, and the thunder and explosions that the eruptions provoked, as well as the darkness produced by the volumes of ash and smoke that enveloped the island . . . On 28 October, the livestock all over the area nearby suddenly dropped dead, suffocated by the noxious gases that had condensed and rained down in fine droplets over the whole district.

Pico Partido, Lanzarote.

This time, Melchor de Arvelos was quick to report the new destruction to the *Regente* in Gran Canaria. On 17 October he wrote:

> ... and now another volcano has burst out on the tenth of the current month [October] at about five in the evening ... [with] two mouths, a good musket shot apart [*c.* 600m], one is very close to the burnt church at Santa Catalina and the other near Mazo.

The first mouth built the Santa Catalina cone and the second formed the black, cloven pyramid of the Pico Partido, the most distinctive volcano in Lanzarote. The villages of Santa Catalina and Mazo had already been abandoned. Now they were buried and were never seen again.

> So much fire [lava] and sand [ash] were expelled [wrote the *Alcalde*], that the discomfort was felt three or four leagues away [12km or 16km], damaging roofs and fields ... all the best land in the area [has] been lost ... The land cannot be cultivated or worked: the cisterns and wells are without water and totally lost; the refuges and houses almost covered, the barns in difficulty ... In our misfortune, birds, rabbits, mice and other little animals run wild over the volcanic sands, without any means of feeding themselves – although all that is but naught compared with the pain caused by the tears and lamentations of men, women

and children under the onslaught of this hostile element [who have been] deprived of their property and exposed in the fields to the inclemency of the weather . . . [The people are] searching for hollows in the wilderness where they can shelter, at such an inconvenient time as the present – on the verge of winter . . . There is no doubt that all the [unprotected] grain will be lost when it rains . . . There are no houses near those that have been lost, nor any further away, in which people could shelter . . . Thus there is an urgent need to assist those who have lost everything [and] . . . allow them to leave for other islands with their grain stocks . . . [In addition], in order to encourage and console those who have been disheartened by their horror of the fire, we have determined to detain the boats that have arrived [to stop them from taking any grain away] . . . [At the same time], the continuous tremors, that never cease throughout the island and make it palpate incessantly, have made the inhabitants – especially the womenfolk – succumb to fear.

At this stage, the *Alcalde* clearly wanted to allow the people to leave the island if they wished because they obviously felt helpless and terrified. He concluded his litany with a polite request that the *Regente* should issue his recommendations with the briefest possible delay. In fact, Juan Francisco de la Cueva can have been in little doubt that something was seriously amiss in Lanzarote. As he later recounted on 4 April 1731 in his letter to the Crown:

[The eruption] was prodigious both in the quantities of fire [lava], stones [cinders], and sand [ash] expelled, and in its duration – for it still continues to destroy the island today. The fire was so strong and so high that it could continually be seen, from this island [Gran Canaria] and others for a distance of more than 50 leagues [*c.* 200km]. The stones were in such quantity and of such size that they formed many high mountains during the eruption, and a noise like thunder was heard whenever they entered the water. For several days the eruption shook buildings, doors and windows as far away as the mountains of this and other islands. The quantity of sand was such that, as well as causing as much, if not more damage than the fire to houses, lands and water cisterns, it also formed an islet deep in the sea which was almost one league [*c.* 4km] long and over three leagues [*c.* 12km] in circumference. The sand was also blown by the wind and the fire as far as 15 leagues [*c.* 60km] away to the interior of Fuerteventura, without, however, causing notable damage there.

The People Shall Remain on Lanzarote

In October 1730, the *Regente* did not expect the crisis to continue for much longer. The best way to guess how volcanoes might behave in the future is to get to know how they have behaved in the past. This is what guided the *Regente* at first. He probably knew that eruptions in the Canary Islands were usually brief, and believed that the crisis might not last too long in Lanzarote. (The longest of the four eruptions that had taken place in Tenerife between 1704 and 1706 had lasted only twenty-four days.) His prime concern, in the interim, was to protect the grain stocks on Lanzarote from both the eruption and thieves; and to stop the panic-stricken people from leaving the island and, perhaps, creating public disorder elsewhere. Thus, on 31 October 1730, the *Regente* issued orders to the *Alcalde Mayor* in exactly this vein. Melchor de Arvelos should continue to administer justice, 'to prevent grave prejudice to the public weal, if the people were left to themselves, which might run counter both to the universal good of all these islands and to His Majesty's service'. On pain of severe penalties, no families were allowed to leave for other islands; and boat owners were forbidden to transport them. Under no pretext or motive whatsoever should grain of any species be removed from the island. A census should be taken forthwith of the food, water resources and available arable land on Lanzarote. All grain and herds that could not be adequately protected should be transferred to neighbouring Fuerteventura. Juan Francisco de la Cueva, however, showed remarkable concern for the plight of the poor and dispossessed, and he ordered that they should be given alms, shelter and a daily ration of food. In order to maintain local communities, he urged that what the fires had destroyed should be restored. Given the new and miserable state of the island, the *Regente* believed that the people would then be able to resume their normal way of life as soon as the eruption stopped. At first, the *Junta* agreed with this policy.

The *Regente* also ordered the *Alcalde* to increase the membership of the *Junta* in order to control the civil turmoil that seemed bound to arise. Six of the Great and the Good of Lanzarote were co-opted to help Melchor de Arvelos in his unusual task – two judges, the Commissioner of the Holy Inquisition, a soldier, and 'two men of honour and conscience'. Most of them were distantly related, and descended from Jean de Betancourt, who had first settled the Canary Islands. All but two were military men and they increasingly faced the crisis with military solutions. They might not know much about volcanoes or economics, but they could recognize a military threat when they saw one. As time went on, the defence of Lanzarote became their obsession.

From the purely military point of view, their reaction was not without its merits. If everybody had abandoned Lanzarote, they would have got the blame if an enemy had then invaded. On the other hand, if they had obliged everyone to stay put, fear might have forced the people into a revolt. To their ordered, hierarchical, minds, revolt would have seemed much worse than any eruption.

In fact, the *Junta*'s stance was supported at first by the Governor-General of the Canary Islands, the Marqués de Villahermosa. On 5 November, he wrote to the *Junta* from Tenerife supporting the measures outlined by the *Regente* and commanding them to take the utmost precautions for the defence of the island. The feared outside intervention could have come either from pirates and freebooters operating from the nearby Barbary coast; or from the British, who were certainly not to be trusted. They had seized Gibraltar in 1704, and a fourteen-month siege in 1728 had failed to wrest it from their villainous

The Montañas del Señalo from the edge of the crater of Pico Partido.

clutches. Although the two countries had just signed the Treaty of Seville, the old foe could well take advantage of the crisis to steal Lanzarote – even if it were shaking and covered with ash! That would then give them a base from which to attack Tenerife and Gran Canaria.

This world view must have been far from the minds of those in the front line in Yaiza. Hopes rose when Santa Catalina and Pico Partido stopped erupting on 30 October. They were dashed again when Pico Partido resumed its efforts alone on 1 November and gave off great clouds of ash and smoke. More lavas appeared on 10 November, but the lava-flow that erupted from Pico Partido on 27 November was altogether more terrifying. Father Curbelo described how it 'rushed down to the coast at an incredible speed, reached the [northwestern] shore on 1 December, and formed a small islet, all around which many dead fish were found'. Although the lava was very fluid, its average speed over the 7.5km from the volcano to the shore can only have been about 75m an hour. The exaggeration shows how terrified those who saw it must have been. But the ash was now spreading farther and farther afield, destroying crops and threatening more and more fertile land.

A Map and Recommendations of Repentance

Meanwhile, as the enlarged *Junta* in Lanzarote was no doubt doing what committees do, a more significant event was taking place in neighbouring

Fuerteventura. The authorities in Fuerteventura had a vested interest in the problems of Lanzarote, for people were fleeing there without permission: by the end of November no fewer than 363 illicit refugees had been discovered in Fuerteventura. They had no doubt bribed the boatmen of Lanzarote to defy the *Regente*'s orders. Such behaviour was a warning of possible chaos to come; in the Spanish Empire in those days, people could not just move about whenever they felt like it.

The Military Governor of Fuerteventura, Pedro Sánchez Umpiérrez, had the bright and original idea of commissioning an oil-painted map of the devastation of Lanzarote 'to bring to light the places lost by the action of the volcano, and those places lost because of the sands'. He sent it to the *Regente* 'so that His Excellency can envisage the island in the best possible way, and execute his ordinances with the best possible focus'.

This was probably the first volcanic hazard map ever produced. It is not known whether the authorities in Lanzarote knew of this initiative, or realized its importance if they did. But, obviously, the Military Governor of Fuerteventura was of a different mettle from the rather supine *Junta* in Lanzarote, who were neither leaders of men nor tamers of eruptions. Indeed, the Governor-General had already remarked to the *Regente* that the natives of Lanzarote were 'timorous and dumb in the utmost degree'. But he took good care not to visit Lanzarote himself.

When Juan Francisco de la Cueva acknowledged the Military Governor's map, he also included a note from the Dean of Chapter in the church in Gran Canaria. The Dean proposed a different way of overcoming the 'deplorable state' of the island and the 'lamentable sufferings' of its inhabitants. 'Kindly continue your Rogations,' he urged, 'and encourage all churchmen and members of the Religious Orders to do likewise. Those doing continuous religious missions should insist on public penitence to placate Divine Justice.' Perhaps the people of western Lanzarote had been particularly sinful. Perhaps, also, the local clergy, like Father Curbelo, were more helpful and soothing, but it was not a subject that the parish priest of Yaiza mentioned in his diary. Anyway, sin or no sin, repentance or no, the eruptions went on for another five years.

By 25 November 1730 the eruptions had already lasted longer, and had done more damage, than any previously experienced in the Canary Islands. The people felt that they were trapped on an increasingly dangerous island. Fear gave way to panic. The only salvation seemed to lie in flight. Boat owners were cajoled, and probably bribed, to take refugees to Fuerteventura against the express orders of the *Regente* and the *Junta*.

Departures to Fuerteventura Allowed, December 1730

The map had revealed the extent of the devastation of Lanzarote, and the eruptions were showing no signs of stopping. Indeed, they were starting to multiply. The *Regente* realized that he had to change tack if Lanzarote were to avoid deaths by volcanic action, famine or civil unrest. He had also to prevent a shortage of grain that would cause prices to rise and might precipitate an economic crisis to add to the volcanic emergency. In short, Juan Francisco de la Cueva faced an administrator's nightmare.

Thus, on 9 December the *Regente* reversed his earlier decision and decreed that the poor and homeless should now be allowed to depart; and that they could take their own grain and chattels with them. But they should only be permitted to emigrate to Fuerteventura. The *Regente* was probably trying to limit any possible civil unrest to the two islands. Juan Francisco de la Cueva also added that enough people should stay on Lanzarote to protect it from invasion. But, by the beginning of December, the lassitude of the *Junta* was starting to irritate the *Regente* and he warned them that public disturbances could well break out if the crisis were not properly handled.

The situation on the spot was certainly not improving. The *Junta* had no cause for complacency. In Yaiza on 16 December, Father Curbelo noted that

> The lava that had hitherto been rushing towards the sea had now changed direction ... Turning to the southwest, it reached Chupadero, which was soon [on 17 December] no more than a vast fire. Then it ravaged the fertile Vega de Ugo [1km east of Yaiza].

On 29 December the *Junta* again wrote to the *Regente*, but, for some unknown reason, their letter took a month to reach Juan Francisco de la Cueva in Gran Canaria. The delay cannot have improved his opinion of the *Junta* – and, indeed, he had already asked for more information on 12 January 1731. The delayed letter did, in fact, give details of the population distribution, the water supply and the areas of arable land and pastures. It also noted that some puzzling fumes had killed the herds near Chupadero, but 'some members of the *Junta* and many other persons, had crossed on foot, or on horseback, without coming to the slightest harm'. They survived because the lethal gas was probably carbon dioxide, which would lie close to the ground because it was denser than air. It did not become thick enough to asphyxiate humans, who naturally held their noses higher above the ground than their beasts. In the same letter, Melchor de Arvelos also described the latest lava-flows:

> The last mouth that opened near Mazo [Pico Partido] gave out fire in distinct branches, discharging as fast as the Betis [the River Guadalquivir], but with the difference that, whereas the waters carry light wood along, piles of incandescent rocks are being dragged along here in the flames vomited by the Infernal Fire-Dragon that is destroying the island.

The *Junta*, he added, had seen this with their own eyes and heard it with their own ears! They may genuinely have believed that they had been in the thick of the battle – escaping noxious gases and witnessing fluid lava-flows. No doubt they had done their modest best, and they were not impervious to the distress of the islanders. They foretold that the 'trembling and rumbling noises in the earth' and the 'fire and ash' seemed bound to bring 'great melancholy' and 'discouragement' in their wake, which could only herald 'a tragic end' and 'prospects of mourning'.

People May Leave for Any of the Canary Islands, January 1731

The *Junta* probably felt just as scared and helpless as the rest of the population. They were certainly just as bamboozled by the apparently erratic progress of the eruptions. They were, nevertheless, able to assess some of the needs of the inhabitants. They estimated that 600 families could still be supported on Lanzarote. The remaining 400 families must needs leave. The *Junta* warned against channelling all the refugees onto Fuerteventura, as the *Regente* had decreed, because it would place an unbearable strain on that island. The *Regente* saw the merit of this view and at once issued a further decree allowing 400 families to leave for any island of their choice, other than Fuerteventura. They could take all their goods and grain with them, so that they could sustain themselves without draining the resources of their future hosts.

Events in the New Year, if anything, took a turn for the worse. At Yaiza on 7 January 1731, Father Curbelo reported that

> new eruptions [from Pico Partido] completely altered the features formed before. Incandescent flows and thick smoke emerged from two new openings in the mountain. The clouds of smoke were often traversed by bright blue or red flashes of lightning, followed by thunder as if it were a storm. On 10 January 1731, we saw an immense mountain grow up, which then foundered with a fearsome racket into its own crater the selfsame day, covering the island in ash and stones . . . [Pico Partido then stopped erupting at the end of January.] But on 3 February, a new cone grew up [Montaña Rodeo]. The lava burnt the village of Rodeo . . . reached the sea coast . . . and continued to flow until 28 February.

The islanders were terrified and clamouring for help. Volcanoes seemed to be springing up all over the place without warning. Nobody had the slightest idea when, or where, the eruptions would strike again. Nobody could guess when the next village would be burnt. Nobody could foretell when the eruptions would stop. All that anyone could do was to try to palliate their effects. In the meantime, village after village was being destroyed – and over a dozen were eventually buried. Ash was blanketing some of the best agricultural land on the island. Crops were being devastated. Animals were starving – when they were not being gassed. The whole island was shaking and often covered in swirling volcanic dust. The 'Infernal Fire-Dragon' was attacking from all sides.

As Melchor de Arvelos wrote to the *Regente* on 19 February 1731, 'the neighbourhood is quite incapable of providing any bread, or vegetables, or any foodstuffs for the herds'. And not only that. A tremendous storm inaugurated Lent on Ash Wednesday and appropriately swept ash all over the shaking island. The devil seemed to be gaining the upper hand. His disciples, the British, might not be far away . . . The *Junta* thought that the British could easily take advantage of the plight of Lanzarote, and use it as a base from which to invade the other islands. But, by the middle of February, the *Junta* was thinking of keeping only a fortress garrison of 200–300 men to defend the island. They even dared to suggest that it should be maintained at the expense of the Royal Ministry of Finances.

The events of March can only have reinforced the impression of doom. Father Curbelo observed that another volcanic cone had grown up on 7 March, and sent out a lava-flow that had destroyed the village of Tíngafa and swept beyond it to the sea. Then, yet another outburst, beginning on 20 March and lasting eleven days, built up a small group of cones that formed the Montañas del Señalo, just to the south of the still-fuming Pico Partido.

Reports of Chaos, March 1731

The *Alcalde Mayor* and his *Junta* were not really up to their task. It seems, indeed, that the *Regente* received complaints about their inefficiency. But, to some extent, they obeyed the *Regente*'s orders, when, for example, they made a quite thorough geographical census of the needs and state of Lanzarote in the autumn of 1730. But, judging by the *Regente*'s later letters, they forsook the people in the end. At times, too, they begged for help and guidance. When they got it, they did nothing with it. They proved incapable either of implementing the *Regente*'s decrees or of offering leadership themselves. Reading between the lines of the letters, it is obvious that the situation on Lanzarote in the winter of 1731 must have been chaotic. The *Junta* must take much of the blame for this. They had tried to stop boats from evacuating refugees from the island and aid had been badly distributed. They added a lack of imagination to their incompetence.

On 8 March the *Regente* expressed the hope that the *Junta* had executed his latest measures 'with promptness, equity, and justice that would dissipate the repeated complaints expressed by the citizens'. A certain needle crept into his next letter, on 25 March. He ordered that:

> without protest, interpretation, or sundry other delay, boats should be brought to port, so that all those families . . . with their remaining grain, could leave for the island of their choice, as had been ordered already . . . [and] that the boat owners should comply, without fail, with the contracts established with the citizens for the evacuation of their persons, goods and grain.

The *Regente* acknowledged that it was, indeed, hard to strike the correct balance between all the varied vested interests on the island, but he complained that:

it was certain that the poor had not been looked after with the unceasing care which the Royal Court of Justice had commanded . . . Abuses have been without number, and the tyrannies and crimes of the transporting boatmen have gone unpunished . . . and the distribution [of aid], for which [the *Junta*] has been so often responsible, has not been observed.

Just in case the *Junta* had not yet got the message, the *Regente* added that it was 'irrational to sacrifice produce and population to defend the island and thereby probably lose everything'. The *Regente* had the power and most of the ideas. He followed a pragmatic policy, and altered his orders when circumstances dictated. Juan Francisco de la Cueva, then, gets high marks for his intelligent reactions to the changing nature of the emergency as well as showing compassion towards its victims. But even he threw in the towel after seven months.

The Regente *Appeals Directly to the Crown, 4 April 1731*

The *Regente* soon realized that threats could do no more, and he decided to appeal directly to the Crown. He sent the whole dossier of letters to Madrid for 'gracious and Sovereign approval' on 4 April 1731. The dossier reached the Marqués de la Compuerta at the palace, and he signified his approval of the *Regente*'s action on 12 May 1731. It is very doubtful if King Felipe V ever knew of the eruption. At forty-eight, he had gone mad – it was said – as a result

The *Regente*'s appeal to the Crown (detail).

Montaña Rajada, with the Montañas Quemadas beyond and Timanfaya on the skyline.

of continual erotic activity. He also did more for the royal aroma than the royal aura by neither washing, shaving, nor changing his linen. He usually thought he was a frog. The famous Neapolitan castrato, Farinelli, sang to him practically every night for nine years to bring solace to his troubled mind. The autocratic monarchy, the apex of a vast intercontinental empire, had more pressing problems than an eruption on a little Canary island.

Continued Tribulations at Yaiza, Summer and Autumn 1731

Father Curbelo stayed at his post with his flock in Yaiza at least until the end of 1731. The torment continued:

On 6 April, [the eruptions] started up again with even greater violence and ejected a glowing current that extended obliquely across a lava field that had previously formed near Yaiza. On 13 April, two mountains [of the Montañas del Señalo] collapsed with a terrible noise . . . On 2 May, a quarter of a league farther away, a new hill arose and a lava-flow threatened Yaiza. [This activity ended on 6 May, and a month of calm once again raised the hopes of the belea-guered villagers.]

On 4 June, three openings occurred at the same time, accompanied by violent earthquakes and flames that poured forth with a terrifying noise . . . and once

again plunged the inhabitants . . . into great consternation . . . On 18 June, a
new cone was built up between those that already masked the ruins of the villages of Mazo, Santa Catalina, and Timanfaya . . . [Pico Partido] then gave off
a white gas, the like of which nobody had ever seen before.

Then the focus of the eruptions suddenly switched 12km to the west, frightening the people as much by their unpredictability as by the disturbances that
they caused. These eruptions took place under the sea. A great mass of smoke
and flames, which could be seen from Yaiza, burst out with violent detonations from many places in the sea off the whole west coast; and the coast was
covered by enormous quantities of dead fish of all kinds, including some that
had never been seen before, probably thrown up from depths not previously
fished by the local fishermen. Soon afterwards, the eruptions resumed on land
again, but in yet another place. They formed the Montaña Rajada in July and
the Montañas Quemadas in the autumn. Once again, the outbreaks seemed
to be creeping closer and closer to Yaiza.

On Christmas Day 1731, the whole island was affected by the most violent earthquake yet experienced during the crisis. Three days later, a new cone was
formed; and another lava-flow was expelled that destroyed the village of Jaretas,
burnt the Chapel of San Juan Bautista, near Yaiza, but just failed to reach Yaiza
itself.

It seemed only a matter of time before Yaiza would be destroyed, so the people
decided to follow the example of many of their fellow islanders. They con-
ceded victory to the volcanoes. Father Curbelo and his parishioners emigrated
to Gran Canaria. Their subsequent fate is unknown, but they may well have
returned to Yaiza when the eruptions stopped in 1736. In fact, Yaiza itself was
spared. The flows that came closest to the village still missed it by about
100m.

1732–6

In 1732 and 1733 eruptions were concentrated in the area north of Yaiza and
they built up the Timanfaya and Montañas del Fuego volcanoes. Activity must
have simmered on for many months in this area, because these cones are
amongst the biggest formed during the whole period. It is not known exactly
how long the eruptions lasted, but they were still going on in January 1733,
when Bishop Dávila y Cardenas visited Lanzarote. He found the spectacle
rather disappointing:

The volcano was not uncovered during the three days that I was there [near
Yaiza]. All that could be seen was a light, as if it were from a candle. I did not
stay longer because my chest was affected by the dust from the sands.

Cultivated fields of *picón* in central Lanzarote.

The eruptions had their last fling in the spring of 1736. It happened very close to the place where they had first started, five and a half years before. In late March 1736, Las Nueces volcano was formed; and in early April a ten-day eruption built up the Colorada cone about a kilometre to the east. The eruptions stopped on 16 April 1736.

Three small eruptions, lasting barely two months all told, took place almost as an afterthought at Tinguatón, near Pico Partido, in 1824. Then . . . silence.

Written records are equally silent about the last years of the eruptions. It is certain that many of the people of Lanzarote suffered five and a half years of distress. They can scarcely have been consoled by those churchmen who urged little but prayers and repentance for the sins that, they believed, must have brought the eruptions to Lanzarote. The *Alcalde Mayor* and the *Junta* were incompetent, but the *Regente*, at least, had a pragmatic policy, although he was perhaps too quick to throw in the towel and pass the problem to Madrid.

Several tantalizing questions remain. What did the *Regente* or the *Junta* do after the whole dossier was sent to Madrid? Was the *Junta* dismissed? Did it regain the *Regente*'s favour? Or did inertia reign supreme until the volcanoes exhausted themselves in 1736? As for the practical lessons that might have been passed on to posterity, perhaps the main problem now is to decide if the emergency could have been handled any better. The only available recourse was to evacuate as many victims as possible from central Lanzarote to the safety of all the neighbouring islands. But this could only have been a provisional solution, for jobs would have had to be found for the evacuees for the best part of five years. Unemployed, they would have been a great potential source of unrest. With an empire headed by an incapable monarch, Spain at that time was probably less well equipped to tackle such a problem than any of the rivals with whom it so often went to war.

The Revival of Lanzarote

This great eruption, which caused such an administrative crisis and terrified the unsophisticated people, had a paradoxical result. The population grew. The island prospered as never before. Lanzarote had had about 4,967 inhabitants in December 1730. Perhaps as many as 2,500, or 3,000 people had left the island at the height of the eruptions. But, by 1744, the population had risen to 7,210, and it had reached 9,075 by 1768.

The eruption had enriched the soils of the central parts of the island in particular, leaving a fertile surface layer of fine ash and dust called *picón*. It was rich in nutrients, easy to handle and to plough, and it preserved valuable humidity from the sea air. With the careful husbandry that the people of Lanzarote were well able to bestow upon it, the land could now produce a wider range of crops than ever before. The farmers also learnt to plant their crops in individual small holes, about a metre deep, where they would be sheltered from the desiccating east winds from the Sahara. The farmers broke out from their previous dependence on cereals, sheep and cattle, and began to cultivate vines, onions, figs, almonds, potatoes, tomatoes and melons. Recently they have added other vegetables and flowers to their repertoire. Of course, the intractable lava-flows and the steep new volcanoes could not be handled in this way and still form the most brutal landscape in all the Canary Islands. They have now become a tourist attraction and part of a National Park. Dromedaries take visitors up the great cone of Timanfaya. The visitors return from their ordeal usually more enlightened about volcanic activity – and sometimes 'seasick' as well. They can seek consolation in the restaurant at the Islote de Hilario, where guides make much play of the steam and gases that arise from fissures nearby and set newspapers on fire with the heat. Much of the cooking in the restaurant is done using a similar source.

This heat provides more than just the raw material for a geothermal trick. It is a reminder – if not yet a threat. Temperatures of 600°C have been registered only 13m below ground, showing that molten rock is waiting for the next eruption. The eighteenth-century outburst killed nobody. Lanzarote, with its increased population and its flourishing tourist developments, might not be so lucky next time.

8

Laki, 1783

The eruption at Laki gave out the largest volume of lava recorded in historic time and, like the eruption on Lanzarote, the events were described by a parish priest. But Laki produced different, and far more widespread, disasters, including a famine, an unusually hot July, three very cold winters, and a wierd blue haze over much of Europe.

1783 was a terrible and amazing year. In February, a dreadful earthquake in Calabria, in southern Italy, claimed about 80,000 victims. In June, a prodigious amount of lava began to gush from a fissure on Laki ridge in Iceland. In July, exceptional heat and a dry blue haze spread over northwestern Europe. In August, 1,377 people died in Japan when Asama erupted. In September, the United Kingdom formally acknowledged the independence of the United States at Versailles. In November, Pilâtre de Rozier and d'Arlandes inaugurated human air travel with a trip over southern Paris in Montgolfier's hot-air balloon. December marked the start of one of the coldest winters of the century in many places in the northern hemisphere, and famine was already raging in Iceland and Japan. The eruption at Laki has been held responsible for some – if not, of course, all – of these events.

*

The southern coast of Iceland is an isolated, thinly populated expanse of tree-less meadowland, interspersed with rather boggy deltas. It is hemmed in by an arc of mountains stretching between two glistening ice-caps. To the north-east lies Vatnajökull, the largest ice-sheet in Europe, which culminates in the peak of Öraefajökull; and to the southwest lies its more modest counterpart, Myrdalsjökull. Both ice-caps partly mask systems of volcanic fissures that burst into life from time to time: Katla lies under Myrdalsjökull; and Grímsvötn is the most active of several systems beneath Vatnajökull. The Katla and Grímsvötn systems also stretch out to run alongside each other on the bare Sída uplands between the two ice-caps. Here, both Katla and Grímsvötn have had their hour of glory. Katla's came in AD 934 when the Eldgjà, the 'fire-fissure', spewed out 19.6km³ of lava – the largest flood of lava that has occurred on Earth during the last two thousand years at least. Grímsvötn's turn arrived in 1783, when some of its fissures opened parallel to the Eldgjà and only 5km away.

The row of cones along the Laki fissure.

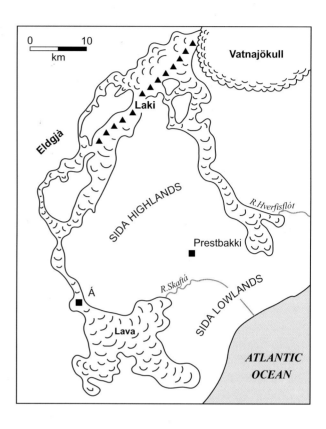

Laki and the Skaftár Fires.

This eruption has had a little problem with its name. The fissures split open across the flanks of the old volcanic mountain ridge of Laki. This is why, outside Iceland, it was called the Lakagígar, or 'Laki Fissure' eruption. But, in Iceland itself, where, after all, they ought to know, they call it the Skaftárel-dar, or 'Skaftár Fires', after the River Skaftá, whose valley was choked by the lavas. The fissure from which they erupted is thus called the Skaftáreldagígar. Such a tongue-twister for those unfamiliar with Icelandic no doubt led for-eigners to call the eruption after Laki.

The eruption had an experienced eye-witness. The Reverend Jón Stein-grímsson, minister of the Sída district from 1778 until 1791, lived at Prestbakki farm, on the coastal lowlands, about 40km south of Laki mountain. He had already witnessed the eruption of Katla in 1755 and he left by far the most reliable and detailed accounts of the events of 1783. Unfortunately for the international community, they were in Icelandic. But Thorvaldur Thordarson has recently translated them into English, along with other original sources, as part of his detailed studies of the eruption. This chapter thus owes much to his work – and also to Sigurdur Thórarinsson and John Grattan who analysed some of the major effects of the eruption.

The eruption began on 8 June 1783. The fissures eventually cracked open for 27km and built up a row of at least 140 cones of ash and cinders that com-monly rose about 90m high. This was nothing compared with the size of the lava-flows. They reached $14.7km^3$ – a volume exceeded only by Eldgjà in modern times and almost fifteen times as much as Etna expelled in 1669. Nearly two-thirds of the materials gushed out during the first seven weeks, and 90 per cent before the end of October. Then, as if exhausted by so much effort, the fissure spluttered on feebly for another three months before it whimpered to a close on 7 February 1783. But the eruption produced far more than spectacular volumes of molten lava. It set in motion the greatest natural catastrophe ever to strike Iceland. A strange blue haze covered the country; wildlife perished; farm animals died in their thousands; and famine in the land dragged droves of people to an early grave. Farther afield in Europe, the blue haze spread and persisted for many weeks; the sun glowed red like burning embers; and leaves shrivelled as if they had been nipped by frost, although July 1783 was one of the hottest months ever recorded there. The two winters that followed seemed exceptionally cold both in Europe and in North America.

Warnings

The first warnings of the eruption were only vague. About 20 May 1783, the vessel *Torsken* sailed past southern Iceland on its way from Denmark to the port of the Hafnarfjördhur. When the ship docked, the crew declared that they had seen 'a column of fire in the mountains or in the glaciers' lying to the north of the Sída district. This may have been the first of a series of eruptions of the Grímsvötn volcanic system in the part hidden beneath the Vatnajökull ice-cap. More cogent warnings soon followed. Earthquakes started, and after Ascension Day, on 29 May, they became so strong and frequent that many people in the area slept outside in the safety of their tents. In those days, they would have had no reason to suppose that the earthquakes might be heralding an eruption, but they had only to wait until Whitsun to find out.

The Skaftár Fires

Some eruptions have a proper sense of theatre: they know how to make an entrance. Thus, an outburst on any beautiful Whit Sunday morning stands a good chance of being remembered. In Iceland, where cloud so often hides the summits and volcanic activity is quite commonplace, the eruption that began on Whit Sunday, 8 June 1783, had no prospect of ever being forgotten – especially when its consequences were so serious.

At nine o'clock on Whit Sunday morning, Jón Steingrímsson and his parishioners noticed 'a black volcanic cloud' rising up beyond the hills on the northern skyline. The ground cracked and rumbled as the fissure opened southwest of Laki mountain. Soon the cloud of ash spread over the coastal lowlands on the gentle northwesterly breeze, and made it dark inside the houses. Fine ash, 'like the remains of burnt coal' and 'glittering hairs that could easily be crushed between the fingers', showered down lightly for a few hours. But, that afternoon, a southerly breeze sprang up which blew the ash northwards throughout the next day.

The weather changed for the worse on 10 June. The ash erupted in several columns as the fissure lengthened. Rain began to fall, mixed with sandy ash, inky mud and fine hairs of lava. It smelt 'like a mixture of nitrate and sulphur'. It was acid rain, burning bare skin, making eyes smart and scorching leaves. The ash lay about a centimetre deep on the ground, so that footprints were visible in it. On 11 June an easterly wind brought a cold snap and a snowfall. The following day, the snow lay knee deep near the River Skaftá gorge.

Nobody had yet approached the source of the eruption, 40km away in the hills to the north. Instead, the eruption came to them. On 10 June, the River Skaftá dried up: the lava had cut off its headwaters near the Vatnajökull icecap. The next day some farmers from Síða went wood-cutting in the River Skaftá gorge. Suddenly, that afternoon, they saw a glowing red-hot lava-flow come surging down the gorge towards them. They grabbed their belongings and ran off just in time, then stood and watched the molten lava splashing against and bouncing off the walls of the gorge like a stream in flood. It had no trouble in overwhelming the logs that they had just cut, nor all the forest trees that they had left standing . . .

Away on the uplands the fissure lengthened, and more lava spewed out and careered down the gorge. On the evening of 12 June the snout of the flow, glowing like molten copper, emerged from the gorge and spread over the wet lowland, steaming, spitting and hissing, and cracking like gunfire. It soon destroyed the meadows of the farm called Á, 35km from the fissure. The unusually fluid lava had advanced by an average of at least 7km a day. As lava flows go, this is very fast.

Nevertheless, on 13 June, a party of farmers braved the elements and trekked up to inspect their summer pastures in the hills. They were rewarded with a splendid display from the molten lava. It was a sight fit to warm the heart of the devil himself. They counted a line of twenty-seven vermilion fountains spurting skywards, and one mighty lava-flow racing down into the River Skaftá gorge. Chastened and awe-struck, they returned home convinced that the seething mass of molten lava must soon swamp their farms.

The flow resumed all its old vigour on 14 June, rumbling down the gorge and shaking the ground. Volcanic earthquakes and thunder and lightning from the column of erupting ash, visible 250km away, kept everyone awake for most of the following night. They had good reason to be on the lookout. The River Skaftá gorge, 35km long, 500m wide and 160m deep, was already almost choked with lava. In the lowlands, the snout of the advancing flow seemed to be as much as 40m high as it swept over the valuable Brandaland timber-cutting area, covering good pastureland and the farms of Á and Nes. It was said that each farm had been worth 1,200 silver coins. Their inhabitants had just enough time to load their movable property onto their carts and abandon

Laki lava flows in the Skaftá gorge.

everything else. Volcanic earthquakes were shaking the ground and making the timbers of the houses creak and groan as if they were about to collapse. Ash showered onto the farmlands, and with it fell curious hairy lava fragments that shone bluish-black and looked like seal-hair. Sometimes the wind rolled them into hollow bundles like miniature tumbleweed blowing across the Nevada desert. A strange blue fog and the nauseating smell of sulphurous fumes began to hang over the lowlands, and those with bad chests soon could scarcely breathe. It started to rain heavily. The surviving birds abandoned their eggs, but they 'were hardly edible because of their bitter and sulphurous taste'. Prospects looked bleak. As one farmer later confessed, everyone was convinced that Trinity Sunday, 15 June, 'would be their last day alive'. In this, at least, they were unduly pessimistic.

Still, events took a gloomier turn during the next few days. The earthquakes, the thunder and the spurting lava-fountains continued. On 17 June, Jón Steingrímsson saw a lava-fountain from his home at Prestbakki, which meant it must have been shooting over 800m skywards. On 18 June, the blue fog also appeared in central and northern Iceland; and the sun now often looked blood red, even at noon. During the next five days, more molten lava gushed from the fissures, filled the River Skaftá gorge to its very brim, rushed southwards over the coastal lowlands in a steaming black delta, destroying the farming hamlets of Hólmi, Fljótar, Hólmasel and Botnar, and almost reached the sea. Sometimes, the lava even pushed under the soil and rolled it up like a carpet as it advanced.

On 20 June, several farmers took courage again and went up to the hills to see how the summer pastures had fared. They realized that meat, milk and eggs would soon be in short supply. Lava had swamped two-thirds of their valuable grazing land, and, with it, the fields of Icelandic moss and angelica roots that helped to vary the people's monotonous diet, as well as the nesting-grounds of swans and other birds that provided them with eggs. At mid-summer, Saturday 21 June, Jón Steingrímsson recorded that 'a huge amount of ash fell on Sída, followed by sleet and snowfall so that the mountains became white'. At about the same time a pale coating of 'sulphur' fell along with the ash over northern Iceland.

On 23 June, stronger earthquakes began again. On 25 June, the fissure duly lengthened, explosions built up cones of ash and cinders along it, and the finer ash and dust rose up in a column perhaps 12km high. On 27 June, the largest of all the ashfalls showered onto the coastal lowlands, forcing farmers in Fljótshverfi, to take refuge farther to the west. Haymaking was impossible. In Sída itself, the farmers had to rake the ash from the pastures so that their livestock could reach their food. When most of the gases had exploded from the fissures, the molten lava swished upwards in great fountains, many of them licking more than 1,000m skywards. A strong sulphurous smell often spread throughout the area. Then, as the fountains waned, the lava gushed forth in blazing torrents into the nearest valleys. On 29 June another molten mass surged from the Skaftá gorge onto the lowlands.

This was the pattern – of ash, lava-fountains and flows – that was to be repeated throughout the first five months of the eruption. But none of this regularity was obvious to the anxious folk on the coastal lowlands, who had no idea what would happen to them next. And the Icelanders did not realize that death had not yet served them its most urgent notice.

Then on 25 July, eruptions more or less completely stopped on the fissures southwest of Laki. The truce did not last. On 29 July, 'with rumbles and a boiling sound', an entirely new fissure cracked open on the northeastern flank of Laki, directly in line with its predecessors. Ash eruptions, lava-fountains and lava-flows followed as before, but this time the flows took a new route to the lowlands via the River Hverfisfljót gorge, which drained the area to the north-east of Sída. This gorge was 15km long, but just as deep and wide as the gorge of the River Skaftá. It suffered the same fate. The flows filled the gorge to the brim before the end of the month and also oozed across the coastal lowlands, but, once again, they failed to reach the sea.

From mid-August, the eruption began to decline. So, apparently, did the reporting diligence of Jón Steingrímsson and the other witnesses. Henceforth, they limited their remarks to the major events. There were, however, similar, but rather smaller, surges of molten lava, and showers of ash, and 'sandy rain' as the northeastern fissures cracked open further during September and October. But most of the far-reaching eruptions were over by 25 October 1783 and no flows reached the lowlands after 30 October, although ashy rain did shower down upon them throughout November. Afterwards, the fissures extended as far as the edge of the Vatnajökull ice-cap, but the eruptions became weaker and weaker until they finally petered out on 7 February 1784. But throughout 1784, the north wind often blew a sulphurous smell over the coastal lowlands, and Grímsvötn volcano itself continued to erupt at intervals under Vatnajökull until 26 May 1785.

The lava had killed nobody, but it had covered, or badly damaged, perhaps as many as twenty-one farming hamlets. Two complete parishes were uninhabitable for two years. Sinister black lava buried churches, farmsteads, woodlands and meadows. Luckily, the area had had a small population, but this was little consolation to those who suffered great hardship. Nevertheless, the people did not give in. Within a few years, fourteen farming hamlets were rebuilt on new sites close to the edge of the solidified lava-flow. Perhaps only three hamlets were abandoned for ever.

But long before the eruption ended, the problem had changed scale altogether, and was soon to become a major social and economic crisis. Its impact in 1783 was all the greater because Iceland was then a poor agricultural country on the very margins of viable farming. Denmark ruled Iceland and ran it as a dependent colony, exploiting its agriculture and restricting its trade. The population of Iceland may have exceeded 100,000 during the balmy days of warmer climate and independence during the Middle Ages, but it had probably never risen above 50,000 since the Danes had taken over in 1380. Conditions had worsened during the seventeenth and eighteenth centuries because the climate had become colder and wetter during what scientists now call the 'Little Ice Age'. Crop yields in Iceland diminished, and upland farms and marginal lands had to be abandoned. The subsistence farming that had enabled the people to eke out an existence for centuries was now becoming a desperate struggle for survival.

In 1778 there were 49,863 Icelanders; and many of them were already poverty-stricken and undernourished. The slightest epidemic, environmental mishap, or even any whim of the weather might kill them. The eruption of Laki provided this environmental mishap; and it caused a crisis without precedent. It did not spring from the lava or the ash, but from the toxic gases, especially fluorine and sulphur dioxide, that hissed from the fissures along with the lava.

The eruption liberated about 8 megatonnes of fluorine; and the sulphur dioxide combined with the humidity in the air to form an aerosol of sulphuric acid amounting to some 150 megatonnes. Apparently, such sulphurous exhalations have only been matched in recorded history by two eruptions: at Tambora, in Indonesia, in 1815, and by Laki's Icelandic neighbour, Eldgjà, in AD 934. The effects of the fluorine were concentrated in Iceland, but the sulphuric aerosol formed the curious dry blue fog that spread not only over

Iceland, but all over Europe and beyond. In Iceland, it gave its name to the great disaster that it brought – the 'Haze Famine'.

The Haze Famine

Within ten days after the start of the eruption, the thick, acrid, blue haze of the sulphuric aerosol had spread all over Iceland. The sun was the colour of glowing charcoal for most of the day; the air was heavy and smelt of sulphur; and visibility was reduced to one kilometre or less. Raindrops were often acid enough to burn dock leaves and exposed human skin. The blue haze made people's eyes smart, made them cough and exacerbated their asthma. Metals tarnished, and, sometimes, a precipitate of sulphurous compounds coated the land in a white dust. Jón Steingrímsson reported that

> the hairy sand-fall and sulphurous rain caused such unwholesomeness in the air and in the earth that the grass became yellow and pink and withered down to the roots. The animals that wandered around the fields got yellow-coloured feet with open wounds, and yellow dots were seen on the skin of newly shorn sheep, which had died.

The farm animals died of malnutrition, starvation – and chronic fluorosis. When fluorine reaches concentrations of 250 parts per million of the dry mass of grass eaten by animals, it causes chronic fluorosis that will kill within a few days. Smaller concentrations, of some 20–40 p.p.m. for instance, will kill animals after a few months. In either case, they develop 'bone-sickness': their bones go soft and grow tumours; they cannot stand up; and they lose their teeth and cannot eat. Death is inevitable. The animals contracted fluorosis first in the summer on the upland pastures where the fluorine was most con-centrated, but those on the lowlands only succumbed during the autumn. The beasts that had not developed fluorosis had to eat withered grass covered with a layer of ash, which ground their teeth to stumps and choked their lungs and kidneys. There was no fodder to replace the dead grass. Milk yields from both sheep and cattle soon dwindled to much less than half their average. Then these animals also began to die. Their masters were already coughing and spluttering. They, too, soon started to feel the pangs of hunger, for mutton, milk and beef were the mainstays of their diet. Little by little, these sources of food were eliminated. Even the fish seemed to have vanished; and, in any case, the strange fog was often so thick that the fishermen could not find the fishing grounds out at sea. The people also developed dysentery and scurvy, caused by a lack of vitamin C. They, too, started to die before the year was out.

The summer had been dark, dank and drear. There had even been thick snowfalls on 11 and 21 June 1783. Often, fine ash lingered in the air to darken the gloomy, hazy days still further. When the haze thinned as the eruption declined in the autumn, the winter of 1783–4 provided the knock-out blow.

In Iceland, it was one of the most severe in a century in which harsh winters had not been rare.

In Iceland during 1783 and 1784, over 10,000 head of cattle (half the total stock), 27,000 horses and about 190,000 sheep (three-quarters of the total stock of each) perished. These were the vital elements upon which the rural community depended almost totally. Hunger, malnutrition, disease and death cut through the hapless, isolated and almost defenceless population. Iceland became a land of mourning. Before the famine came to a lugubrious end in 1785, one fifth of all the population of Iceland – 10,521 people – had died. The 'Haze Famine' directly caused 9,300 of these deaths. There were only about 39,000 bereaved survivors, who formed probably the lowest population in Iceland for 500 years. Perhaps the most sensible thing for them to do would have been to emigrate to the newly independent United States, rather than remain on the verge of starvation under the yoke of an uncomprehending Denmark. Most Icelanders, however, had other ideas. They had children instead. The catastrophe provided an opportunity and a spur. From 1786 to 1800, the birth-rate averaged 4 per cent a year and the average annual death-rate just 2.5 per cent. By 1824, the losses caused by the famine had been made up, and the population had risen to 52,630 by 1830. Just as had happened in Lanzarote half a century before, the volcanic onslaught produced a positive and lasting human reaction. The prophets of doom were confounded again.

'An Almost Universal Perturbation in Nature'

There were prophets of doom a-plenty in Europe in 1783. Long before news of the eruption had filtered from Iceland, its effects spread across the continent and on into Asia and north Africa. Ash, the blue sulphuric haze, a red sun, uncommon gloom, oppressive heat, violent thunderstorms and scorched vegetation were puzzling, worrying, and sometimes even frightening Europeans from Hampshire to Moscow. As the *Leeds Intelligencer* remarked on 15 July 1783, 'there seems lately to have been an almost universal perturbation in nature . . . All Europe has been shaken by some uncommon convulsions'. In France, people were 'talking very seriously of the end of the world'. Nobody could be sure whether these events were symptoms of a great calamity that had happened in some distant land, or worrying portents of yet worse to come. It was, perhaps, just as well that 1783 was not the millennium.

The clouds of ash, steam and gas from the Laki fissures soared between 7km and 13km skywards, especially during June and July 1783. They were much smaller than the likes of Vesuvius could produce, but they rose high enough, at times, to reach the stratosphere. The upper winds could then carry their nasty effects far beyond Iceland.

During the first week of the eruption the ash and aerosols were swept northwards over the Arctic Ocean. Then the upper winds changed direction and swirled towards Europe. Black, gritty ash thinly crusted ships sailing across the

North Sea. It blackened the fields and spoilt the crops in the Faeroe Islands, western Norway and in Caithness in northern Scotland, where they remembered 1783 as 'the year of the ashie'. The wind carried the finer particles on to Denmark, Holland and Germany; and, in Venice, an impalpable dust fluttered down like manna onto the *Serenissima*, and proved to be so rich in iron that it was attracted to magnets.

But far more widespread was the curious, persistent pall of dry blue haze which had spread all over Iceland by 17 June. Between 16 June and 19 June, it made its first appearances in Scandinavia, Holland, France, Germany, Switzerland and Poland. It was first reported in Britain on 22 June, and it arrived in St Petersburg on 26 June, in the Middle East at the end of the month and in North Africa and Central Asia in early July. Sailors docking at Le Havre, said that they had run into the fog out in the Atlantic Ocean, well before they entered the English Channel. For more than two months thereafter, it scarcely cleared; instead it thickened notably over Europe in the later parts of June, July and August, as more gas apparently gushed from the Laki fissures.

The effects of the acid aerosol in Europe were less severe than in Iceland. The cocktail was usually too weak to kill animals, but strong enough to scorch leaves, grass and cereals. Wherever the haze persisted, pre-industrial Europe got a foretaste of the pollution that was soon to scar manufacturing areas such as the German Ruhr and the English Black Country in the following century. Some 3,000kg of sulphuric acid precipitated onto every square kilometre in the northwestern half of Europe in July 1783. This is four times the average concentration per square kilometre over the earth at present. Nobody had seen anything like that in 1783.

Its effects in England were typical. The Reverend Gilbert White of the village of Selborne, in Hampshire, remarked that 'the sun, at noon, looked blank as a clouded moon, and shed a rust-coloured, ferruginous light on the ground and floors of rooms, but was particularly lurid and blood-coloured at rising and setting'. Often, indeed, neither sun, nor moon nor stars could be seen less than $20°$ above the horizon. The poet, William Cowper, observed that the sun rose and set 'with the face of a red-hot salamander'. His more prosaic contemporaries compared it to hot pewter, molten copper or glowing charcoal. The 'thick and heavy air' often reduced visibility to less than one kilometre and trees and other objects seemed distorted. This was no normal fog. It was notably dry, often smelt distinctly of sulphur, and the 'uncommon gloom' did not disperse when the wind or weather changed. Sometimes, a white dust precipitated from the sky and carpeted the ground like a hoar frost.

The Reverend Sir John Cullum described events in his parish near Bury St Edmunds, in eastern England, on 23 June 1783 in a letter to the Royal Society of London. Barley and oats turned brown, rye seemed mildewed, but wheat was less affected. Hardy Scots pines and larches were 'damaged and looked shabby'. Ash trees, walnuts, cherry trees and hazelnuts all shed their leaves plentifully, and 'vegetables appeared exactly as if a fire had been lighted near them that had shrivelled and discoloured their leaves'. Nevertheless, some del-

icate plants, such as mulberry and fig, were unhurt where they were growing
on a protecting wall. Sir John attributed this damage to an 'unseasonable
frost'. Indeed, some claimed to have seen a white frost at 3 a.m. on 23 June
and others said that they had seen ice in water-butts. The evidence, though,
better fits the effects of acid pollution. The Reverend Baronet was probably
misled: a frost severe enough to damage Scots pine would certainly harm fig
trees, however protective their wall. If there really had been a frost, it was inci-
dental. But the conflicting evidence shows how equivocal even quite detailed
testimony from a less scientific age can be. Nevertheless, there is overwhelming evidence from much of Europe that the acid aerosol damaged the vegetation in 1783.

The dry blue haze persisted throughout Sweden, Holland, Belgium,
Germany, Bohemia, Poland, France and Hungary virtually until the end of
1783. Hungary offered a more general exception to the woeful tales of
damaged crops. The yields of wine, wheat, peas and beans were abundant –
perhaps because they had been so well watered by the two dozen storms that
occurred between the arrival of the haze on 23 June and the end of September 1783. In France, too, irreparable damage was far from universal. For
instance, July had been so boiling hot at Dreux, 75km west of Paris, that the
harvest had all been safely gathered in on 14 August 1783. Other areas were
not so lucky. In Grenoble, the fog in July was as dense as in winter. In the
nearby Alps of Upper Provence and Dauphiné, the haze lurked above the
summits; the summer warmth never arrived; and life was very unpleasant for
the transhumant sheep and cattle that had come from Provence to feed on
the usually lush pastures. Back in lower Provence, conditions must have been
dire indeed, for 'many people even lost their appetites'. An anonymous contributor to the *Journal de Paris* on 9 July 1783 recommended a diet for those
forced to live in the acid haze. They should drink mineral waters; eat red, acid
fruit; drink water with a little added vinegar, which had given vigour to the
troops of Ancient Rome; eat vegetables whenever possible; take one or two
glasses of pure wine with meals; and not venture out on an empty stomach.
(No doubt they would then have felt fit enough to tuck in to Provençal cuisine
as soon as the fog lifted.)

The blue haze bleached and altered the colours on painted canvases at
Neuchâtel in Switzerland, which proved that the haze really was what would
later be called an acid aerosol. It upset the houseproud Dutch ladies of
Groningen when it turned their polished brass door-knockers white. In Italy,
in July, boatmen did not dare venture out into the obscurity of the Bay of
Naples without taking a compass with them. Laki was even daring to taunt
Vesuvius . . .

On 29 July 1783 the *Leeds Intelligencer* revealed British provincial fears, by
describing those abroad:

The foreign papers mention that the haziness, which has lately prevailed here,
is general throughout all the southern part of Europe. It is even observed upon

the most lofty of the Alps. In Italy, it has occasioned great consternation, as the same appearance of the air was remarked in Calabria and Sicily a little previous to those dreadful earthquakes that have destroyed so many cities. The people of France, too, began to forbode some dire calamity. The Paris Gazette mentions that the churches are most unusually crowded, and the shrines of their saints uncommonly frequented.

As befitted the most intellectual nation in Europe, the French savants quickly sought precedents and explanations for these strange happenings. On 4 July, in the *Journal de Paris*, an unnamed member of the Académie des Sciences expressed his regret that irrational fears had spread through enlightened France. He condemned 'the conjectures which begin amongst the ignorant even in the most enlightened ages, proceed from mouth to mouth until they reach the best society, and even find their way into the public prints'. He offered a perfectly rational – and totally wrong – explanation that the haze was the natural result of the effect of hot sunshine on the ground that had been previously drenched by prolonged heavy rains. There was, therefore, nothing to fear now.

The Provençal geologist, Paul-Robert de Lamanon, assured readers of the *Journal de Paris* on 9 July 1783 that cities like Paris, Madrid and Vienna were protected from a calamity on the Calabrian scale because violent earthquakes only took place where very high mountains, the sea and volcanoes occurred together. There was, it must be said, more than a grain of truth in this assertion. (De Lamanon, incidentally, was soon to see many volcanoes. In 1785 he joined the La Peyrouse expedition to the Pacific Ocean, saw Hawaii and was one of the first Europeans to set eyes on the Cascade Range from the sea. He was killed and probably eaten on the island of Vanikoro in 1787.)

Enlightened France did, however, enjoy something of an intellectual triumph in the end. It was on 7 August 1783, in Montpellier in southern France, that the French naturalist, Mourgue de Montredon, first suggested the link between the dry fog and an eruption in Iceland. It was only during the following year that Benjamin Franklin, American Ambassador to France, put forward a similar link in an article revealingly entitled 'Meteorological Imaginations and Conjectures', read in 1784 to the Literary and Philosophical Society of Manchester, England. Franklin believed that the haze had either come from 'Hecla' volcano in Iceland – or that it had occurred when the earth had passed through a 'smoky region in space'! Nobody could be certain. So how could anyone be sure what else was in store?

After-effects?

Whatever the doubts and speculations of the time, the way that the sulphuric dry blue fog spread, with its retinue of red suns, uncommon gloom and withered crops, now leaves little doubt that the eruption of Laki was responsible.

Two other contrasting features of the weather have also been added to the dire dossier of the eruption: a hot and stormy July in parts of Europe in 1783; and three successive severe winters in 1783–4, 1784–5 and 1785–6 in Europe and eastern North America – if not throughout the whole northern hemisphere. But the late eighteenth century was a period of climatic extremes, and the two possible climatic effects of the Laki eruption are hard to prove, leaving room for doubt, speculation and, sometimes, ingenious arguments. Quantitative records were still defective at this time so that earth scientists are forced to rely on qualitative weather reports and sporadic statistics, which are notoriously unreliable and often exaggerated. The 'worst', 'coldest', 'hottest' or 'wettest' weather 'in living memory' seems to crop up every few years. This is why careful analysis of European weather in the 1780s has been so valuable. What, then, might have been the climatic effects of the eruption of Laki beyond Iceland?

STORMY WEATHER

July temperatures in northwest and central Europe were between 1°C and 3°C higher than the 1768–98 mean. Temperatures were over 3°C warmer in Holland and Denmark; over 2°C warmer in England, Belgium, northeast France and northwest Germany, southern Sweden and southern Norway, and over 1°C warmer in central France, central Germany, Switzerland and Austria. But in all these places, the August temperatures were about average – although the dry fog still persisted.

The heat was notably unpleasant in England, where daily temperatures often exceeded 24°C in July. As Gilbert White reported from Selborne,

> The heat was so intense that butchers' meat could hardly be eaten on the day after it was killed, and the flies swarmed so [much] in the lanes and hedges that they rendered the horses half-frantic and riding irksome.

If the horses were affected, then things in England were serious indeed . . . July 1783 was to prove the warmest month in central England from the start of records in 1659 until 1983 and the global warming of the 1990s. The mean temperature reached 18.8°C, some 2.7°C above the July mean for 1770–95. (However, the mean temperature for the summer as a whole was 16.5°C, whereas it had reached 17°C in 1781.) July 1783 was also the warmest month recorded in Copenhagen between 1768 and 1893 and the second warmest in Edinburgh between 1764 and 1896; it was also unusually hot in Stockholm, Geneva, Grenoble, Berlin and Vienna.

The persistent dry fog seemed to be irritating the overheated atmosphere and the fearsome thunderstorms might have been an obvious consequence. These raged over vast areas of Britain, for example, on 2 July, 10 July and 17 July. At least twenty-four people and dozens of farm animals were killed – chiefly struck by lightning. The delightfully named *Exeter Flying Post* reported that during the storm in Gloucester on 2 July, 'the women, shrieking and crying, were running to hide themselves, the common fellows fell down on their knees in prayers and the whole town was in the utmost fright and consternation'. On 15 July, the *Leeds Intelligencer* reported that the storms had even caused consternation in Yorkshire. People were 'apprehensive that the time of the grand consummation of all things was at hand', and some clergymen took the chance to urge their flock to repent before the Day of Judgment dawned.

Summer storms in continental Europe are common because of the convection caused when the land heats up. In July 1783, many places recorded over half a dozen unusually fierce storms which were damaging enough to have made the headlines – if headlines had then been in vogue. In spite of the evident attraction of lightning to church steeples, it was an old-established central European custom to ring church bells during a storm. This was a custom that was clearly in need of review, for a German scientist calculated that, between 1750 and 1783, lightning had struck 386 steeples and killed 103 bell-ringers. Thus it was that, on 4 July 1783, at Dobraken church, near Pilsen in Bohemia, lightning killed six bell-ringers, and badly scorched another four. The storm then swept on into Hungary and thirty people died in Eger. During another storm near Amalfi in Italy, lightning killed forty – apparently rather unwise – reapers in the fields. Almost sixty people met their deaths in storms in Provence and the French Alps. To cap it all, lightning killed some of King Louis XVI's horses at Versailles at the end of the month. And, in spite of all this dreadful sacrifice, not one of these storms dispersed the dry blue haze.

But not all the areas covered with the sulphuric haze were warmer than usual in July 1783. At the very source of the haze, Iceland was 1.3°C cooler than the 1768–98 mean temperatures; and Russia, Siberia and the Balkans were about 1°C cooler. On 19 July, for instance, heavy snow fell around Moscow, although the haze persisted unabated throughout the month.

The best explanation for this weather pattern seems to be that a high pressure system stayed over central Germany in July 1783. The resulting clockwise circulation of the winds would bring warm southerly air to northern Europe and pull cold northerly air over Russia. Thus, indeed, southerly winds occurred four times more frequently than average in Britain in July 1783. Did the Laki eruption cause the high pressure, or just help to maintain it, or have nothing to do with it at all? There must be a distinct possibility that the abnormal July heat only coincided with the eruption. After all, the haze did not coincide with the region of abnormal heat: it covered a much *wider* area, and lasted for several months *longer* – into the autumn of 1783. The heat is more closely linked to the high pressure system in July than it is to the sulphurous fog from Laki. On the other hand, the dry fog could well have helped the storms to develop. One ingenious line of recent research has suggested that the high pressure system concentrated the aerosol near the ground, absorbing both the incoming solar energy and the outgoing radiation from the earth to cause the abnormal July heat. Once the high pressure system declined, so did the heat. Thus, the high pressure would be the prime cause of the heat; the Laki sulphurous aerosol would only be a secondary contributor.

COLD WINTERS

Many volcanic aerosols have been accused of causing cold weather, including those erupted from El Chichón in 1982 and Pinatubo in 1991. But they were violent eruptions that expelled vast clouds of aerosol and dust into the stratosphere, and caused cold weather by preventing some of the sun's heat from reaching the earth's surface. The three winters of 1783–4, 1784–5 and 1785–6 were amongst the most severe in the past 250 years – virtually wherever records were kept in Europe and North America. Their harshness was much more widespread than the heat of July 1783. Spring droughts were also long and frequent; and, in France at least, the wine vintages were drenched and ruined by continuous autumn rains. Iceland itself suffered temperatures of minus 15°C for most the winter of 1783–4, whereas, since 1900, the mean winter temperature for northern Iceland has been only minus 1.7°C. The next two Icelandic winters were only slightly warmer.

In eastern North America, temperatures from December 1783 to February 1784 were 4.8°C below the 225-year means; the winter of 1784–5 was still 3°C below the mean; and the winter of 1785–6 was 2°C lower. Mean temperatures were often cooler by similar amounts in Europe, too. And the winters were depressingly long. Unremitting frost prevailed from 21 December 1783 until the end of February 1784 in Copenhagen. In Trondheim, Norway, temperatures rose above freezing on only four days between 21 December 1783 and 5 April 1784. At Selborne in Hampshire, Gilbert White lamented that the winter had become established by 16 November 1783 and the frost had continued for weeks. On New Year's Eve, ice had formed under people's beds, water-bottles had burst in bedrooms, and meat had frozen solid. On 25 January 1784 the turnip stocks had turned to mush, and on 29 January dung and stable litter had frozen under the horses. There were frequent snowfalls until the end of April 1784 – and by December 1784 the next winter was well under way.

It was just the same across the English Channel. In the Paris basin, the long winter stretched from 9 December 1783 until after 20 February 1784. Snow lay over 60cm thick in the fields; and temperatures were 4°C colder than average in Paris. Then came a long spring drought, lasting from April to June, that halved the yields of fodder, cereals and vegetables. A wet autumn followed and reduced the wine vintage. The next winter, 2°C colder than average, lasted from 20 December 1784 until April 1785, and brought in its wake yet another spring drought, a rotten autumn, and a third long winter in 1785–6, when, at least, the temperatures remained about average. By now there was widespread misery in rural France; hungry peasants flocked to the towns in a vain hope of finding food and jobs. They became a desperate, famished and malleable underclass instead. For two years, however, the weather seemed to relent. Then, on 1 November 1788, began yet another harsh winter; it was 3°C colder than average, and it lasted over five months until 11 April 1789. The people were on their knees – if not in their sickbeds or in their coffins – when the States General met at Versailles on 4 May 1789 and marked the first act of the French Revolution. But it takes more than a revolution to stop harsh winters: the winter of 1794–5 proved to be the coldest of the series in Paris and, for good measure, in central England as well. (To counterbalance the swing, however, the winter of 1795–6 was the warmest during the last thirty years of the eighteenth century, with temperatures some 3°C above average in France.) Geography and climate do not dictate the course of history, but they can some-times limit the choices or opportunities that are available to people. Clearly, for instance, the French and British did not adopt the same course of action at the time. Nobody – not even the most ardent historical revisionist – would, of course, claim that the Laki eruption caused the French Revolution.

Studies of the influence of eruptions on past weather have only come to the fore since the 1970s, and it seems that violent eruptions that are also rich in sulphur compounds have the most marked cooling effects on the weather. The eruption of Laki in 1783 gave off plenty of sulphur, but most of the aerosols stayed below the stratosphere and fell to earth within about a year. Thorvaldur Thordarson, who has made the most detailed studies of the whole problem, suggests that the eruption could well have been responsible for the cold winter of 1783–4. It might, then, have taken a further two years for normal climatic patterns to be resumed, because of the knock-on effect in the Arctic Ocean. The eruption of Laki aerosols would have kept the Arctic Ocean unusually cool during the summer of 1784, when frost stayed in the Icelandic soil until July and ice was far more common than usual in the nearby ocean. The ice would cool the air – which then spread over the northern hemisphere. This more stable, cold, dry, air would also sustain high pressure systems for longer periods. In turn, this would block the progress of low pressure systems that would normally bring westerly winds and warmer, wetter conditions to Europe. In fact, westerly winds did blow far less often than average just after the eruption. But this knock-on effect gradually wore off and 'normal' condi-tions returned in 1786. Thus, the eruption of Laki could have caused the cold winters of 1783–4, 1784–5 and 1785–6.

But, on the present scientific evidence available, the eruption of Laki cannot be held responsible for the very severe winters of 1788–9 and 1794–5. Did vol-canic eruptions – at present unidentified – cause these? On the other hand, when the shivering sufferers during the winter of 1783–4 looked for historical precedents, they often referred to the awful winters of 1708–9 and 1739–40, although neither of them has yet been attributed to volcanic activity. So it is *just* possible that the three cold winters after the eruption of Laki were a coincidence.

It is also possible that another volcano – Asama, in Central Japan – con-tributed to these harsh winters. Asama began erupting on 9 May 1783; its intensity increased on 26 July and it rose to a violent climax on 4 and 5 August. The Japanese summer was unusually cold. The rice harvest failed and there was a famine. However, the volcanic materials that Asama ejected into the stratosphere were relatively poor in sulphur dioxide, which implies that this eruption would have had little effect on the climate. On balance, therefore, it seems that the eruption of Laki probably did cause all those odd meteorological events between the autumn of 1783 and the spring of 1786.

9

Cosegüina, 1835

For 150 years, the eruption of Cosegüina was believed to be one of the greatest in recorded history. It was 'full of sound and fury', but its importance seems to have been rather inflated, perhaps because a civil war was raging at the time. Indeed, one of the best accounts came from a distinguished army commander. The importance of this eruption, then, lies more in its vigorous image than in its impact.

The Stupendous Convulsion, January 1835

The Central American republic of Nicaragua has packed an impressive amount of turbulence into a history of less than two centuries; and only earthquakes and eruptions appear to have been more violent than its political and social quarrels. It seems entirely appropriate that thirty volcanoes should stand in a threatening line across the state. Cosegüina lies at the northwestern end of this chain, and crowns the peninsula that juts out into the Pacific Ocean to enclose the Bay of Fonseca. Cosegüina owes its prominence more to its striking situation than to its height, because it rises a mere 862m above sea-level. It is amongst the smallest of the world's more violent volcanoes – but then, of course, Krakatau was even smaller.

When Cosegüina erupted in 1835, it could boast of an unusual distinction: it made so much noise that it was mistaken for a participant in a civil war. After the Spanish Empire in the Americas collapsed in 1821, the new Central American states of El Salvador, Nicaragua and Honduras formed a federation that was loosely modelled on the USA. They were joined for a time by Guatemala and Costa Rica, but the arrangement proved so unsatisfactory that a complicated civil war soon broke out between many rival factions. The Federal army fought to put down these revolts and preserve unity, but the tottering Federation collapsed altogether in 1839.

The eruption of Cosegüina created an enormous stir in Central America. It soon became notorious as the 'great' eruption. Some of the exaggerations associated with the outburst were undoubtedly caused by the civil war. All over Central America, the eruption had sounded like noisy gunfire, but nobody could quite make out where it was coming from. This uncertainty can only have heightened the tension, increased the bewilderment and excited the imagination of the marauding bands and the hapless townsfolk and villagers in the Central American forests. Thus, when news of the eruption was confirmed, everyone was only too keen to believe that it had, indeed, been more violent than it eventually proved to be.

Cosegüina.

124

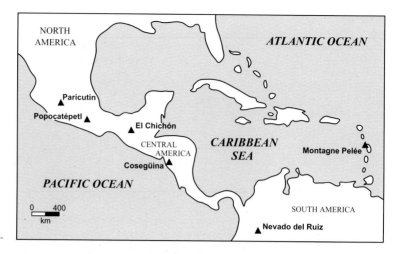

Volcanoes of
Central America.

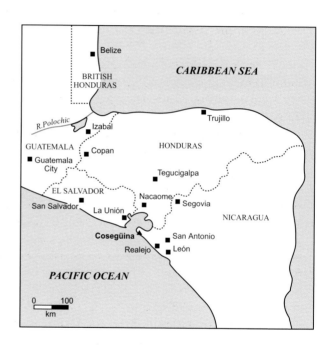

The location of Coseguïna.

One of those who was inadvertently responsible for establishing this inflated reputation was Colonel Juan Galindo. He would have been well worth meeting. One of the leading commanders in the Federal army, he was also a man of culture, and one of the few people in Central America then interested in its ancient Mayan ruins. Even better, Juan Galindo was also a corresponding member of the Geographical Society of London. He took time off from his military duties to send vivid eye-witness accounts of what he described as 'one of the most stupendous convulsions of the globe ever known in America'.

Alexander Caldcleugh – our man in Chile – added to its glamour when he compiled a report on the eruption from faraway Santiago de Chile for the Royal Society of London in 1836. He even compared the outburst of

Coseguïna with the eruption of Vesuvius in AD 79. 'No volcanic eruption in modern times,' he wrote, 'has been recorded that reached the frightful extent of the one which I have now had the honour of laying before the Royal Society.' He believed that it had even surpassed the enormous explosion of Tambora, in Indonesia in 1815, which is still considered to be perhaps the greatest eruption of the past 2,000 years.

John L. Stephens provides a flavour of the view of the eruption that had already become established by 1840. He was the author of the very successful *Incidents of Travel in Central America,* in which he described his epic journey through the wars and forests of that area in 1839–40 as the unofficial envoy of US President Van Buren. Politics may have been his prime concern, but, like Juan Galindo, he was also interested in the Mayas. When he was trekking through the forests of Honduras, he had bought the site of the great Mayan ruins at Copan for $US50. Volcanoes, for him, were a mere sideline, but Coseguïna impressed him nevertheless:

> Before me was the volcano . . . with its field of lava and its desolate shore, and not a living being was in sight, except my sleeping boatman. Five years before . . . I [had] read in a newspaper an account of the eruption . . . Little did I then ever expect to see it; the most awful in the history of volcanic eruptions . . . The face of nature was changed; the cone of the volcano was gone; a mountain and field of lava ran down to the sea; a forest old as creation had entirely disappeared, and two islands were formed in the sea; shoals were discovered, in one of which a large tree was fixed upside down; one river was completely choked up, and another formed, running in the opposite direction; seven men in the employ of my *bungo*-proprietor ran down to the water, pushed off in a *bungo,* and were never heard of more; wild beasts, howling, left their caves in the mountains, and ounces, leopards, and snakes fled for shelter to the abodes of men.

Some of this was true. But such an episode in a best-selling book was enough to establish the reputation of Coseguïna amongst the cultured public. John Stephens, of course, was only repeating what others had reported. One very early rumour, which he did not repeat, even claimed that three large towns and several villages had been submerged and that eruptions and earthquakes had occurred near the Caribbean coast of Honduras as well as near Belize. Far-fetched indeed – in more senses than one . . .

So it was that, for 150 years, practically everybody who knew anything about volcanoes thought that Coseguïna had produced an outburst of fearful size, worthy to rank with the greatest eruptions in recorded history. Recent reappraisal has downgraded this outburst. It was powerful, yes, but not quite up to the standards of Krakatau or Vesuvius. This revision is even borne out by careful reading of the contemporary accounts – once the obvious fantasies and scenes of horror and panic have been eliminated. Coseguïna, in fact, caused relatively little damage to settlements – and even less loss of life.

Eye-witness accounts suffered from an exaggerated vocabulary, which tended to obscure the facts. This was not Central American bombast – after all, one of those who reported the eruption was a British Fellow of the Royal Society of London. The eruption was certainly more powerful, and probably noisier, than any in that area within living memory. Those who saw it, therefore, had little else with which to compare it. And the country was at war . . . The story of the 'great eruption of Coseguïna in 1835' has to be viewed not only through the eyes of its contemporary witnesses, but also through the harsh spectacles of hindsight.

What did Coseguïna really do? The volcano erupted mainly from 20 January to 23 January 1835 and then whimpered along afterwards until the end of the month. The explosions made a fearful noise and pulverized the molten rock into very fine fragments which formed huge clouds of volcanic dust with the consistency of flour that quickly rose over 25km into the air. The upper winds winnowed the dust from the clouds and scattered it widely around Coseguïna. At the height of the eruption, nuées ardentes surged down the slopes of the volcano and completely swept away the luxuriant tropical forest that had clothed the cone and the peninsula around it.

A Prologue?

It is not absolutely certain when Coseguïna began to erupt . . . Before the eruption apparently started, Colonel Juan Galindo was camping at Salama, deep in the forests between Guatemala City and the Caribbean seaport of Izabal. He reported that

> On the night between 16 and 17 January, I distinctly heard continued noises similar to those produced by volcanic eruptions, yet with something particular in the sounds, which made them rather resemble the discharge of single large guns.

It may well have been real gunfire that he heard. If the experienced Colonel could not tell the difference, how could common mortals be reassured?

20 January 1835

The eruption seems to have started with no more than 'a slight noise and smoke' on 19 January. By 6.30 on the following morning, a magnificent and expanding pyramidal cloud was already soaring up from Coseguïna. From San Antonio, 80km to the south, it looked 'like an immense plume of the whitest feathers'. First it became tinged with grey, then with yellow, and finally it changed to crimson as glowing red-hot ash shot from the summit. From El Viejo, a sheet of fire seemed to rise straight into the air. At Nacaome, some

64km to the north in Honduras, fine ash began to fall at about 11 a.m. and at noon the cloud of many colours had plunged the city into such darkness 'that nothing whatever could be distinguished'. Alexander Caldcleugh reported that at 5 p.m. the ash there was 8cm deep, although the shower soon abated and 'respiration became relieved'.

Spectators had the best view of events in La Unión in El Salvador, 48km across the Bay of Fonseca. The local Commandant, Manuel Romero, sent a report to the Federal authorities, which Colonel Galindo transmitted to the Royal Geographical Society in London soon afterwards:

[On 20 January], the day having dawned with usual serenity, at 8 o'clock, towards the southeast, a dense cloud was perceived of a pyramidal figure, and accompanied by a rumbling noise . . . It covered the sun . . . [and then] the whole firmament about eleven, and enveloped everything in complete darkness, so that the nearest objects were invisible. The melancholy howling of beasts, the flocks of birds of all species that came to seek . . . asylum amongst men, the terror which assailed the latter, the cries of women and children, and the uncertainty caused by so rare a phenomenon – all combined to overcome the stoutest heart, and fill it with apprehension. [At 4 p.m.], the earth also began to quake, and continued in a perpetual undulation, which gradually increased. This was followed by a shower of phosphoric sand, [which lasted until 8 p.m.], when a heavy and fine powder, like flour, also began to fall.

The sea was no safer. On 20 January, an inshore vessel, a *bungo*, with seven men aboard vanished without trace. The Colombian galleon, *Boladora*, left Acapulco in Mexico and sailed into darkness and dust as it passed Coseguïna on its way to Realejo in Nicaragua. The crew believed that they would soon be suffocated and spent forty-eight desperate hours shovelling dust from the decks. They were unable to reach Realejo, but eventually arrived at the port of Caldera. The incessant shovelling must have gone to their heads, because they had convinced themselves by then that the whole of Nicaragua had disappeared.

That evening, Coseguïna calmed down a little, but more explosions during the night sent out shock waves that made the land rock like a drunken sailor for 80km around the volcano. Thunder and lightning went on all night. The noise of the explosions reverberated through Central America like a fusillade.

21 January 1835

At Nacaome on 21 January, Alexander Caldcleugh reported that the morning had started clear, but had become 'thick and hazy' by 8 a.m. as the ash poured down on the city. The dust showered over El Salvador, southern Guatemala and southern Honduras throughout the afternoon. Much nearer the volcano, pumice the size of chick peas rained down on Tigre Island in the Bay of Fonseca. About 3 p.m., earthquakes described as 'undulations of the earth' rocked the whole area stretching from Realejo and San Antonio, in the south, to beyond La Unión in the north. In La Unión, the Commandant reported that the earthquake, at 3.08 p.m., had lasted an unusually long time, and that

> Many men, who were walking in a penitential procession, were thrown down. The darkness lasted forty-three hours, making it indispensable for everyone to carry a light, and even with their aid, it was impossible to see clearly.

Other violent explosions shook the earth at about midnight, but it seems that no buildings collapsed. The nearest main settlement was, after all, 48km from the volcano. The people were terrified, nevertheless. The explosions constantly reminded them that the civil war was not, perhaps, the greatest of the dangers that they had to face.

22 January 1835

A glimmer of pale light returned to La Unión on 22 January, but the sun could still not be seen. The thickest part of the dust cloud seems to have spread southwards that day. Alexander Caldcleugh described how fine, white ash began to fall on San Antonio on the morning of 22 January. A great black cloud spread across the sky, and

> within half an hour, it was more utterly dark than during the most clouded night. So intense was this darkness that men could touch without seeing each other, the cattle came in from the country with all the signs of alarm and uneasiness, and the fowls went to roost as on the approach of night. This state of complete darkness prevailed until the following morning.

Back in the forests of eastern Guatemala, Juan Galindo was camping on the night of 22 January with his men on the banks of the River Polochic. The apparent firing began again.

> Both my men and myself had been accustomed, during our whole lives, to hear volcanic eruptions in all parts of Central America; yet for some hours, we entertained not the least doubt that the noise was produced by artillery, and that it proceeded from the direction of Izabal. I could not, therefore, but conclude that a [military] action was taking place in that port; though, again reflecting on the improbability of such an event, a conjecture occurred to me that the Commandant, in some extraordinary state of inebriation, was celebrating his installation, his birthday, or some other event. I thus continued in the utmost uncertainty, being more and more puzzled by the long continuance of the firing. Towards morning, it is true, the noise became confused, and consequently more resembled ordinary volcanic eruptions.

No wonder Colonel Galindo was becoming rather paranoid. Next day, when the company was sailing downriver, they met some fishermen canoeing upstream. The Colonel immediately suspected that they were either troops in disguise or arms smugglers. He confessed later, however, that his men had eventually managed to dispel his doubts.

At that time, Juan Galindo could have had no idea which volcano was erupting. In any case, his main problem was not to identify the culprit, but to decide if a skirmish really had taken place. It is still puzzling, nevertheless, that the noises seemed to be coming from Izabal, to the east, whereas Coseg̈uina lay to the south. However, unless the forests had generated some peculiar echoes, it seems most likely either that fighting had started in Izabal, or that the Commandant was, indeed, as drunk as the Colonel suspected.

23 January 1835

Once again, Coseg̈uina made a fearful noise throughout the night. Near dawn at La Unión, a sober Commandant Romero heard 'tremendously loud thunderclaps coming from the volcano . . . like the firing of pieces of artillery of the highest calibre'. Then dust deluged the town.

When a veiled light returned at La Unión on 23 January, the town presented 'a melancholy spectacle'. The dust was so thick that it had completely covered the rockiness of the streets – a great novelty in an area unused to snow. The people, themselves, were so thickly coated with dust that they could not recognize each other except by the sound of their voices. The dust-shrouded houses and trees looked macabre. But just as everyone was starting to feel a little better, intense darkness returned to the town. Explosions boomed out. Yet more volcanic dust fell. This time there was panic. As Commandant Romero noted,

> although leaving the place was attended with imminent risk from the wild beasts which sallied from the forests and sought the towns and high roads . . . yet another terror [from the volcano] was superior: and more than half the inhabitants of La Unión went forth on foot, abandoning their homes, well persuaded that they should never return to them, since they prognosticated the total destruction of the town, and fled with dismay for refuge to the mountains.

These conflicting migrations must have caused some very interesting encounters in the suburbs . . .

There was just as much terror in León, which was then the capital of Nicaragua, and was situated 88km from the volcano. A violent earthquake had accompanied the rumblings from Coseg̈uina on the night of 22 January. The following day, the whole area was 'in the most fearful darkness', the explosions were 'terrific', and about 25cm of ash fell. The official report of events in the capital described how some citizens proposed a different solution to the crisis:

> This scene . . . produced in the minds of all the most terrible impression. It was attributed to the Divine anger; and the people ran in crowds to the temples to implore the mercy of Heaven. The garrison of the town at the same time kept up incessant discharges of cannon and musketry, which was done by order of the government, on the advice of some intelligent chemists, who thought that the atmosphere might be cleared by letting off rockets, lighting fires, and causing all the church bells to be rung.

Some of these antics had been tried before elsewhere. Rumour had it that they had succeeded. Rumour was wrong. The eruption did, indeed, wane the next day, but probably not because of the initiatives taken in León. Nevertheless, the hullabaloo can hardly have soothed taut Nicaraguan nerves. Explosions and earthquakes also rocked Nacaome that day and the dawn light was soon replaced by total obscurity, enlivened only by lightning. The dismayed citizens firmly believed that the Day of Judgment had arrived. An impalpable white dust covered everything. It was so fine that the 'slightest breath of air drove it into every interstice'. What is more, it was giving off a nasty, 'fetid, sulphurous smell'.

Further afield, at Segovia in Nicaragua, and in Tegucigalpa, 130km away in Honduras, for instance, falls of evil-smelling dust were followed by torrential rains. Such storms were almost unheard of during the dry season in Central America. Truly the harmony of nature had been upset. What was the world coming to? Perhaps they should not have revolted against the Spaniards after all?

24 January 1835

On 24 January, the eruption quickly began to lose its power and long calm intervals soon separated the explosions. Weak daylight returned to the stricken towns around Cosegüina, although clouds of fine dust still veiled the sky. As early as 3.30 a.m. the moon and the stars could be seen at La Unión, but 'as though through a curtain'. For the next three days the volcanic dust fell incessantly, masking the sun and eventually lying 13cm deep in the streets. Frequent earth tremors kept the citizens in a high state of nervous tension. The buildings rocked, but none fell down. In Nacaome, improved visibility revealed that many birds and little animals had been suffocated and lay dead in the dust that was now 20cm deep in the streets. Wild animals that had sought refuge in the town were roaming the streets. Streams, choked with ash and dust, had 'cast upon their shores an innumerable quantity of fishes in a torpid state, and some dead'.

Noise

If darkness and dust were the two main characteristics of the eruption, its third – and most widespread – aspect was the noise it made. Coseg̈uina was full of sound and fury. It was heard from as far as Oaxaca, 1,100km away in Mexico to the north, and at Bogotá, 1,750km to the southeast in Colombia. All those who heard it thought that the noise was coming from close at hand. Where the eruptions could not be seen, the explosions were taken for gunfire, or war – even when they seemed to be coming from some strange places. When the noises continued, puzzlement often turned into fear of a surprise attack by armed gangs. In Guatemala City, for instance, troops grabbed their weapons and rushed out from their barracks, believing that an approaching enemy had fired off a cannonade. They could just have been rather over-excited – but, even so, they were 640km from the volcano.

Because noise travels faster than rumour, and both travel faster than the truth, the last ten days of January 1835 in Central America were fraught with fear and worry, even well beyond the area where two or three days of darkness had prevailed.

Those who were showered with dust or rocked by earthquakes at least knew what they were afraid of. The people in La Unión, San Antonio and Nacaome, the main towns nearest to Coseg̈uina, realized that the volcano was the source of their misfortunes. In more distant cities, such as Trujillo on the Caribbean coast of Honduras, where volcanic dust often accompanied the noise, the inhabitants thought that the volcano responsible must be close by. Some 175km northwest of Coseg̈uina, in the Federal capital, San Salvador, imaginations were, of course, more sophisticated. Rumour there had it that the culprit was San Vicente volcano, a day's journey to the east. What was more, some even claimed that 'the heart of the indigo-producing country had been destroyed and 40,000 people had perished'. But, as Colonel Galindo drily remarked, 'subsequent accounts have shown the falsity of these conjectures'. There had been no such catastrophe.

Some 560km from Coseg̈uina, in Belize, the capital of British Honduras, the officers of King William IV could not decide whether the bangs were coming from a warship in distress, or from a naval battle in the Federal civil war. Just to be on the safe side, the port superintendent fired off the guns of the fort to answer a possible distress call. There was no reply. He did not have to interfere further: a war outside British territory was no concern of His Majesty's troops.

Colonel Juan Galindo was also honoured with some of the most picturesque rumours ever associated with anyone reporting a volcanic eruption:

In the interior of the forests [of British Honduras], the inhabitants universally believed that it was myself attacking their port with a Central American [Federal] force. At Petén [in northern Guatemala], it was likewise supposed to be myself at the head of an independent insurrection in the British settlement.

Epilogue

Coseguïna quickly calmed down after 24 January. But near the volcano, daylight came back slowly because the dust was so fine that it lingered on in the atmosphere until the end of the month. The dust that reached the stratosphere travelled at a speed of about 270km a day and probably spread throughout the northern hemisphere. Noticeable amounts fell 700km away in southern Mexico, and 1,280km away in Jamaica. Some experts in the nineteenth century believed that between 50km^3 and 150km^3 of dust had fallen, but these rather wild estimates have now been reduced to about 5.6km^3. Even a few decades ago, the dust was still reputed to have masked the sun's heat and thereby lowered average world temperatures for several years after the eruption. Some estimated that the dust veil had been four times greater than that expelled by Krakatau in 1883. This also is now considered to be very doubtful. It was, indeed, cooler than usual during the late 1830s. But it now seems that average temperatures began to fall as early as 1828, well before the eruption. Coseguïna, then, was not to blame for this cooler decade.

When the air finally cleared at the end of January 1835, a bare and fuming Coseguïna was revealed. Part of its summit had collapsed into a crater, 600m deep and 3km across, in which nestled a steaming lake. All the surrounding forests had been stripped away. Two new islands of 'pumice stone and mineral earth' now arose in the Bay of Fonseca, one 730m and the other, 180m long, and both had a 'coppery smell'. A tree had been rammed upside down into a shoal. The flanks of Coseguïna were still fuming so much that it was hard to make out where the land ended and the sea began. Ash had completely choked up the River Chiquito and the small stream that had replaced it was now flowing in the opposite direction. All this fuming mass was the remains of the nuées ardentes that had surged down the slopes of the volcano at the climax of the eruption and had killed the seven men who had tried to escape from the peninsula in the small *bungo* boat. At the southern foot of the volcano, the nuées ardentes had completely destroyed the Hacienda Sasamapa and all its livestock. Don Bernardo Benevio's Hacienda Coseguïna, 8km from the crater, hardly fared any better. At least 3m of pumice had destroyed, and partly buried, all the dependencies, fields and woodlands. About 300 head of cattle were in such a 'weak and wretched condition' that many died soon afterwards. At the edge of the devastated area skirting the foot of Coseguïna, farm animals and wild beasts roamed around for days suffering from shock, with their flesh scorched red-raw. Their luckier companions had died quickly and their decaying bodies, along with the corpses of thousands of dead birds, were cluttering every path and stream and floating out into the Bay of Fonseca.

The main settlements had been well beyond the reach of the nuées ardentes. Their main problem was the falling dust, although it does not seem to have piled up thickly enough to make roofs collapse. The seven unlucky men killed in their *bungo* in the Bay of Fonseca were joined by only one other casualty: a little girl in La Unión.

As the Commandant of La Unión later recorded,

> Many of our people are afflicted with catarrhs, headaches, sore throats, and lung
> infections, resulting, doubtless, from the dust. Several persons are thus seriously
> unwell; and yesterday a girl of seven years old died with symptoms of an inflamma-
> tory sore throat. The cattle in the neighbourhood are also suffering.

All this was sad, but it was scarcely the greatest volcanic disaster of the era.
Indeed, the Governor of León even reported good news from his province:

> It does not appear that the damage was anywhere so great as was imagined at
> the period of the catastrophe. The sand and ashes which were scattered over
> the plains, rather contributed to fertilize them . . . [Where] rain fell a few days
> afterwards . . . the plants showed a most luxuriant appearance, the pasture rose
> rapidly, and everything seemed to promise a forward spring.

Colonel Galindo added a parting shot to his own account, which may, or may
not, also qualify as good news. At the height of the eruption, 'the terror of the
inhabitants of Alencho, anticipating the approach of the Day of Judgment,
was so great that 300 of those who lived in a state of concubinage were married
at once'.

Married bliss, and the repose of Coseguïna did not, alas, end the civil
war, which dragged on for another five years. At length, at Tegucigalpa, in
Honduras, in February 1840, the Federal army was routed by the insurgent
separatist troops in a battle that marked the death-knell of the Central
American Federation. The Colonel fled from the battlefield with a couple of
dragoons and a servant boy. They were recognized in a native American
village. It was there that someone hacked Juan Galindo to death with a
machete.

Nº 4. About 4.40 P.M.

Nº 5. About 5 P.M.

W. ASHCROFT DEL.

Nº 6. About 5.15 P.M.

10

Krakatau, 1883

Although the reputation of Cosegüina has been punctured, the eruption of Krakatau has suffered no such fate. It is still rightly regarded as one of the most spectacular eruptions in recorded history, whose effects were felt the world over. Much of the uninhabited island of Krakatau sank into the sea, and most of the thousands of victims met an unexpected form of death across the Soenda Straits.

Krakatau erupted for 100 days. The climax started on a Sunday lunchtime and continued for fifty hours. Its most ferocious and devastating outburst lasted for about five hours on a particularly nasty Monday morning. The noise of the explosions reached farther than any sounds hitherto recorded. The eruptions occurred near, or under, the sea and they generated powerful sea-waves, or tsunamis, that swept away almost everything on the low-lying coasts of the Soenda Straits. Noticeable waves then spread across all the oceans in the world. Erupted ash caused widespread, total and suffocating darkness. Floating pumice clogged the seas for several months. Fine ash, dust, gas and shattered fragments of Krakatau were thrown into the stratosphere, where they formed an aerosol that encompassed the globe several times. The aerosol caused sunsets so beautiful that artists took out their easels, journalists and scientists produced their most purple prose, and some conscientious citizens called out the fire brigade.

*

Krakatau lies in the Soenda Straits, between Java and Sumatra in Indonesia. In early 1883 it was an uninhabited, thickly forested island, 4km wide and 9km long, that was made up of a line of about half a dozen volcanic cones. Rakata, in the south, formed the highest point, at about 822m; Danan rose in the centre; and, in the north, the even lower cone of Perboewatan had been the site of the last previous eruption in 1680–1. By the end of August 1883, two-thirds of Krakatau had vanished, and 36,417 people were dead.

In 1883, Indonesia was the Dutch East Indies, then in their colonial heyday; and the capital, Jakarta, was then called Batavia. The Soenda Straits formed one of the most concentrated international shipping lanes in the world, funnelling trading vessels between Europe and the Far East. However, apart from the helmsmen, nobody needed to take much notice of Krakatau. Yet, in a country of volcanic giants, this inconspicuous little island produced the most famous eruption of the nineteenth century and its effects were amongst the most widespread of any volcanic outburst in recorded history.

Sunsets painted by Ascroft at Chelsea, London, 26 November 1883.

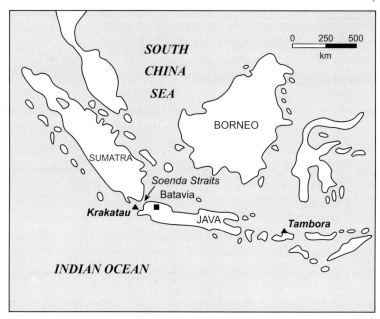

The location of Krakatau.

In all, Krakatau ejected about 20km³ of ash and pumice. This was a very large eruption indeed, and was especially interesting because it was so varied. Yet it is full of paradoxes and ironies. Ash and nuées ardentes killed only about 4,500 people. Krakatau drowned most of its victims. Experts still differ greatly – and sometimes angrily – about exactly how the tsunamis were caused. Was it by the explosions themselves, by the collapse of northern Krakatau when the crust weakened, or by the gigantic landslides that ensued? Or all three? Although many thousands of people witnessed the culminating outburst over a vast area, nobody saw what exactly took place on Krakatau itself. No dispassionate observer was present. A ship approached within 18km of the island, but the eruption was revealed only briefly through the swirling ash. Not a single photograph of the climax exists and survivors rarely timed events accurately. The eruption produced deafening explosions, violent air waves, hurricane force winds, suffocating darkness, lightning and gigantic sea-waves that induced deep shock, anguish, terror and death throughout the Soenda Straits. The victims had little time to consult their watches or jot down notes. They ran for their lives, not for their diaries. And most of them were at least 40km from Krakatau. The geological evidence is often fragmentary and ambiguous. Much of the ash and pumice ejected now lies below sea level, and, when two-thirds of Krakatau collapsed, it carried much of the material evidence with it into the abyss.

In 1885, Dr Rogier Verbeek analysed the eruption in a classic monograph, *Krakatau*, in which he assembled the testimonies of survivors and correlated them as best he could with time controls established in Batavia. The pressure gauge at the gas works in Batavia registered the explosive shock waves from

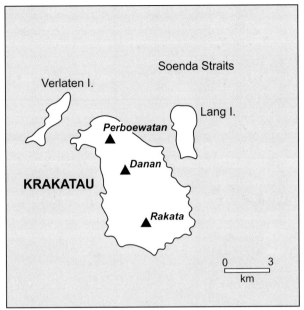

Krakatau before the eruption in 1883.

Krakatau after the eruption in 1883.

Krakatau and the tidal gauge at Tandjong Priok, the port of Batavia, recorded many of the sea-waves. Logs from ships in and around the Straits also helped to time the ashfalls and storms. Learned monographs have been devoted to several major eruptions, but few have also been honoured with an investigation sponsored by such an eminent body as the Royal Society of London – not to mention a centenary volume, *Krakatau 1883*, published by the Smithsonian Institution of Washington. Nevertheless, more than a century after the event, the story of the paroxysm of Krakatau must still remain a flickering cinematographic impression.

Krakatau, 20 May–26 August 1883

There had been some rather weak spluttering from Perboewatan at the northern end of Krakatau in 1680–1. It was Perboewatan, too, that started everything again in 1883, when it burst into life at 6 a.m. on 20 May. A column of ash and steam shot 11km into the air in thirty minutes. Explosions reverberated 155km away in Batavia and, for a few days, ash fell on southern Sumatra. Then there was a lull. On 27 May mining engineer Schuurman chartered the steamer *Gouverneur Generaal Loudon* to take sightseers from Batavia for 25 guilders. A new crater on Perboewatan, 1km wide, rewarded them with explosions every five or ten minutes – 'and all experienced a festive and pleasant day'. The vessel was to approach Krakatau again in rather less festive circumstances before August was out.

The eruption resumed – revitalized – in mid-June. The crest of Perboewatan was blown off, and two more erupting centres burst into action, probably on Danan cone in the middle of the island. By mid-July, banks of pumice were floating in the Soenda Straits. During a calm interval on 11 August, a government surveyor, H. J. G. Ferzenaar, became the last person to set foot on old Krakatau. It was fuming, murky and shrouded in ash, and its luxuriant forests had been burnt. In the third week in August, bigger and more frequent explosions expelled dark columns of ash and steam that impressed the multitudes of spectators on the coastal plains of Java and Sumatra fronting the Soenda Straits. All this was but a portent for one of the largest eruptions of historic time. At noon on Sunday, 26 August 1883, more than 36,000 people thronging the coastlands of the Soenda Straits had already begun their last twenty-four hours on earth.

The coastal plains along the Soenda Straits were rarely more than 5km wide or rose 50m above sea-level. They were backed, especially in Sumatra, by thickly forested hills. These intensely cultivated plains formed an intricate patchwork of paddy-fields and stands of sugar-cane. Hundreds of kampongs, or villages, full of hens cattle and children, emerged from clusters of coconut palms, breadfruit trees, banyans and mangoes. The local people lived in flimsy huts made of rattan wickerwork and thatched with palm leaves. The main towns on the Straits were Teloeq Betoeng and Ketimbang in Sumatra, and Merak, Anjer and Tjiringin in

Krakatau erupting on 27 May 1883.

Java. Each had a population of about 10,000, mostly composed of indigenous people. Each also had a Chinese and, perhaps, an Arab quarter. The few Dutch colonial administrators lived in villas of white-plastered brick or stone, with red-tiled roofs. They were built on small knolls, as befitted the status of their owners. Overseers oversaw. 'The Dutch flag flapped happily in the sunshine.'

Anjer was generally thought to be the prettiest town, but all enjoyed fine views over the islands and promontories of the blue Straits. All these settlements were at least 40km from Krakatau. Only the pepper cultivators on the islands of Sebesi and Seboekoe Ketjiel lived any closer, some 20km and 30km, respectively, north of the volcano. Nobody lived on Krakatau. When the eruption ceased, nobody was left alive on Sebesi or Seboekoe Ketjiel either.

Batavia and Buitenzorg, 26–27 August

Dr Verbeek was at home in Buitenzorg, in western Java, when the climax of the eruption started on 26 August. Krakatau delivered its opening salvo at 12.53 p.m. The noise of the explosions took nearly fifteen minutes to travel the 155km to Buitenzorg and to the capital, Batavia. They sounded just like distant rumbles of thunder. At that moment, the *Medea* was nearing Batavia. Captain W. Thomson saw Krakatau emit 'a black mass rolling up like smoke in clouds'. He measured its height. The crest soon rose 25km into the air. Four hours later, the column was much wider and over 36km high. The following day, it must have soared well over 50km skywards.

As afternoon turned into evening, explosions became louder and more distinct throughout western Java. In Batavia, the Night Gun was fired at 8 p.m., as usual, from Fort Prins Frederick. Its noise used to irritate some of the citizens. Now, for once, it sounded like a child's pop-gun amid the din. During the night, the explosions 'became so severe that almost nobody in West Java dared to go to sleep'. Many people, fearing an earthquake, spent the night in their gardens or walking in the Koningsplein in Batavia.

Monday, 27 August dawned with a bang in western Java. In Buitenzorg, Dr Verbeek's house was amongst those facing west: lamps burst and plaster fell from the shaking walls at 6.45 a.m. In Batavia it also felt cold; the temperature had dropped to 18°C instead of the usual 27°C. The explosive crescendo was recorded in Batavia with some precision in an unexpected way. It was noticed later that the explosions had sent the pressure gauge at the gasworks into frenzied oscillations, with the most violent shocks recorded at 6.36, 9.58 and 10.45 a.m. All these powerful explosions beat out the rhythm marking the ejection of 20km^3 of ash and pumice, the collapse of part of the earth's crust, and the foundering of two-thirds of Krakatau into the resulting abyss. Then the explosions became weaker and more sporadic and only a few dying spasms were recorded after noon.

But few in Batavia were watching the gauge at the gasworks. It began to grow dark at noon. It was eerie. Ash muffled the sounds. Business and traffic were abandoned. What on earth was going on? At about 12.30 p.m. when the darkness was deepest, a sea-wave over 2m high suddenly flooded into the Batavia Canal. Two people were drowned in the confusion and many small craft were smashed. This was the largest of eighteen waves registered during the next thirty-six hours on the tidal gauge at nearby Tandjong Priok.

The general sense of foreboding only lessened a little after 2 p.m. when the ash stopped falling and the cocks started crowing again to celebrate the return of daylight. By then, the ash lay 10cm deep in the streets and a distinct smell of sulphur filled the air. Everyone wanted to go home; even after the explosions seemed to have come to an end. Sensible people were still convinced that these calamities must have come from a volcano much closer than Krakatau. They could not have realized, then, that the cold, the darkness, the ashfalls, the odd sea-wave, and all the confused poultry were events on an entirely different scale from those occurring in the Soenda Straits.

Soenda Straits Coastlands, 26 August

In the Soenda Straits on Sunday, 26 August, it was quite obvious where the noisy culprit lay. Krakatau had been erupting since lunchtime. A succession of very loud detonations just after 5 p.m. was followed by a rain of ash and warm lumps of pumice that lasted for an hour. Thereafter fine ash showered down more or less continuously over a gradually widening area. The ash

Krakatau and the Soenda Straits in 1883.

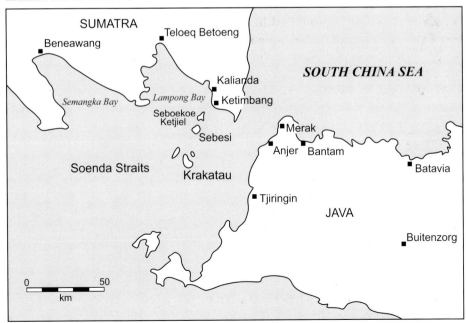

spread fastest towards Sumatra. It began to fall on Lampong Bay at about 6 p.m., but only reached Anjer in Java about 9.30 p.m. Throughout the Straits, however, the increasingly vigorous explosions made the sea 'behave unnaturally' after six o'clock. One minute it was violently agitated and the next it was quite calm. Occasionally, the waters surged up almost 2m, and then ebbed away just as much, and just as quickly, smashing many small craft in the process. Tjiringin on Java and Teloeq Betoeng in Sumatra both witnessed such floods about 6 p.m.. Unknown to anyone elsewhere at the time, a larger flood at about 7.30 p.m. completely washed away the Chinese workers' camp at the stone quarry at Merak, in Java. It was 65km from the volcano.

That Sunday evening in Anjer, roaring explosions were shaking the ground and the sea had become very rough. There was a violent thunderstorm to add to the fiery glare shining above Krakatau. Telegraph-master Schruit was gallant enough 'to reassure several ladies who were alarmed and excited by the surrounding phenomena'. Things – and, no doubt, the ladies as well – calmed down at Anjer after 9.30 p.m., just as the ash began to fall on the little town.

Ketimbang, Sumatra, 26–28 August

On Sunday, Krakatau was apparently concentrating its efforts in a northerly direction, over Sebesi island and around Ketimbang, 40km away in Sumatra. No witnesses survived to tell of their agony on Sebesi. Controller Beyerinck and his wife recorded their experiences in Sumatra. Mrs Beyerinck proved to be remarkably resilient.

Sunday afternoon was much more turbulent in Ketimbang than in Java. Pea-sized pumice fell for hours and heavy waves crashed farther and farther up the shore. Upstairs at her home about 8 p.m., Mrs Beyerinck and her three children were trying to concentrate on their evening meal amidst the noise. Their appetite was not improved when a servant rushed in to tell them that 'the sea had gone' and that the coral reefs had been laid bare along the coast. Something was clearly amiss. Soon, the 'frightful roaring' of an advancing sea-wave rose above the din of the eruption. Controller Beyerinck and his assistant, Mr Tojaka, who were working in the office next to the house, just had time to escape. The wave wrecked the office, but halted and then ebbed before it reached the upper storey of the house. Mr Beyerinck decided at once to take his family and followers to their hut up in the interior of the island. The decision saved most of their lives, but it cost them six days of horror. They were never to see their home again. They struggled through paddy-fields and then got lost in the jungle. Under a deluge of torrents of pea-sized pumice, more and more local people joined them and, together, they found their hut about midnight. They were in the small village of Oemboel Balaq, 120m high on the slopes of Mount Radja Bassa. The Beyerincks and their servants settled for the night in the little room. Their hut was surrounded by a motley assembly of 'thousands of terrified natives, moaning, and crying, and praying to Allah for deliverance'. They did not realize that they were very lucky to be alive.

At five the next morning, 27 August, falling ash was smothering the forest and many trees were ablaze. The Controller sent some local people to find out what was happening elsewhere. They returned an hour later with the news. Ketimbang had vanished. At about 2 a.m. a tsunami had crashed onto the shore, destroying the lower parts of the town, and had completely wrecked the Beyerincks' home. As it swept onwards to Sumatra, this had probably destroyed the coastal villages, and drowned many of the islanders on Sebesi and Seboekoe Ketjiel.

At about 10 a.m. they heard some very loud explosions. Pumice rattled down. Darkness fell again – as it had fallen in Java. There was a choking smell of sulphur. Suddenly a nuée ardente of burning-hot ash and dust blasted northwards from Krakatau. On its 40km journey across the Soenda Straits, it burnt all the vegetation, all the peppers, and all the remaining people on Sebesi and Seboekoe Ketjiel. Within minutes, it surged onto southeastern Sumatra and killed hundreds of people before it lost its impetus on the thickly forested mountainsides. As Mrs Beyerinck described later, its outermost edges enveloped her family and their followers, killing some and sparing others in a searing lottery:

> Suddenly, it became pitch dark. The last thing I saw was the ash being pushed up through the cracks in the floorboards, like a fountain. I turned to my husband and heard him say in despair 'Where is the knife? . . . I will cut all our wrists and then we shall be released from our suffering sooner.' The knife could not be found. I felt a heavy pressure, throwing me to the ground. Then it seemed as if all the air was being sucked away and I could not breathe . . . I felt people rolling over me . . . No sound came from my husband or children . . . I remember thinking, I want to . . . go outside . . . but I could not straighten my back . . . I tottered, doubled up, to the door . . . I forced myself through the opening . . . I tripped and fell. I realised the ash was hot and I tried to protect my face with my hands. The hot bite of the pumice pricked like needles . . . Without thinking, I walked hopefully forward. Had I been in my right mind, I would have understood what a dangerous thing it was to . . . plunge into the hellish darkness . . . I ran up against . . . branches and did not even think of avoiding them. I entangled myself more and more . . . My hair got caught up . . . I noticed for the first time that [my] skin was hanging off everywhere, thick and moist from the ash stuck to it. Thinking it must be dirty, I wanted to pull bits of skin off, but that was still more painful . . . I did not know I had been burnt.

Mr Beyerinck brought his wife back to the hut. She tried to breast-feed her baby son. She couldn't. Then she realized that he was dead. Mrs Beyerinck was too stunned to cry. She could not even speak, because the hot ash was still choking her throat. Mr Beyerinck himself had lost the use of his hand. They were all suffering badly from thirst – partly from dehydration caused by fluid loss from their burnt skin, and partly from the mixture of ash and mucus in their throats. The Beyerincks were also afraid for a time that some local people might attack them to get water. Later, other villagers arrived, claiming that Radja Bassa itself was about to erupt. Controller Beyerinck decided that they ought to flee from this new – and unverifiable – threat. They trekked downs-lope in the pitch darkness of that Monday afternoon and met a few survivors from the nearby village of Kalianda. Cold mud now began splattering down upon them. This would, in fact, have been a good insulating compact against their burns, and probably helped them to survive. The family sheltered for the night under a large table. It was not before Tuesday afternoon, 28 August, that 'the strong wind tore the mass of ash apart and we saw the wonderful glit-tering sun'. But then they had to wait and wait until Saturday 1 September before the *Kedirie* came and rescued them. When the captain saw their piteous condition, he thought he would never get them back to Batavia alive. He was wrong. They recovered.

Vessels in the Soenda Straits, 26–27 August

The ships in the Soenda Straits got nearest to Krakatau, but it is astonishing that they did not run for safety as the climax of the eruption started. To judge, too, by their adventures, it is even more astonishing that so few of those on board were killed or injured. Even south of the Straits, hot ash rained down upon the *Berbice*. It began to burn holes in the sails nailed over the hatches to protect the cargo. The crew had to shovel it away in frenzied anguish all night. They were terrified that the ship might blow up – the *Berbice* was carrying petro-leum. The *W. H. Besse* prudently anchored about 80km north of Krakatau when the crisis developed. The explosions on Monday morning set the bar-ometer jumping up and down. A black bank from Krakatau soon enveloped the ship, and ash, swirling in hurricane-force winds, brought darkness for six hours. An odd quirk gave the *W. H. Besse* a casualty. A seaman walked off the forecastle in the darkness and succumbed to his injuries after the vessel returned to Boston.

Captain Watson of the sailing-ship *Charles Bal* chose to pass alongside Krakatau on the night of 26–27 August *en route* from Belfast to Hong Kong. Courage or folly? The vessel would surely have been destroyed had it sailed passed the volcano just after 10 a.m. the next day. The crew witnessed Krakatau's early onslaught on Sumatra, which nobody, at the time, even sus-pected in Java. At 4.15 p.m. on 26 August, Captain Watson saw 'a furious squall of ashen hue . . . being propelled [from Krakatau] with amazing velocity to the northeast'. Although the vessel still lay south of the island, warm, blind-ing pumice and ash soon started to rain down on it. At 11 p.m. the wind changed, and gave the crew a unique glimpse of Krakatau, 18km away. The volcano was in full fury. 'Chains of fire appeared to ascend and descend between it and the sky, while on the southwest end, there seemed to be a continual roll of balls of white fire.' These were quite small nuées ardentes, incandescent clouds of ash and pumice, cascading down the flanks of the volcano. Then darkness closed in upon them again. They spent a terrifying night, zigzagging erratically through the straits. The pitch blackness was broken only by lightning and the electrical discharges of St Elmo's fire that played about the masts in 'peculiar pink flames from fleecy clouds'.

A curious lull followed the dawn of 27 August, and, for a time, the sea was like glass. By about 10.15 a.m., the *Charles Bal* had travelled 48km northeastwards beyond Krakatau. Luckily. Suddenly a 'fearful explosion' broke the tranquillity. 'We were enclosed in a darkness,' said Captain Watson, 'that might almost be felt, and then commenced a downpour of mud, sand and I know not what . . . we could not see each other.' (This was the same huge nuée ardente that destroyed Sebesi and Seboekoe Ketjiel and killed Mrs Beyerinck's baby in Sumatra.) When the tumult abated at about four o'clock, ash had encrusted the ship, but it was otherwise undamaged. Even more remarkably, nobody had been hurt.

Meanwhile, the *Gouverneur Generaal Loudon* of the Netherlands–Indies Steamship Company left Batavia at 8.10 a.m. on 26 August on a routine trip to Padang, 1,000km away in western Sumatra. The vessel only reached its destination five days later, because it was forced to make an unscheduled voyage around Krakatau at the height of its destructive spasm. One of its passengers, N. H. van Sandick, a public works engineer, described an odyssey that would have made Odysseus himself quake.

The steamer carried a full complement of passengers. The way in which they were grouped together – and described – offers a glimpse of the perceived order of merit in that colonial society. Europeans, chiefly Dutch officials, occupied the First Class. The 'colourful mixture of races in the fore of the ship' included: 'His Majesty's troops' (about 160 in number); some 300 'exiles' (convicts sentenced to hard labour, often Dutch – and often in chaingangs); 'Arabs, Chinese, and natives'.

The ship made an unaccustomed call at Anjer on 26 August to pick up 111 additional passengers, including 100 local people hired as coolies to build a lighthouse off western Sumatra. At 2.45 p.m., the *Loudon* set off for Teloeq Betoeng, on Lampong Bay in Sumatra. As the ship crossed the Straits, Krakatau 'gave the passengers a free performance . . . we saw a high column of black smoke rise above the island'. Light ash powdered the boat. The *Loudon* anchored off Teloeq Betoeng at 7.30 p.m. on 26 August. Ash soon started to fall more thickly and the sea became rough. Strangely, however, no boat arrived to disembark the passengers for Teloeq Betoeng . . . In fact, this saved the lives of those who would normally have left the boat and stayed in the town that night. Captain Lindemann discovered only about midnight that a boat had, indeed, set off from the town, but the waves had wrecked it. The captain wisely decided at once that it would be safer to anchor farther offshore for the night. He considered that the small steamship, the *Berouw*, was moored far too close to the shore for its own safety in such conditions. And so it was to prove – in a most dramatic fashion . . .

At daybreak on 27 August, Captain Lindemann saw how right he had been. The *Berouw* was already stranded on the shore. Then, at about 6.30 a.m., four sea-waves came in at 'tremendous speed'. The captain steered the *Loudon* directly into these waves to prevent it from capsizing. The stranded *Berouw* was helpless. The waves washed it right over the pier and dumped it in the wreckage of the Chinese quarter. Within a few moments, the lower parts of Teloeq Betoeng were almost completely destroyed. Captain Lindemann realized that his passengers were now in even greater danger; and that he was powerless to help those left in the town. He therefore decided to return to Anjer and report the disaster. The *Loudon* set out at 7.30 a.m., but darkness enshrouded the ship about 10.30 a.m. before it could leave Lampong Bay. The vessel was to remain in darkness for eighteen hours. Ash, pumice, and then muddy rain poured down and was soon 15cm deep on the decks. From time to time, flashing lightning showed that the whole ship was encrusted with grey mud. It looked just like the Flying Dutchman's phantom vessel. But the passengers were in no mood to reflect on Wagner's opera: some could hardly breathe; some heard buzzing in their ears, others felt pressure on their chests; and still others became sleepy. Mr van Sandick drily noted that 'the circumstances left something to be desired, since it would have been quite natural if we had all choked to death'.

The sea was mountainous, the wind of hurricane force. Captain Lindemann dropped anchor and steered as best he could into the advancing waves. St Elmo's fire played about the masts. 'The natives' believed that it was a sure sign that the ship would be wrecked. They climbed up to put out the flames with their bare hands, but the fire merely sparked up elsewhere. In rare moments of calm, the first-class passengers could hear the chain-boys and coolies praying for help, whilst the Muslims amongst them intoned 'La Ellaha ela Allah' (There is no God but Allah).

It took superhuman efforts to control the *Loudon* as it bucked and plunged throughout the morning. Captain Lindemann seems to have well deserved the gold medal that he was later awarded by the government. He had to be roped to the controls to save him from being thrown overboard, and the second engineer had to be tied down in the engine-room so that he could work the machinery. At last, a measure of calm returned on the afternoon of 27 August. The cook even managed to prepare dinner, which, as Mr van Sandick added ruefully, was spiced with ash, mud and pumice.

Soenda Straits Coastlands, 27 August: Enormous Waves

The people on the coastal fringes of the Straits had even more alarming worries on that dreadful Monday morning. These were the areas flooded by the great tsunamis, which proved to be by far the most lethal agents that

A tsunami wave at Krakatau after a small earthquake.

Krakatau unleashed. The tsunamis formed broad swells, imperceptible to vessels on the open sea, that bulged up into huge waves, perhaps 30m high, as they approached shallow water near the shore. These waves scythed down the coastal settlements as if a giant and implacable hand had swept them aside. Different waves crashed onto the shore in different places at different times. Their onrush was rapid. They killed most of the people that they surprised on low ground. Those who were lucky enough to see the big waves coming, ran as they had never run before. The survivors escaped, not through ingenuity, but merely because they were luckier than their neighbours.

Telegraph-master Schruit was up early in Anjer on 27 August. At 6.30 a.m., he saw

an enormous wave . . . like a mountain rushing onwards . . . Never have I run so fast in my life . . . death was at my heels, and it was the thought of my wife and children [back in Batavia], who would be left destitute by my losing my life, that gave me superhuman strength . . . I fell, utterly exhausted . . . and, to my amazement, I saw the wave retreating.

As soon as he recovered, Mr Schruit dutifully reported the calamity to the Dutch authorities. As darkness returned about 10 a.m., he reached the untouched village of Jahat, where some of the survivors soon began to gather. Everyone was very thirsty. Mr Schruit took charge and rationed the water:

'I sat upon the water vat and quenched the thirst of the crowd by means of small draughts.'

That morning, at least three tsunamis hit Beneawang at the head of Semangka Bay in Sumatra. After the first wave ebbed, Controller P. L. C. Le Sueur invited over 200 villagers to shelter in his house on the hill. But more waves crashed on shore as darkness increased between 10 and 11.30 a.m. Water smashed the front of the house and rushed in. With the phlegm that empires are built on, Mr Le Sueur 'advised everyone to go to the rear'. He was soon to need all the phlegm he could muster. Another wave destroyed the house completely and swept everyone along. He managed to keep afloat in the turmoil only by clutching onto a passing shelf until the waters retreated. Mud from Krakatau rained down on him in the darkness. He was in a state of shock, exhausted and afraid. Local people around him were crying for help, but he could not even see them, let alone help them. Then an even bigger wave took hold of him. It wedged him for a while between two floating houses, but, just before he suffocated, the houses parted, and he grabbed hold of a banana trunk. At last, when this wave receded, Controller Le Sueur sat in the dark, splattered with falling mud. He realized that the swirling waters had stripped him naked except for his vest. Eventually he struggled across an area of thorny bushes until he met some local people who gave him a modicum of clothing. They reached succour together some eight hours later.

There can, however, be few more graphic accounts of any struggle for survival than that of a Javanese rice cultivator who was working in the paddy-fields some 8km inland near Merak in Java about 10.30 a.m. on Monday morning.

> . . . all of a sudden there came a great noise. We . . . saw a great black thing, a long way off, coming towards us. It was very high and very strong, and we soon saw that it was water. Trees and houses were washed away . . . The people began to . . . run for their lives. Not far off was some steep sloping ground. We all ran towards it and tried to climb up out of the way of the water. [The wave] was too quick for most of them, and many were drowned almost at my side . . . There was a general rush to climb up in one particular place. This caused a great block, and many of them got wedged together and could not move. Then they struggled and fought, screaming and crying out all the time. Those below tried to make those above them move on again by biting their heels. A great struggle took place for a few moments, but . . . one after another, they were washed down and carried far away by the rushing waters. You can see the marks on the hill side where the fight for life took place. Some . . . dragged others down with them. They would not let go their hold, nor could those above them release themselves from this death-grip.

Many were even less lucky. At about 10.30 a.m. in Tjiringin, south of Anjer in Java, a tsunami drowned fifty-five members of the local Rajah's family who had gathered for a feast. The Dutch Assistant Controller also died, conscientiously protecting the government cash-box that had been his responsibility for forty-

The steamship *Berouw*, marooned in the River Koeripan Valley.

eight years. In Beneawang, 250 local chiefs were drowned as they waited to meet the Dutch Provincial Governor. Four convicts wearing iron rings were severely burnt when they were struck by lightning at the First Point Lighthouse in Java. The litany of death and injury was almost endlessly varied . . .

The stranded steamer, *Berouw*, had one of the more extraordinary adventures on 27 August. Teloeq Betoeng was shrouded in darkness and swirling ash when another great tsunami crashed onto the shore at 10.30 a.m. It just failed to reach the Residency that stood 37m above sea-level, but those sheltering within it never even heard the wave above the roar of the hurricane ripping through the trees. Those on the *Berouw* were not so lucky. The wave swept the vessel bodily up the River Koeripan valley, 3.3km from its original anchorage, and 2.5km from the Chinese camp where it had been dumped at 6.30 that morning. All the crew of twenty-eight on board were killed.

Soenda Straits, 28 August

To the 'unbounded joy of all on board' the *Gouverneur Generaal Loudon*, the sky began to clear about 4 a.m. on 28 August. Captain Lindemann weighed anchor at once and resumed the journey to Anjer, but he found that the

Anak Krakatau with Rakata in the background in 1989.

passage between Seboekoe and Sumatra was blocked by floating pumice and tree-trunks. The captain, therefore, decided to sail southwards around Krakatau. The northern parts of the island had vanished. Rakata had been sliced in two. 'A steep crater wall could still be seen,' said Mr van Sandick, 'while the other half of the mountain had completely disappeared and had become sea.' Between Krakatau and Sebesi, smoking pumice floated on the swell as if the sea was sighing. In Java, the waves had swept the coasts almost completely bare, and coated the shore with grey or yellowish slime. Little was left of Anjer. A few Dutch officials, pottering about the ruins, were picked up and dropped off again at the undamaged town of Bantam. Then, called by duty, Captain Lindemann resumed his interrupted schedule at 7.30 p.m. and set out for western Sumatra. *En route*, the *Gouverneur Generaal Loudon* passed a now calm, but still smoking, Krakatau yet again.

Shock and Disorientation, Soenda Straits, September–October

Similar scenes greeted all those who rushed to the devastated coastlands. Lighthouses and European villas on the higher knolls remained intact, but, below the immense tidemarks, only a few age-old trees and the foundations of the more substantial buildings had survived. The lowlands were a morass of uprooted trees and the chaotic vestiges of many thousands of modest lives – smashed furniture, broken crockery and cooking utensils, doors wrenched from their hinges, torn and tangled garments, farming implements, house adornments, knick-knacks, and animal carcasses and human corpses.

Most of the survivors of the eruption were in deep shock. Their traumatic anguish lasted many hours. They were isolated, disorientated and uncomprehending, thirsty, homeless and bereaved, with no means of calling to the outside world for help, and no way of guessing what calamity might befall them next. News travelled slowly before the radio, they could not see the pattern of events – and, for many hours, could not often even see a hand in front of their faces. Krakatau had spread its shroud far more widely than most erupting volcanoes – even those of familiar violence in the Dutch East Indies. The tsunamis were totally unexpected. Survivors suffered immense deprivation, losing family, home, work and possessions. The structures of their lives as well as their houses and villages had been completely destroyed. But little seems to have been reported about their fate. In any case, the Dutch authorities had more pressing problems: evaluation of the damage and the casualties, and burying the dead.

Dr Sollewyn Gelpke described Tjiringin a week after the catastrophe. 'Thousands of corpses . . . and also carcasses . . . still await burial, and make their presence apparent by an indescribable stench . . . they lie in knots . . . impossible to unravel . . . among all that had served these thousands as dwellings.' The waves had scooped out the market place and the Chinese quarter of Tjiringin. Controller Tromp conscripted neighbouring villagers to bury the dead at a fee of 5 guilders per corpse. Survivors returned to the town to search – largely in vain – for their own property. Others came to loot. Some apparently found a few government cash-boxes, but made the mistake of flaunting their newly won wealth, and were soon arrested and severely punished.

On 7 October 1883 the Reverend Philip Neale, Anglican chaplain in Batavia, journeyed to the Straits with the Lloyd's agent Mr McColl. Near Merak, the tsunamis had obliterated the road and they were forced to *walk* in the hot midday sun. This was such an unusual thing for Europeans to do in Java that it seems to have impressed Mr Neale almost as much as the devastation. By then, most of the 3,000 or so corpses recovered had been buried, but the confusion of wrecked forest and villages remained just as the waters had left them. Not a single house survived in Merak. At the quarry nearby, the engineer's house had been sliced off at ground level, the railway lines had been twisted like wire, and engines had been thrown hither and thither.

Towards Anjer, the tsunamis had wrenched great chunks of coral from the sea-bed and carried them over 5km inland. Mr McColl had spent all his life in Anjer, but now he could not even find the street where his home had stood. Although the Residency survived on its hillock, the only recognizable building in the wave-swept zone was the long-ruined fort. The waves had washed open the graves in the European cemetery and had disinterred the dead. Their corpses joined most of those drowned at Anjer. They were sucked out

The remains of Merak after the tsunamis.

together into the Straits, where they floated ghoulishly for days amidst the pumice.

Unlike the floating corpses in other areas, many of those in Lampong Bay, in Sumatra, had been scorched to death – probably by the nuées ardentes blasted northwards from Krakatau. Pumice, dead fish, tree-trunks and corpses cluttered every bay in southern Sumatra. Teloeq Betoeng itself could not be opened to shipping again until 15 December 1883. There was also apparently more civil unrest in Sumatra too. The local people averred that Krakatau had brought this disaster upon the land to punish the Dutch because they were fighting the indigenous people in Achin in northern Sumatra.

Well beyond the areas devastated by the tsunamis, falling ash, pumice and mud had defoliated crops, badly affecting coffee trees and young rice in particular. But, eventually, the ash added much porosity and fertile nutrients to the soil; and grasses and root crops especially were soon flourishing again both in Java and Sumatra. During the following seasons, higher crop yields offered a meagre consolation to the bereaved survivors.

World-wide Spectacle, August–December

One of the remarkable features of the eruption of Krakatau was that it devastated such a wide area of the Soenda Straits. Some minor effects, but still spectacular in their way, had a world-wide compass. The explosions were inter-

The remains of the old fort at Anjer after the tsunamis.

preted as distant gunfire, muffled, violent detonations, outbreaks of local hostilities, or as signals from ships in distress. Such interpretations were not particularly unusual – except that the noises were heard more than 2,000km away,
in northern Sumatra and central Australia. On the afternoon of 27 August
they sounded like rumbling gunfire as far away as Rodríguez Island, in the
Indian Ocean, 4,653km from Krakatau. The tsunamis generated waves
throughout the Indian Ocean and much of the Pacific Ocean. On Tuesday
morning 28 August at Bandora near Bombay, some 4,800km from Krakatau,
the sea retreated and gave the citizens an ephemeral bonanza of stranded fish
before it rushed back again. In Auckland, New Zealand, 7,767km from the
volcano, a wave 2m high was recorded.

Pumice banks, often containing clusters of over fifty corpses at first, choked
parts of the Soenda Straits until December 1883. They floated out especially
into the Indian Ocean. Swarms of insects and flies, and shoals of small fish
abounded around them. Crabs and barnacles colonized the larger lumps and
finally caused them to sink. But these banks often persisted for many months,
and one accumulation floated 8,170km from Krakatau until it reached
Durban, South Africa, in September 1884.

The intense explosions also ejected masses of volcanic dust and gases that
formed a sulphuric aerosol in the stratosphere. The aerosol travelled westward
and completed its first trip around the world on 9 September and its second
on 22 September. The results were lurid, often beautiful, and world-wide. Blue
moons – and blue suns – were seen. Green suns and moons appeared two

weeks later. Soon afterwards, the sun developed the pinkish halo, later called a Bishop's Ring, after the Reverend Sereno Bishop who first described the feature in Hawaii in December 1883.

The last months of 1883 were graced by the most beautiful sunsets ever described. They were even the subject of a special weekly section in the scientific magazine, *Nature*, in December 1883. A particularly brilliant sunset celebrated St Andrew's Day, 30 November 1883, in Edinburgh. Even the staid newspaper, the *Scotsman*, was ecstatic: 'emerald . . . deep blood-red . . . crimson . . . luminous orange . . . bluish grey . . . resplendent blue . . . fiery-red, as if a huge conflagration were raging below'. Small wonder that these sunsets in more excitable New York City should have induced public-spirited citizens to call out the fire brigade. Remarkable afterglows developed in the hour following these incomparable sunsets, when the whole spectacular series of colour-changes was displayed all over again. William Ascroft painted these sunsets over the River Thames in Chelsea and they formed the subject of a special exhibition in London.

Aftermath

Although events in Java were best documented, it was really southern Sumatra that bore the brunt of the eruption. Krakatau attacked Sumatra first, more severely and for longer than western Java. Sebesi lost its whole population. Uninhabited Krakatau naturally suffered the greatest material losses. Perboewatan and Danan foundered into a great hollow in the crust, or *caldera*, which was flooded by seawater 300m deep. Rakata balanced for a moment, or an hour or so, unsupported on the edge of the hole. Then all the northern half of the cone sliced off and avalanched into the abyss. The southern half of Rakata is now all that remains of old Krakatau.

The northern two-thirds of Krakatau had disappeared; pumice blanketed nearby Lang and Verlaten Islands as well as the more distant Sebesi and Seboekoe Ketjiel Islands. Pumice also accumulated so thickly in the sea that it formed two temporary islands, called Steers and Calmejer. However, they were too insubstantial to last, and the waves soon eroded them down to shoals. All this pumice and ash went on steaming and exploding in the Soenda Straits until November 1883.

Krakatau caused 36,417 fatalities, of which 37 were listed as 'European' and the rest as 'other'. About 4,500 deaths were caused by falling ash, and especially by nuées ardentes. The tsunamis claimed the remaining 32,000 victims. In Sumatra, the deaths were concentrated in the areas of Ketimbang (8,038), Teloeq Betoeng (2,260), and Semangka (2,160). In Java, the deaths were concentrated in the areas of Tjiringin (12,022), Anjer (7,610), Tangerang (2,340), and Serang (1,933). The European fatalities occurred mainly in Anjer (14), Merak (13) and Tjiringin (5). In all, Dr Verbeek calculated that 132 villages had suffered damage and a further 165 had been utterly destroyed.

Krakatau then stayed quiet until December 1927, when Anak ('child of') Krakatau first erupted in the sea-flooded hollow, created when part of the island collapsed in 1883. It has erupted in most years ever since, but its activity has seemed a mere caricature of the overwhelming outbursts of August 1883.

11

Montagne Pelée, 1902

Montagne Pelée annihilated a whole city with a type of volcanic eruption that came as a complete surprise because it had never been studied before. Although the effects of the eruption were much more limited in area than those of Krakatau, they were still remarkably intense. Most accounts of the event claim that there were only two survivors, but this is only one of several myths that have fastened themselves to this eruption.

'The Pearl of the West Indies'

Christopher Columbus had been the first European to discover the island, that the local Caribs called Madanina, on 15 December 1502, but the native peoples were then left alone for over a century. Early in July 1635, the French colonized the island, called it Martinique, and established the fort that became the kernel of Saint-Pierre. Martinique has had some famous daughters. One of the first French women to set eyes on Montagne Pelée was Françoise d'Aubigné, who lived in Martinique from 1645 to 1647. She was later to become Madame de Maintenon, the secret, stern second wife of Louis XIV. She was almost equalled by Marie-Josèphe-Rose Tascher de la Pagerie, who spent her youth in Martinique before becoming Napoléon's Empress Joséphine. Aimée Dubuc de Rivery took an even more exotic path: to the harem of Constantinople, where she became the mother of Sultan Mahmoud II. No subsequent islander rose to such heights, although one man was to win fame as a circus exhibit.

*

Martinique became one of the jewels of the French colonial empire, rich in sugar-cane plantations and rum distilleries. Its capital was Fort-de-France, but the commercial and intellectual focus of the island was Saint-Pierre. It stood in the centre of a beautifully proportioned bay, which curved from the southern headland at Le Carbet round to the low green pyramid of Montagne Pelée that formed its northern arm stretching out to Le Prêcheur. This was the site of the most terrifying and lethal eruption of the twentieth century. On the left was the aggressor, Montagne Pelée, and on the right the victim, Saint-Pierre. In about two minutes, on 8 May 1902, the volcano killed some 27,000 people.

It is a tragic story. People were caught up in events that they could neither understand nor control, and they died, not through incompetence or negligence,

Montagne Pelée and modern Saint-Pierre.

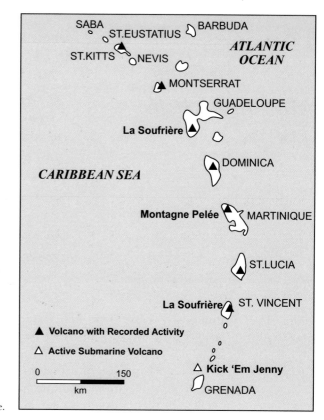

The location of Montagne Pelée.

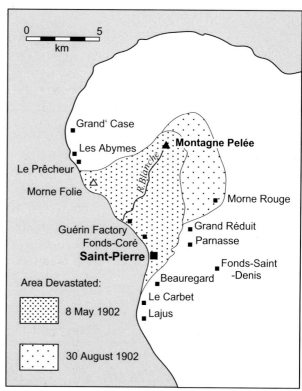

Montagne Pelée, 1902.

but because they tried to do their rational best. Masters and maids, teachers and tradesmen, intellectuals and ignorant, black and white died together in a few awful moments. Most of their bodies were never recovered.

The very extent of the catastrophe perhaps incites those who have tried to recapture the old atmosphere of the city to exaggerate its graces. But Saint-Pierre was a charming place and, by common consent, the 'Pearl of the West Indies'. In 1902 it was the vibrant commercial capital of Martinique, with a vigorous trade in rum, sugar, cocoa and coffee, in spite of an economic crisis during the last decade of the nineteenth century, brought on when the price of sugar fell. There was no harbour: vessels anchored offshore in the sheltered roadstead. Most of the population of 26,011 was of Afro-Caribbean origin, originally imported to harvest the sugar-cane, together with some Asian-Indian groups, but many people in the island were of mixed parentage. In Saint-Pierre, one quarter of the population was under 14; and 47 per cent could neither read nor write. Virtually all the power lay in the hands of about 4,000 *békés* – white administrators and plantation owners, who formed a substantial Creole middle and upper class. Strongly catholic and conservative, they disliked the new democratic ideas that had been in vogue in France since 1871. After leaving local politics disdainfully in the hands of those of mixed parentage for many years, they had just started to take an interest in public affairs again. Only a small proportion of the islanders cared about politics, but they cared passionately. These antagonisms help explain why some politicians and journalists recklessly flung about unjustified charges after the eruption – to the great disadvantage of the island.

Saint-Pierre was a throng of shops and bazaars, and had sixteen mechanized distilleries. It had fine, tree-lined squares, a botanic garden, mosquito-free streams, and a very busy roadstead, as well as municipal electricity, telephones, a piped pure water supply and public fountains. The buildings were constructed of stone and painted yellow – unlike those of the much less elegant and earthquake-prone capital, Fort-de-France. The main square, the Place Bertin, was dominated by a lighthouse 20m high and was always full of people and rum casks. Allegedly it often smelt of garlic and sugar, which, for some, might have diminished its charms. Two main streets running parallel to the shore contained the chief commercial offices, the chamber of commerce, the Grand Hotel, the theatre, built in 1787, and the town hall. A horse-drawn tram plied back and forth to the prosperous villas in the northern suburb of Fonds-Coré. The city itself had three fairly distinctive quarters: the working-class Fort district in the north; the Centre; and the Mouillage in the south, which was hotter and rather less salubrious. The city was restricted – some might have said hemmed in – by the low, wooded hills, or Mornes, that covered most of the interior. Here some of the wealthier classes had their plantations, or their second homes, away from the hurly-burly of the city. North of Saint-Pierre, the River Roxelane valley opened out to the promenade of the Grande Savanne, the botanic gardens that had been founded in 1803, and the airy suburb of Trois-Ponts which led up to the lower slopes of Montagne Pelée. Life in

Martinique, however, was not an unbroken idyll. The great hurricane on 18 August 1891 had claimed 700 lives, and an earthquake had killed 400 people in Fort-de-France in 1839.

Montagne Pelée formed the northern horizon some 7km away, a pale green pyramid with a rather ill-defined, hummocky summit about 1,300m high. It was close enough to be the object of a traditional Whit Monday ascent through the forests of guava trees that were decked with begonias and orchids. The summit cradled a circular hollow, known as the Etang Sec because it so rarely contained water. Its rim was notched on the southwest by the headwaters of the Rivière Blanche, which flowed down to Dr Auguste Guérin's factory on the coast. This notch could be clearly seen from Saint-Pierre; and an extreme pessimist might have feared that it would direct any large eruption straight towards the city.

The type of eruption that caught Saint-Pierre was a major element in the city's tragedy. The citizens could not have foreseen their fate, for what Montagne Pelée launched upon them was then unknown to science. It had occurred before – as recently, for instance, as at Krakatau in 1883 – but it was here that the phenomenon was first named and described as a nuée ardente – an incandescent, scorching cloud. There was a great blast, accompanied by gas, steam, hot ash, pumice and shattered bits of mountain, that cascaded across the ground and through the air at speeds of 500km an hour and at a temperature between 200°C and 450°C. This was the first nuée ardente to win international fame. Many people saw it. Few survived.

The great French geologist, Alfred Lacroix, was appointed by the French government to investigate these extraordinary events. His account of *La Montagne Pelée et ses éruptions* has become a classic work of volcanology. More recently, the build-up to the catastrophe has been analysed by Simone Chrétien and Robert Brousse in *La Montagne Pelée se réveille*, and Léo Ursulet has concentrated on the aftermath of the eruption in *Le Désastre de 1902 à la Martinique*. Thus, many of the myths accreted to the tragedy may have been dissipated at last.

Devastation has been so commonplace in the twentieth century that it is hard to imagine the enormous impact that the destruction of a whole city had in those self-confident years. As Lacroix remarked in 1904, 'a comparable human hecatomb has rarely been produced by a natural phenomenon in such a short space of time'. Even human action in modern times has scarcely ever managed to do it so quickly.

Prologue

The violent spasms during the geological history of Montagne Pelée were almost completely unknown in 1902. The Caribs had called it the 'Fire Mountain', either because of an eruption about 1600, or of another that had formed the hollow of the Etang Sec about 1300. After the first French colonization,

An eruption of a nuée ardente from
Montagne Pelée.

Montagne Pelée masked its hand for nearly 200 years. In 1792, there were a
couple of spluttering explosions of fumes and hot water that killed birds and
nineteen manicous (opossums) on the summit. Nothing worth remembering
in such revolutionary times . . .

The eruption of 1851 was more worthy of the name. The smell of 'rotten
eggs' from escaping hydrogen sulphide spread to Le Prêcheur on the west
coast. Then, at 11 p.m. on 5 August, there was a loud rumbling explosion and
all the southern flank of the volcano as far as Saint-Pierre was dusted with
white ash as if there had been a frost. A few similar explosions followed. Some
people were frightened into confession, and a few couples married to
legalize their sexual arrangements. The Governor, Rear-Admiral Vaillant, set
up a commission to investigate, comprising a doctor and two pharmacists.
Mainly to calm public disquiet, they concluded that Saint-Pierre had nothing
to fear. Indeed, they thought that a white erupting plume might be just the
kind of picturesque decoration that the mountain needed to give it a touch
of majesty. Since the volcano quickly calmed down, these reassuring aesthetic
considerations were fixed in local folklore long after memories of the less
pleasant emissions had become blurred.

Father Vanhaecke, a local priest, first noticed new sulphurous fumes emerging from the Etang Sec when he visited the summit 'about 1889'. He temporarily lost his voice; and his manservant ran away, fearing that he, too, would become a victim of sorcery. It seems, however, that neither sulphur nor sorcery made any further appearances – on the volcano at any rate – for over a decade.

Fumes, 4 June 1900–23 April 1902

Now, at the dawn of the new century, Montagne Pelée seemed to be extinct – or at least very somnolent. Everybody knew that. Of course, the volcano was giving off a few fumes again, but that was just like an old man snoring. Nothing to worry about.

Those who made the traditional annual trip to the summit of the volcano on Whit Monday 1900, saw fumes coming from the Etang Sec. By next year's trip, half a dozen sulphurous holes had formed. Even worse, in February 1902, recently married Madame Emilie Dujon discovered that the fumes had tarnished the silver at her home near Le Prêcheur. By the end of March the odour of rotten eggs wafted on the trade winds was making life unpleasant in villages around the volcano. It even upset the horses. Some people got colic when they drank spring waters from just below the summit. Meanwhile on 11 April the *Roddam*, under Captain Edward Freeman, left London for the West Indies.

Gaston Landes, a natural sciences teacher at the *lycée* and one of the intellectuals in Saint-Pierre, climbed the volcano on Sunday, 20 April. He noticed that two further sulphurous vents had opened. Although he – like everyone else on the island – knew little about volcanoes, he suspected that Montagne Pelée might be embarking on another eruption. On 22 April, an earthquake cut the submarine telegraph cable to Guadeloupe. On 23 April, more earthquakes shook the flanks of the mountain and threw dishes from their shelves in Saint-Pierre.

Steam and Dust, Thursday, 24 April–Friday, 25 April 1902

On 24 April, Montagne Pelée exploded columns of steam and old volcanic rocks that it had shattered to dust and ash. After a bigger explosion at 8 a.m. the next day, fine grey dust fell on Le Prêcheur for two hours. People could hardly recognize each other in the streets. Old wives' tales about 1851 began to cause unease in the village.

Seen from Saint-Pierre, the steam formed an attractive white plume that the Commissioners of 1851 could not have failed to admire. But Gaston Landes and some friends, who were inspecting the mountain through the telescope at the chamber of commerce on 25 April, were disconcerted to see that rocks were being thrown 300m skywards from the Etang Sec. The suspicions of

Monsieur Landes were confirmed: the eruption was under way. That same day, the steamer *Roraïma* left New York for her last voyage to the West Indies.

Other Activities, Saturday, 26 April–Wednesday, 30 April 1902

Montagne Pelée then taunted its victims with a pause and threw out no shattered rocks for five days. It stayed calm enough on Sunday 27 April to entice parties of rather foolhardy visitors to the summit to see what was afoot. Eugène Berté published his group's observations in the daily newspaper, *Les Colonies* on 7 May. They had been dumbfounded. The Etang Sec contained a lake looking like quicksilver. Trees, 20m high, had been submerged, and a new cinder-cone was spurting out boiling water from its crater. The fumes had tarnished their silver buttons. They resolved to note any further changes whenever conditions permitted. But Montagne Pelée was to permit no such conditions for quite some time.

Sunday, 27 April also marked the first round of the elections, by universal male suffrage, for the French Parliament. There were three candidates for the constituency of Martinique (North). Fernand Clerc, political leader of the conservative whites, topped the poll with 4,495 votes, but did not obtain an overall majority. Louis Percin, the radical-socialist and a supporter of the outgoing French government, came second with 4,167 votes; while the socialist workers' candidate, Joseph Lagrosillière, polled 753 votes. A second-round run-off, therefore, had to take place on 11 May between the top two candidates. Louis Percin was expected to collect Lagrosillière's votes and win. The abstention rate of 53.6 per cent followed the usual pattern, and it was matched exactly in Martinique (South). On 27 April, the eruption had apparently played a negligible role in the election.

Montagne Pelée contented itself with giving off fumes during the last days of April, but three earth tremors shook Saint-Pierre on Wednesday evening, 30 April. That day, the twice-weekly paper, *Les Antilles*, had greeted the eruption with flippant joy: 'We had never hoped to see an event like it . . . but, in the name of God, don't let [the mountain] start to vibrate . . . but we don't really expect such a nasty thing . . . ' The paper went on to repeat the latest local quip – that Montagne Pelée was just making April Fools of everybody. However, an exciting social event was in prospect. The 'Gymnastic and Shooting Club' was organizing a great excursion to see the new show on Sunday, 4 May. Regrettably, it had to be cancelled.

Retreat to Safety in Saint-Pierre, Thursday, 1 May–Sunday, 4 May 1902

Loud bangs awakened the people of Le Prêcheur in the early hours of 1 May. The eruptions had resumed. The trade winds blew ash and fumes all over the western slopes of the mountain. On Friday afternoon, ash fell so thickly that lamps had to be lit. Montagne Pelée began to rumble ominously, with more violent and more frequent explosions.

At 11 p.m. on 2 May, terrifying detonations awakened all Saint-Pierre. A lightning-riddled column of ash and fumes rose 3km into the air. Immediately, fine dust began to rain down on the city for the first time since 1851. It soon lay 3cm deep in the streets. At Morne Rouge, only 5km from the summit, the ash, noise, shaking and lightning gave the inhabitants a glimpse of Hell. There was a rush to church. Those claiming to be the greatest sinners jumped the queues for the confessionals.

Next morning, 3 May, Morne Rouge was absolved and white as snow – or, at least, blanketed in ash. Some ash even fell on the capital, Fort-de-France. It was perhaps no coincidence that the first official notification of the eruption was immediately sent to Paris. The Governor, Louis Mouttet, took the regular Girard Company steamer, *Rubis*, from Fort-de-France for the hour's journey by sea to Saint-Pierre. He went on at once to Le Prêcheur where the darkness, damage and distress were greatest. He promised the villagers refuge, if need be, in the barracks in Saint-Pierre. Louis Mouttet was 44, and had been appointed Governor in December 1901. He was rather untypically interested in the underprivileged and in the new state education. He was married, with three young children.

Meanwhile, in his last letter to his brother, the primary teacher, Roger Portel, described the start of the 'flight of frightened folk' from the flanks of Montagne Pelée towards the supposed haven of Saint-Pierre. Women and barefoot children carried all they could, their plaited hair dusted with grey ash; and 'great black lads strode along, bent double under the mattresses needed for the coming nights'. As they thronged into Saint-Pierre, 'old women at their windows mumbled their interminable prayers' – for protection either from Montagne Pelée, or from the refugees or, perhaps, from both.

At Grand' Case, north of Le Prêcheur, Charles and Emilie Dujon had awakened on 3 May to find their house enveloped in swirling ash. Charles decided that the household should abandon the plantation forthwith and go to stay with Emilie's parents in Saint-Pierre. They had to protect their eyes and mouths with wet handkerchiefs all the way to the city. 'I prayed, with my crucifix in my hand,' she said, 'and expected death at any moment.'

Ash fell on Saint-Pierre virtually throughout 3 May. It was very disconcerting, for, as a wealthy white Creole declared, ' the ash turned the blacks white'. The birds could no longer fly. The schoolchildren were given a holiday. Factories, shops and businesses closed. The churches opened, and the priests hardly stopped baptizing, confessing, or simply comforting their flocks. Thus many people had now nothing to do but to throng the streets and spread every alarming tale that they had heard or invented. The mayor ordered the firemen to hose the ash from the streets. Watching wits advised them to 'Go and put Montagne Pelée out instead!'

Many of the citizens, however, were more nervous. Emilie Dujon described a chilling glimpse of things to come during evening service at the Cathedral on 3 May. Fearing another big ashfall when the sky suddenly darkened, some worshippers moved to leave the building. Somebody sent a bench crashing to the ground. Without further ado, the startled faithful rushed to the altar, shouting that they were about to die. The priests only just managed to calm their panic-stricken flock.

From 3 May onwards, attitudes to the eruption changed. It was now no longer a firework display, but was becoming a fearsome threat. Then the volcano erupted much less ash on Sunday, 4 May. Hopes were raised, but only for a time. Emilie Dujon recounted how those leaving mass had asked each other whether they were afraid. 'The bravest amongst them laughed.'

A Mudflow, Monday 5 May

The relative volcanic calm of Sunday prevailed throughout Monday 5 May. Saint-Pierre had only an evening shower of ash. It was the Rivière Blanche that caused the trouble that day. Although it had hardly rained, the stream had been behaving oddly for a week; suddenly drying up, then flooding in warm and smelly torrents. By 8 a.m. on 5 May, the Rivière Blanche had attracted 200 spectators. A worried Gaston Landes estimated that it was discharging five times as much as its usual floods. Dr Auguste Guérin's country mansion and his sugar and rum factory at the mouth of the river seemed in great danger, but Dr Guérin, his son and daughter-in-law calmly ate lunch as their yacht, the *Carbet*, was prepared for departure. Suddenly, a neighbour rushed in to tell them that 'an avalanche' was on the way. Monsieur and Madame Eugène Guérin and their heavily laden servants hurried towards the yacht. Dr Auguste Guérin turned back to the house for his hat, or to leave a message for his foreman. Whatever the reason, it saved his life. It was then that the mudflow arrived. It was about 12.45 p.m.

> Then I heard a noise that I can't compare with anything else – an immense noise – like the devil on Earth! A black avalanche, beneath white smoke, an enormous mass, full of huge blocks, more than 10m high and at least 150m wide, was coming down the mountain with a great din. It . . . rolled up against the factory like an army of giant rams. I was rooted to the spot.
>
> My unfortunate son and his wife ran away from it towards the shore . . . All at once, the mud arrived. It passed 10m in front of me. I felt its deathly breath. There was a great crashing sound. Everything was crushed, drowned and submerged. My son, his wife, thirty [*sic*] people and huge buildings were all swept away . . . Three of those black waves came down . . . making a noise like thunder, and made the sea retreat. Under the impact of the third wave, a boat moored in the factory harbour was thrown . . . over a factory wall, killing one of my foremen, who was standing next to me. I went down to the shore. The desola-

A devastated rum distillery in Saint-Pierre.

tion was indescribable. Where a prosperous factory – the work of a lifetime –
had stood a moment before, there was now nothing left but an expanse of mud
forming a black shroud for my son, his wife and my workmen.

Gaston Landes was probably the only person who fully realized what had
caused the mudflow. The notch on the fragile rim of the Etang Sec had given
way, releasing its waters into the Rivière Blanche. Ash, rock and trees mixed
into a mudflow that swooshed down the valley at 120km an hour and pushed
down the buildings in its way. All that could be seen of the Guérin factory was
the top of the giant scales and the chimney. Up the hill, half of the Isnard
plantation had vanished too. Montagne Pelée had claimed its first victims. On
6 May, the newspaper, *Les Colonies*, listed twenty-three fatalities, including
Monsieur and Madame Guérin, one English and two West Indian maids, and
four unlucky men who just happened to be passing at the fatal moment.
Next day, the newspaper added the names of two young children to the
death-toll.

When the mudflow swept into the sea it generated a small tsunami, which
reached Saint-Pierre fifteen minutes later. The sea first retreated 50m from
the shore, then flooded 20m inland. Smaller oscillations continued for fifteen
minutes before the sea returned to normal. The citizens did not link the sea-

wave with the mudflow, but both were worrying because they had been unpredictable and inexplicable. Fonds-Coré seemed much too close to the Rivière Blanche for comfort. The inhabitants abandoned the suburb, shoving their laden carts as best they could through the deepening ash towards the safety of Saint-Pierre.

Governor Mouttet requisitioned the naval cruiser *Suchet*, which had just arrived in Fort-de-France, for his second visit to the disaster area. They left at 4 p.m. His main preoccupation was with Le Prêcheur. Food and water were scarce. Ash was falling and the flooding river had cut the road to Saint-Pierre. The only escape was by sea – which had just produced a weird wave. In Le Prêcheur, intelligent leadership from the mayor, Monsieur Grelet, and the priest, Abbé Desprez, just kept the people calm. The Governor promised a rapid evacuation, 'if the village were to be seriously threatened'.

That evening, the mudflow in the Rivière Blanche was the talk of the town, and sang-froid was certainly not boosted when the electricity supply failed and plunged Saint-Pierre into darkness because ash had clogged the generators.

A Poster, Tuesday, 6 May

As Montagne Pelée rumbled threateningly during the early hours of 6 May, false rumours spread that the rivers in Saint-Pierre itself were flooding. Some left their homes to check these tales – and returned to find that they had been burgled. Others, often thought to be refugees living up in the hills, paraded the streets shouting anti-religious slogans echoing the current political debate. Mudflows continued to rush down the Rivière Blanche throughout the day, offering a diverting and terrifying show to hundreds of spectators from Saint-Pierre.

The Governor took the *Topaze* on 6 May for a further visit to Le Prêcheur. Morale was lower in the village, although he had sent 6,000kg of cod, beans and salted meat to sustain the population. The mayor had even issued food coupons to ensure fair distribution. Nevertheless, so many people piled onto the *Topaze* to escape – to Saint-Pierre – that it had to leave hurriedly to avoid being swamped.

On 6 May, too, Rodolphe Fouché, the mayor of Saint-Pierre, issued a tranquillizing poster urging the citizens to resume their normal activities and not to succumb to groundless panic; there was no immediate danger; the lava would not reach the city; and events would be localized in those places that had already suffered. So, everything was all right then ...

The most important event of 6 May – and of the eruption so far – passed almost unnoticed and was certainly not understood. In the last letter that Eugène Berté wrote to his brother, Emile, at 11 a.m., he described 'gigantic columns of fumes ... gushing up ... clearly lit up by the fire inside'. Watching through a telescope, Monsieur Landes saw that Montagne Pelée was throwing out huge blocks. That evening, the ejected stones glowed against the night sky. The glows betrayed the truth: Montagne Pelée was erupting molten rock for the first time. A more violent spasm was now inevitable.

'What Better Place is there to be than Saint-Pierre?',Wednesday, 7 May

Abbé Parel, Vicar-General of Martinique, was awakened at 4 a.m. in Saint-Pierre by loud bangs from the volcano. 'Two red craters were spitting out fire like two furnaces.' Lightning was flashing and crackling, and flooding mountain torrents were sweeping hundreds of trees out to sea. Montagne Pelée roared like a rampant lion all day, breaking the monotony with explosions like muffled cannonades. Dark clouds gushed from the crater; ash rained down as far away as Le Carbet. Ash was now so thick in Le Prêcheur that roofs were starting to collapse. During the morning, the first small – and unrecognized – nuées ardentes swept half-way down the Rivière Blanche. They had a 'luminous yellow base and a train of white steam above'.

Nevertheless, those in Saint-Pierre could take some solace from an interview with Gaston Landes in the 7 May edition of *Les Colonies*. He explained how the waters that had burst from the Etang Sec had caused the disastrous mudflow. He warned people, therefore, to leave the valley-bottoms and avoid the fate of the few citizens of Pompeii 'who had not been evacuated in time'. *Les Colonies* then added what seems to have been its own concluding gloss to the interview: 'Montagne Pelée offers no more danger to the inhabitants of Saint-Pierre than Vesuvius to those of Naples.' Experts, armed with decades of research and hindsight, have not only pilloried this comforting view ever since, but have also unfairly attributed it to Gaston Landes. But it is doubtful if anyone with the knowledge then available would have come to a different conclusion. The newspaper also reported that a few hundred people were leaving the city, but went on to ask: 'What better place is there to be than Saint-Pierre?' Nevertheless, when the Neapolitan captain of the *Orsolina* saw the eruption as he anchored off Saint-Pierre that day, he departed *prestissimo*.

Now back once again in Fort-de-France, Governor Mouttet was worried. At 10 a.m. on 7 May, he set up a 'Scientific Commission' to analyse the eruption. It comprised: Lt-Col. Gerbault of the Artillery, Monsieur Mirville, pharmacist at the military hospital in Fort-de-France, Monsieur Léonce, a civil engineer, and two natural science teachers at the *lycée* in Saint-Pierre, Monsieur Doze and Monsieur Landes – no experts on volcanoes. There was none available. Within thirty hours, four of the five were dead.

Georges Hébert, lieutenant on the *Suchet,* spent 7 May in Saint-Pierre testing the atmosphere on a day trip from Fort-de-France. He understood Creole and could pick up all the gossip. People were afraid, without knowing exactly what they were afraid of. The women in the Fort district market were unusually quiet. They instinctively felt that the volcano would kill them all. Suffocating ash was everywhere. All the cats, rats, snakes and birds had apparently escaped southwards – including the boa constrictor confined in the botanical gardens! Lieutenant Hébert tried to persuade a girl he had met at the last carnival to come back with him to the safety of Fort-de-France. 'No,' she replied firmly, 'I'm not leaving because I want to die here with my mother.' Georges Hébert just caught the last boat back to the capital. He was to return to a very different atmosphere in Saint-Pierre the following day.

On the afternoon of 7 May, rumblings and a sea-wave coming from the *south* revealed a complication to the story that few writers would have dared to include in a thriller. Almost 120km to the south, the Soufrière of St Vincent had erupted and killed 1,565 people. The news did not reassure the people when it filtered through to Martinique. Indeed, anxiety was causing panic and disorder in Saint-Pierre. The police could no longer cope, so the mayor, Rodolphe Fouché, asked the Governor for a detachment of thirty colonial infantrymen to help distribute food and patrol the streets to prevent tumult. They were to be dispatched the following morning.

The mayor's request seems to have determined Governor Mouttet's decision to spend the night in Saint-Pierre to calm the citizens and demonstrate his confidence in their future. This time, Louis Mouttet delegated his powers to his Secretary-General, Georges Lhuerre, and took the 4 p.m. Girard steamer from Fort-de-France with his wife, Hélène, and several senior administrators. Montagne Pelée greeted their arrival in Saint-Pierre with a vigorous salvo, exploding blocks big enough to be seen by the naked eye.

Soon after his arrival at 5 p.m., the Governor presided over the meeting of the Scientific Commission. (There was one absentee: Monsieur Mirville had been detained by official duties in Fort-de-France.) The gist of their deliberations was known in Saint-Pierre that evening, although they were not telegraphed to the capital until after 7.05 the following morning. They declared that the features so far produced had been quite normal; there was no danger of earthquakes or landslides; mudflows would be restricted to the Rivière Blanche; and Saint-Pierre was completely safe. In fact, these affirmations did little more than wrap the assertions of the mayor's poster in vaguely scientific fluff. With the possible exception of Gaston Landes, they seem to have wanted, above all, to reassure the citizens – and, perhaps, to calm the fears that men of their position and background could not express.

But the Scientific Commission and the press were anticipating the wrong threats. Lava-flows were no menace: two main valleys would divert them into the sea long before they could reach the city. Many also (wrongly) thought that the eruption was only heralding a devastating earthquake, like that which had caused 400 deaths in Fort-de-France on 21 January 1839. Why, therefore, move to the capital? Those who knew about Krakatau feared a great tsunami – and small sea-waves had already warned of that particular danger. Moreover, a sea-wave (caused by a hurricane) had killed 5,000 people in Galveston, Texas on 8 September 1900. This time, none of these fears turned out to be justified. The cause of the cataclysm was quite different.

Some have claimed that the administration tried to anaesthetize the population with calculated blandishments. Afterwards, Fernand Clerc, and others with a certain political bias, averred that the government's hidden agenda had been to keep people in the city until the second round of the elections on 11 May. But there seems to have been little widespread enthusiasm for the contest: few survivors even mentioned the elections, and over half the electorate had abstained in the first round. The results in metropolitan France on 27 April indicated that the outgoing coalition would win again, and certainly did not need the seat in Martinique (North) for a majority. There was thus no obvious reason to coerce the electorate. The authorities in Saint-Pierre seem to have genuinely believed that the city was in no immediate danger. They voted with their feet and *chose* to stay in Saint-Pierre – and, on 7 May, some of the highest-ranking administrators in the colony joined them.

It is hard to assess the mood of Saint-Pierre as night fell on 7 May. There is probably no general mood in such a crisis. Perhaps the only people who really felt safe in the city were the refugees from the slopes of the volcano. The most widespread emotion in Saint-Pierre after 3 May was probably anguish, compounded by increasing fear and often helpless panic. As Monsieur Degennes, a teacher at the *lycée*, wrote to his family in France on 3 May, 'I'm afraid of a catastrophe, and yet I'd like to go on hoping'. Everybody spent sleepless nights and frantic, bewildered days under the falling ash, listening for every rumble from Montagne Pelée and every rumour from their neighbours. Amongst the totally illiterate half of the population, the wildest tales reigned, unchecked, in the overcrowded streets. And yet, they did not flee. Most were too poor even to consider leaving. Having few 'transferable resources' – that is, virtually nothing – they had to stay put unless the authorities arranged otherwise. In the end, the people seem to have contemplated their fate with resignation. Some wrote apprehensive letters to their loved ones that sometimes had the ring of farewell notes about them. Instinct told them they were doomed. On the other hand, the reassuring logic of available science sincerely persuaded 'informed' and 'sensible' people that the city was in no danger. They considered that Montagne Pelée had shot its bolt with the great mudflow. The Rivière Blanche, moreover, could be relied upon to channel dangerous emissions straight into the sea. So they, too, remained in Saint-Pierre. However, several richer families certainly left the city. Some pessimists took their families to St Lucia, or to southern Martinique. The men then returned alone to Saint-Pierre to look after their businesses, or to guard their property against marauders. Auguste Guérin himself, for instance, who had seen at first hand what the volcano could do, left for southern Martinique. Emilie Dujon and the rest of her family moved out to Beauregard Plantation, 2.5km away in the hills, which her uncle had lent them. Fernand Clerc went to join his family on his plantation at Parnasse. Monsieur Raybaud, managing director of the St James Rum Company, sheltered twenty-six friends in his house at Trouvaillant, in the hills east of Saint-Pierre. There, the ladies spent the terrifying night of 7–8 May at prayer in the salon.

Between the 'informed' and 'uninformed' communities was a third, perhaps younger, group, thrilled by the incomparable spectacle that Montagne Pelée was providing. Every intriguing detour of the unfolding plot forced them to wait for more. As Eugène Berté wrote to his brother, Emile, on 6 May, 'If I had had no children, I would have climbed up myself . . . to watch the marvellous show . . . in the bottom of the furnace.'

Different and cogent reasons thus kept most of the people within the city. They had, in any case, no means of judging the risks they were running and no means of apprehending that they should leave. They were free to go and they stayed. Besides, most of the accommodation provided for refugees was in Saint-Pierre. The people had less than a week in which to decide what to do and to make their arrangements. A mass evacuation would have been virtually impossible to organize in such a short time: the roads were very poor, the available boats were small, and larger vessels would probably have arrived too late. Nevertheless, perhaps a few thousand lives might have been saved.

Nobody knows exactly how many people did actually leave Saint-Pierre, but scarcely more than 5 per cent of the population can have done so. The little steamers of the Girard Company provided the chief means of tranport to and from Saint-Pierre. They usually carried a total of about eighty passengers a day. During the first week in May, however, they transported 1,640 people from Saint-Pierre to Fort-de-France, but only 290 in the other direction – suggesting that 1,350 refugees had left Saint-Pierre. During the same period, on the other hand, Saint-Pierre welcomed some 2,500 refugees from more obviously threatened settlements farther north.

There was a poignant illustration of all these opposing views on the morning of 8 May. The young writer, René Bonneville, off to admire the volcanic spectacle – and to meet his death – waved cheerfully from the *Diamant*, the last steamer to reach Saint-Pierre, to his father, who was fleeing from it on the *Topaze*, the last boat to leave the city before the catastrophe.

Ascension Day, Thursday, 8 May 1902

Throughout the night, Montagne Pelée competed for attention with a storm of unusually awesome violence. Thunder and volcano rumbled in fearsome salvoes. Lightning vied with glowing rocks spurted from the crater. The ground shook. Rain cascaded down. People in Morne Rouge were now so terrified that they clamoured for the last rites. At 3 a.m., floods devastated parts of several villages north of the volcano. At 5 a.m. a mudflow tore through Le Prêcheur, killing 400 people. Then the storm stopped. The volcano hesitated.

In Saint-Pierre, the rain had washed the ash away. The dawn air was fresh and pure. Trees and rooftops glistened in the sun. At about 6 a.m. the first steamer, the *Topaze*, left for Fort-de-France. It carried only thirty-four passengers who had unwittingly diced with death until it was almost too late. At about the same time, the *Roraïma* dropped anchor in the roadstead and, at 6.45 a.m., the *Roddam* arrived from St Lucia. At 7 a.m. the steamer *Diamant* disembarked many passengers from Fort-de-France who had taken advantage of the Ascension Day holiday to see the eruption for themselves. Montagne Pelée did not disappoint them. A magnificent silvery-white column was billowing from its crest. Church bells were already starting to ring for early mass. The *Suchet* should also have arrived at Saint-Pierre at 7 a.m., but engine trouble had delayed its departure from Fort-de-France.

About 7.15 a.m., a skiff set out from Saint-Pierre towards Le Prêcheur, apparently carrying Governor Mouttet and Messieurs Doze, Gerbault and Léonce of the Scientific Commission. Not a trace was ever seen of them again.

By now, however, Ascension Day was not fulfilling its dawning promise. Now and again, impenetrably dark clouds passed over the city. These clouds were a dire and ultimate warning. Montagne Pelée was blasting masses of ash sideways with such force that they were shooting over and beyond Saint-Pierre before falling to earth. The Reaper was about to reap . . .

The Nuée Ardente, 8.02 a.m., 8 May 1902

> And the second angel sounded, and as it were a great mountain burning with fire was cast into the sea: and the third part of the sea became blood, and the third part of the creatures which were in the sea, and had life, died; and the third part of the ships were destroyed. (Revelation 8:8–9)

It was Hélène Lasserre's First Communion. Her parents, older sister and brother were with her in the Cathedral. Before the service started, their estate manager at Morne Rouge came in with the news that some animals had escaped. Edouard Lasserre, the manager and the coachman drove off at once, leaving the family in the Cathedral. When they got to the hills near Grand Réduit, there was a tremendous noise. 'The clouds reached us and overturned our carriage . . . Three minutes later, when we came to . . . we realized that we had been horribly burnt especially on the exposed parts of our bodies . . . Two people, only 10m behind us, were killed.'

At 8 a.m. the telegraph clerk in Saint-Pierre signalled 'Go ahead' to his colleague in Fort-de-France. At 8.01 a.m. – the times were calibrated to the international network – Fort-de-France asked for the morning's news and awaited the reply from Saint-Pierre. At 8.02 a.m. Fort-de-France heard 'a very short trill on the line. Then nothing more.'

There was no warning. Death was often instantaneous. At 8.02 a.m. a businessman in Fort-de-France was on the telephone to a friend in Saint-Pierre. 'He had just finished his sentence when I heard a dreadful scream, then another much weaker groan, like a stifled death rattle. Then silence.'

Montagne Pelée achieved immortality at 8.02 a.m. on 8 May 1902. It was not the most powerful volcanic eruption of the twentieth century, but it was the

The remains of the theatre in Saint-Pierre, with Montagne Pelée on the horizon.

most terrifying and most lethal. A blinding flash lit up the sky. A tremendous cannonade roared out that was heard in Venezuela. Montagne Pelée shuddered and seemed to split open. Then a great blast and nuée ardente shot straight down towards Saint-Pierre at 500km an hour. The infernal avalanche of dark, billowing, reddish-violet fumes, flashing lightning, ash and rocks crashed and rolled headlong southwards, hugging the ground and destroying everything in its path. At first, it was less than 400m thick, and Fernand Clerc could see right over it to the horizon as it surged below him at Parnasse. It seemed like a sea of fire, almost bouncing along as it ignited the workers' cabins and the sugar-cane beside Monsieur Raybaud's house at Trouvaillant. 'We clutched each other tight. We wanted to die together.' The nuée missed them and swept over Saint-Pierre. Untouched, but in deep shock, they ran to Fonds Saint-Denis.

Farther south, a terrified Emilie Dujon saw the nuée rush past Beauregard, stifle the city below, roll out to sea, and then swell outwards and upwards in billowing, cauliflower clouds. Its lethal progress halted just on the outskirts of Le Carbet, 10km south of the crater that it had left two minutes before. Driven almost mad with fear, the Dujon family fled from Beauregard, with the threatening wall of the nuée ardente rising ever higher behind them. Suddenly, Charles Dujon realized that, in their panic, they had left his parents behind. He went to get them, ordering Emilie not to follow him. For Emilie, 'It was a terrible moment. I stood alone moaning, dying of fright, not daring to look at the dark mass, flashing with lightning, that seemed to be rushing towards us with such a deafening noise'. At last, Charles returned with the old couple, and they hurried along, clutching each other in their terror. But soon they fell, exhausted, to their knees to pray and to die. 'Only a miracle could save us.' The miracle came. The great counterblast of gale force halted the nuée ardente. Then they heard the screams rising from Saint-Pierre. But thick, muffling, smoke soon covered the city below. Horrified, they struggled to the hills above Le Carbet. They found a stable on the Lajus Plantation, where about 150 people had already taken refuge. 'We threw ourselves onto the straw. Our throats were on fire.' It was 3 p.m. They had been running from death for seven hours. The priest from Le Carbet gave them absolution because nobody knew what fate still had in store for them. At about five o'clock, the sound of a whistle aroused them from their exhausted torpor. Salvation! They limped to the shore as fast as their lacerated feet would let them – only to see the *Suchet* already leaving for Fort-de-France . . . But other vessels came and sent out rowing boats. In the chaos, the desperate refugees took them by storm. It was only two hours later that the rescue ship could leave behind the sinister red glow which was all that remained of Saint-Pierre. Emilie Dujon never saw her home at Grand'Case again. She and her husband soon left Martinique for good. She lost her home, her homeland, and fifty-seven members of her family.

For the people in Saint-Pierre, the vision of death hurtling towards them was mercifully brief. They had no chance.

The swirling emulsion of gas, steam, scalding mud, scorching ash, hot stones and boulders annihilated Saint-Pierre. On its way, it knocked down trees, huts, public buildings and private dwellings and swept them up into its weaponry. Fonds-Coré vanished completely. The Fort district in the north was razed. In the city centre and beyond, east–west structures were shattered, but some tottering north–south trending walls remained upright, parallel to the direction of the onslaught. Some streets were piled with rubble while others were swept clear. Only a few, very sheltered, roofs remained. The nuée ardente snapped off the lighthouse in the Place Bertin like a matchstick, scythed down the theatre and the prison and reduced the chamber of commerce, the town hall, the Grand Hotel and the *lycée* to rubble. The new market had pillars 30cm thick, built to withstand hurricanes. It disappeared completely. The rum distilleries were blasted apart and their machinery twisted into surreal piles. Little more than the façade survived from the packed Cathedral and its dome was ripped off and dumped into the sea. The clock on the devastated military hospital registered 7.50 a.m., bearing false witness to the time of the cataclysm. Soon a thin layer of hot ash veiled the ruins and the victims.

The nuée ardente passed through Saint-Pierre in two or three minutes, reaching speeds of 500km an hour and temperatures between 200°C and 450°C. The destruction started fires, which soon ignited the countless casks of rum stored about the city. As soon as the nuée ardente was spent, blazing rum and violent winds set Saint-Pierre on fire from end to end. It was then about 8.05 a.m. Most of the people were already dead. The firestorm began.

The blaze generated temperatures as high as 900°C – hotter than the molten rocks that had left the crater. But although the fires raged for many days, they neither destroyed everything nor penetrated everywhere, and the ash layer sometimes proved an efficient insulator. Thus wooden cabins were preserved in the lunatic asylum, but their inmates died. In the Centre church, the fire partly melted the fallen bells, but 10m away, a wooden altar and its lace altar-cloth were found intact beneath a thin coat of ash. The bank, and those inside it, were destroyed, but eight million francs' worth of notes, gold and silver were recovered from the vaults.

Most of the victims in Saint-Pierre died in the space of a few breaths when they inhaled the scorching fumes or ash. Their bodies were often badly burnt. The nuée ardente swept quickly over them – enough to sear throats, lungs and exposed skin, but not always enough to set fire to their clothing.

Suffering was unequal. Some were blessed with instant death, sitting at breakfast, feeding the baby, or waiting for a First Communion. In a house in the main street, the rue Victor Hugo, a man died at his desk, with his daughter's arms around his neck and his son at his knee. Dr Gravier Sainte-Luce, his coachman, his carriage and his horse were struck down as they were leaving home in the rue de Longchamp. Three weeks after the catastrophe, Dr Emile Berté inspected the former home of the Blausse family. The dog had been incinerated. A stable lad had died asleep in his bed, but his body was just starting to decay under a coating of muddy ash. A well-to-do white man and a blonde white girl with a blue ribbon in her hair, a black woman and her year-old child lay in the yard, covered with 2cm of ash. Their bodies were perfectly preserved and they had not a single burn. Dr Berté touched the man's skin: 'I thought my finger would sink into it as if it were dough . . . but it was as firm and cold as marble.' They had been asphyxiated, without warning, perhaps by toxic gas.

Those in the streets of Saint-Pierre had just time to start running. Some were thrown down southwards by the blast or hit and entombed by flying masonry. Many piled up dead in doorways as they scrambled for shelter in the buildings. A cluster of women, entwined in terror, perished in the rue St Jean-de-Dieu, the prostitutes' district. Many victims were burnt extensively, often stripped naked and contorted into grotesque positions by their dying muscular spasms. Then the ash coated them with a crust so that whites could not be distinguished from blacks, granting them an equality that they had not enjoyed in life.

A few dozen people lasted longer. They were seen from ships offshore, badly burnt and dashing in helpless agony for a few minutes about the Place Bertin. In the far south of Saint-Pierre, they saw their fate coming and tried, in vain, to reach the sea before the scorching cloud enveloped them.

In the area covered by the nuée ardente in Saint-Pierre itself, there were only two survivors. Both were partly sheltered by the Morne Abel, the hill on

The stone cell of Sylbaris in the prison in Saint-Pierre.

the edge of the city. A cobbler, Léon Compère-Léandre, was at his door when he was suddenly burnt and darkness fell. When daylight returned, he was surrounded by corpses, including those of his neighbours, the Delavauds. Young Delavaud and his girlfriend, Flavia, had died in each other's arms. The cobbler fled in terror to Trouvaillant.

The other survivor stole the limelight. He was a 25-year-old from Le Prêcheur, with a volcanic temperament and strong as an ox, equally apt as a farmhand or as a sailor, in and out of jobs, in and out of jail. His name was Louis-Auguste Sylbaris, or Cyparis – it didn't matter much in those days. Anyway, everybody called him 'Sanson' (Samson). In early April, he had wounded one of his friends with a cutlass at a fiesta in Le Prêcheur, and he had been sentenced to a month in prison. Towards the end of his time, he was taken into town on a labouring job and learnt that there was another fiesta in Le Prêcheur. He escaped from custody, danced all night, and duly gave himself up again the following morning. He was promptly sentenced to solitary confinement for a week. Thus, on 8 May he was alone in a stone cell built like a bomb-shelter in a deep hollow outside the prison proper. It had only a small, south-facing opening and a thick wooden door.

They hadn't yet brought my daily rations, when, all of a sudden, there was a terrifying noise. Everybody was screaming 'Help! Help! I'm burning! I'm dying!' Five minutes later, nobody was crying out any more – except me. Then, a cloud of smoke gushed through the opening . . . It burnt me so much that I was dancing up and down, left and right – everywhere – to get out of its way . . . I listened and shouted for help, but nobody answered.

Sanson spent his next three days with nothing to eat and only the rainwater to drink. On Sunday 11 May, three men from Morne Rouge were wandering through Saint-Pierre – not, perhaps, wholly with good deeds in mind. They heard Sanson crying out in Créole 'vin sauvé un pauv' prisonnier' – 'come and save a poor prisoner'. They broke down the door with a great rock and released 'the poor prisoner', who was by now delirious with thirst and covered in burns, although his clothes had not ignited. When he asked what had happened to the people from the prison, his rescuers could only reply: 'Pa ni la geôle, tout Saint-Pierre brûlé' – 'There is no jail. All Saint-Pierre is burnt.' His rescuers took Sanson to their priest in Morne Rouge, Father J. Mary, who nursed him and noted down the details of his fantastic survival. Sanson was so grateful that he not only wanted to become Father Mary's servant, but a practising Christian as well. But it was not to be. Sanson became an attraction in a famous American circus, which advertised him as 'the only living object [*sic*] that survived in the Silent City of Death'. Father Mary was to meet a far more dreadful fate before the year was out . . .

The unluckiest citizens of all were those who inhaled the scorching concoction near the edge of the nuée ardente, for they suffered atrociously for

'Sanson' on show.

several hours. Some people may have lived on for a while in the city. Henri Alfred apparently only died on the morning of 9 May. His maid, who was taken to Fort-de-France, succumbed to her burns later that afternoon. The critical boundary of death passed over the Montferriers' home on the northeastern fringe of Saint-Pierre. Monsieur Montferrier was outside and, when he cried out, Madame Montferrier rushed from her kitchen and met the burning blast at her door. They did not feel the dire effects at once. He was to die five days later; but his wife survived because the kitchen had protected her. After the nuée ardente had passed, they set out to rescue their children who had gone to the church at Trois-Ponts. It had been totally destroyed. As they were wandering about under the effects of shock, they noticed that Monsieur Landes' new house was still intact nearby. Gaston Landes, two servants, a pupil at the lycée, Edouard Thouin, and his sister, were all in the garden, severely burnt, bleeding from nose and mouth, and crying out for water. But they could not drink. Over the next three hours they all died. Gaston Landes had massive burns to his skin, throat, lungs and eyes. He was the last to die, about noon, throwing himself about in helpless agony. Amongst the last coherent words that he uttered were: 'What on earth has happened?'

A few people had very narrow escapes. On the edge of the nuée ardente life or death depended on a couple of breaths or a couple of metres. The nuée failed to kill Edouard Lasserre, his estate manager and his coachman by less than 10m at Grand Réduit. Simon Taudilas was in a group of three men and three women near Parnasse, 2km northeast of Saint-Pierre. He fled from the advancing nuée with two friends. They were thrown down and burnt by the blast, but ran on to Parnasse. Simon Taudilas recovered, but one friend died within an hour and the other after three days. All three women survived because they had sheltered in a building nearby. Passioniste Lesage was chatting to two women traders on the road to Le Carbet, 2km south of Saint-Pierre. The blast also knocked him over, rolled him along the ground, drove two stones into his right leg, covered him with wet mud, burnt his hands and feet and choked him with hot ash. The women vanished, but he survived. On the Morne Orange hill at the southeastern edge of Saint-Pierre, two women had barricaded themselves in the Laugier shop. They were sealed from the searing nuée, and were the sole survivors in the district. Luckily the shop was not destroyed and only caught fire after the nuée ardente had passed, so they were able to flee to safety.

The oddest tale of survival concerned two gunners at Colson Camp. Gunners Vaillant and Tribut were on watch when the eruption occurred, but they abandoned their post and went to see what had happened to Saint-Pierre. At 3 p.m. the Camp Commandant sent two men on horseback but they could get no nearer than 400m from the blazing city. On the way back, whom should they meet but Vaillant and Tribut with a seriously injured sailor they had rescued from the beach. He was Raphaël Pons, a stoker from the *Roraïma* that was then ablaze in the bay. When the absconding pair were charged next day at the camp, Vaillant lived up to his name and protested bravely that they had promised to help a badly burnt white family and a black woman in a house in the rue Lucille. Vaillant was so eloquent that he was taken to Saint-Pierre to prove his case. Late in the afternoon of 9 May he found a bemused black woman, who seemed to acknowledge that he had given her water the previous afternoon. The white family, however, had all died and the maid herself died on arrival at Fort-de-France. Astonishingly, the stoker's fate was not recorded, perhaps because he soon succumbed to his wounds.

The Bay of Saint-Pierre, 8 May

The nuée ardente blasted straight out into the Bay and destroyed all but one of the dozen or so larger vessels and scores of smaller craft moored off Saint-Pierre. Most of those on board were burnt, scalded, suffocated or drowned. Several lived because their burnt and dying comrades fell on top of them. Only a fortunate few survived.

The *Teresa lo Vico* was moored close to the southern shore of the city. Most on board died. A falling mast removed the captain's face. The ship's boy, however, only had slight burns because he was below in the engine room and had immersed his head in a basin of water to protect himself from the hot blast. After the nuée ardente passed over, the engineer, Jean-Louis Prudent, dived into the sea, grabbed a small boat, and embarked nine burnt sailors, his wife and their maid, and the dead captain's widow. They struggled to the shore near Le Carbet and waited on the remains of a landing-stage, stupefied with shock.

Saint-Pierre just before the eruption in 1902.

Jean-Baptiste Innocent, ship's boy and sole survivor of the *Diamant*, was tying up to the quay when the nuée ardente blasted him into the sea and exploded the little vessel's engine. He lived because he stayed underwater until the hot ash dissipated. Then he clung desperately to a plank in the water, not daring to approach the blazing shore.

The nuée ardente sank the schooner *Gabrielle* before it could even set it on fire. It threw the mate, Georges Marie-Sainte and four crewmen into the sea, where they clung to floating wreckage for six hours until they could scramble aboard a stray canoe.

When the catastrophe struck, the *Roddam* had been anchored off Saint-Pierre for less than two hours. It still had steam up and it was thus the only vessel that could limp away afterwards. The *Roddam* bottomed, but did not sink because the portholes were shut. Many on board were thrown into the boiling sea and drowned; many others died in screaming agony as they inhaled the scorching, swirling, dust. Captain Edward W. Freeman dashed into the chart-room and saved his life. The red-hot dust of the nuée ardente enveloped him for two minutes that seemed like two years, searing skin and lungs. As soon as the nuée had gone, he decided to make a getaway. But it was dark now and 'All around me, piercing shrieks of agony went up above the roar of the flames'. He could muster only six fit crewmen to effect the hazardous depar-ture with a ship that was badly damaged and scorching hot. The steering gear was blocked so that the vessel 'drifted out of control like a floating furnace' for an hour and a half. The *Roddam* was in no condition to help the *Roraïma*. At length, at 5 p.m. on 8 May, the *Roddam* limped back to Port Castries, in St Lucia, which it had left the previous evening. Captain Freeman was badly burnt; his ship was blanketed in 15cm of ash; and he was one of only twenty who survived, of the forty-six on board.

On the *Roraïma*, Captain Muggha saw the nuée ardente coming and just had time to shout: 'Raise the anchor!' It was his last command. The nuée ardente swept everything clean off the deck and set fire to the *Roraïma* and her captain. The blazing captain jumped into the sea and died. Ellery Scott, the mate, was amongst the four able-bodied survivors who could fight the fires and try to succour the dying. Most of the twenty or so survivors were craving for water, but they could not even take ice-cubes. Some had burnt-out tongues. They were all mortified to see the uncontrollable *Roddam* sail past them without offering help. Then they could only wait for assistance, burnt red-raw and numb with shock, watching corpses bobbing about on the huge waves amidst the thick flotsam of wrecked and smouldering craft.

Rescue? 8 May 1902

Soon after 8 a.m. in Fort-de-France, a big cloud blackened the northern sky, little stones spattered down for a while and a small wave tossed boats about in the harbour. That was all. Only 22km from Montagne Pelée, the physical effects of the eruption were minuscule. But news soon spread that Saint-Pierre had fallen silent.

The Girard Company steamers had been working as usual that morning between the cities. The *Diamant* had left Fort-de-France at 6 a.m. The *Rubis* had left at 7 a.m., but impenetrable ash had forced it to turn back before it could reach Saint-Pierre. Meanwhile, the *Topaze*, which had been the last boat to leave Saint-Pierre at 6 a.m., set off from Fort-de-France on its return journey about 8.15 a.m. Within half an hour, thick fumes and a hail of hot stones from the dark cloud halted the *Topaze*. The returning *Rubis* then came into view. The steamers returned together to Fort-de-France, greatly increasing the disquiet provoked by the silence from Saint-Pierre.

At 10 a.m. the *Rubis* set off to make another attempt to reach Saint-Pierre. It carried Monsieur Labat, a deputy-mayor of Fort-de-France, with an offer to help the mayor of Saint-Pierre with any evacuation that might be needed. The lucky member of the Scientific Commission, Monsieur Mirville, was also on board, as well as the troops that the mayor of Saint-Pierre had requested. Conditions had improved and only fine ash was falling when the *Rubis* turned into the Bay of Saint-Pierre soon after eleven. Montagne Pelée was calm and sated. Wrecked and blazing ships littered the bay. Saint-Pierre was an immense inferno. Monsieur Labat scanned the coast through his field-glasses for any signs of life. In vain. It was far too hot to land. All that they could do was to return and break the news in Fort-de-France.

Meanwhile, in the capital, disquiet was turning into foreboding. Why the silence? Why hadn't the *Diamant* returned? Surely if a disaster had stricken Saint-Pierre, the many survivors would soon start to appear? A woman appeared on the coast road from Saint-Pierre. Could this be the first of them? But she ignored questions and wanted to embrace everybody. She was weeping and kept on babbling 'It was about eight'. She had lost her senses. Nobody else came after her.

Its engine problems solved miraculously late, the cruiser, *Suchet*, left for Saint-Pierre at noon and learnt of the catastrophe from the returning *Rubis*. When the steamer got to Fort-de-France at 12.30, an anxious crowd of 20,000 was waiting on the quayside. Monsieur Mirville hurried to the town hall to tell the authorities. The news soon spread that Saint-Pierre was lost. Everyone had friends or relatives in Saint-Pierre. Surely they could not *all* be dead . . .? Nobody could comprehend the enormity of the destruction and the likely death-toll.

At 2 p.m., the *Rubis* set off yet again for Saint-Pierre. This time it carried an official delegation from Victor Sévère, the mayor of Fort-de-France. It included Monsieur Lubin, the Public Prosecutor, Lieutenant G. Hébert, Lt-Col. M. Tessier, in charge of the thirty infantrymen, Abbé Parel and another priest. At three o'clock, the situation at Saint-Pierre had scarcely changed, but Messieurs Lubin, Hébert and Tessier were able to make two landings by lifeboat. They stood speechless in the midst of the vast solitude that had been the Place Bertin. Less than twenty-four hours after his last visit, Lieutenant

The ruins of Saint-Pierre just after the eruption on 8 May 1902.

Hébert was back in Saint-Pierre. No quays, no trees, no casks of rum, only shattered façades and a few dozen burnt bodies, often in grotesque positions. 'We were sobbing and tears were flowing.' The scorching ash made it impossible to venture inland and they returned to the *Rubis*. The two priests on board 'recited the prayers for the dead . . . The sailors knelt down in grief, crying out the names of their dear ones out there in that fearsome inferno.'

Meanwhile, Commander Le Bris of the *Suchet* had also been unable to get far into the city. Both the cruiser and the steamer turned southwards to Le Carbet to try and pick up any survivors. Even the rescues were difficult because the stormy seas tossed the small craft about like corks as they plied back and forth to the cruiser.

The victims were gathered in the sick-bay on the *Suchet*. Shock affected them differently: some were speechless, some were rambling incoherently, some were crying out in agony, some were singing. All had red-raw burns and an unquenchable thirst, but many could not drink. Nine of those 'who had swallowed the fire' died before the *Suchet* reached Fort-de-France. The nuée ardente had not reached Le Carbet, but its terrified inhabitants had seen it stop just short of the village. They begged to be taken from this forsaken spot forthwith. More boats joined in the rescue, including the *Topaze* and the cable-repair vessel, *Pouyer Quertier*. The convoy eventually returned to the capital at 9.30 p.m. with about 700 refugees, including Emilie Dujon and her family. All looked as if they had come back from Hell. A vast crowd jostled on the esplanade, hoping against hope to see a friend or relative amongst those being taken to hospital.

Commander Le Bris telegraphed to the Navy Ministry in Paris at 9.55 p.m. on 8 May:

Suchet to Navy Paris.
Back from Saint-Pierre, city completely destroyed by mass of fire about 8hr in the morning.
Suppose all population annihilated. Have brought back the few survivors, about thirty.
All ships in roadstead burnt and lost. Eruption volcano continues. I am leaving for
Guadeloupe to get supplies.

Evacuation, Thursday, 8 May–Sunday, 11 May 1902

It was assumed at first in Fort-de-France that all the villages around Montagne Pelée had accompanied Saint-Pierre into oblivion. But the nuée ardente had spread only as far north as the outskirts of Le Prêcheur, missing the village by 100m. Thus the settlement that had suffered falling ash for two weeks, and had been the prime concern of Governor Mouttet, was spared – if only in part.

Dr Emile Berté, ship's doctor on the cable-repair vessel *Pouyer Quertier*, described how thousands were evacuated. When the nuée ardente erupted, the ship was 13km off Saint-Pierre, repairing the broken telegraph link between Martinique and France. Unable to reach Saint-Pierre, Captain Thirion headed the *Pouyer Quertier* for Fort-de-France, accompanied by a band of frantic porpoises. That afternoon, the *Pouyer Quertier* returned to the Bay with the *Topaze* to join in the rescue operations. Emile Berté gazed in horror at his home town. 'Had my people been able to escape? I still couldn't believe that they had all been burnt alive, because my brother [Eugène] was prudence itself.' All his family had died.

At eight the next morning, 9 May, the *Pouyer Quertier* sounded its siren off Les Abymes, just north of Le Prêcheur. All the villagers begged to be taken to the safety of Saint-Pierre . . . Pirogue canoes brought the women and children out to meet the cutters from the *Pouyer Quertier*. Each adult received diluted wine, bread and cheese and each child a bowl of milk. They took 425 people to Fort-de-France.

On Saturday, 10 May it was the turn of Le Prêcheur. The *Pouyer Quertier* was joined by the *Suchet* and Senator Amédée Knight's commodious yacht. Eleven pirogues plied back and forth across the dangerous seas from the shore to the ships. It took five long hours for the forty oarsmen to embark 1,200 women and children. It is said that, as the vessels departed, the exhausted oarsmen respectfully raised their hats and one declared: 'See you tomorrow, Senator – if we are not dead.'

On Sunday, 11 May the rescue vessels, joined by the Danish ship *Walkyrien*, evacuated the remaining 3,000 people from Le Prêcheur. Eventually only two old men remained on the shore to take the last pirogue. Both had given sterling service to the community. 'Go ahead, Mr Mayor,' said the priest, Abbé

Desprez. 'No, Father,' replied the mayor, Monsieur Grelet, 'it is my duty to be the last to leave from here.' And so it was.

It was only when the inhabitants of Le Prêcheur reached the haven of Fort-de-France that the story of the village on the fatal day became known. The raging torrent at 5 a.m. on 8 May had severely damaged the church and the bridge, greatly widened the river mouth, and swept 400 people to their deaths. Many were still convinced that the greatest danger might yet spring from the sea. About 6.30 a.m., therefore, some 400 villagers climbed to shelter at the semaphore at Morne Folie, 100m above the shore, on the flanks of Montagne Pelée. 'Folie' it turned out to be. One young man saw their doom coming.

Monsieur Grelet decided to ask Saint-Pierre for further help, but, because communication links had been broken, he commissioned a boat to take his message. At 7.30 a.m. the 20-year-old Chavigny de la Chevrotière and eleven friends set out to row a pirogue across the Bay. When they were just opposite Morne Folie, Chavigny looked up as Montagne Pelée unleashed the nuée ardente. He had no time to turn away. The hot blast struck him full in the face and tipped them all into the sea. Seven lads were drowned or burnt to death; five managed to reach the shore and lived. Chavigny himself was swept 2km northward to Les Abymes. When the five were rescued on 10 May by the *Pouyer Quertier*, Dr Berté observed that they looked as if they had been scalded by a steam jet, for their burns were widespread, but not deep. Those sheltering at Morne Folie were embraced a fraction more by the searing nuée. All 400 perished. Chavigny de la Chevrotière recovered after spending two weeks in hospital in Fort-de-France.

Survivors of the Nuée Ardente of 8.02 on 8 May 1902

It is often said that only two men survived the nuée ardente. Others who escaped were mentioned in the early accounts but then seem to have been forgotten, perhaps because two survivors made a more dramatic story.

Many more than two people lived after the edge of the nuée ardente had burnt and buffeted them. The *Roddam* took twenty survivors to St Lucia. The *Suchet* rescued twenty from the *Roraïma*, five from the *Gabrielle*, and thirteen from the *Teresa lo Vico* as well as Innocent, the ship's boy from the *Diamant*, and Lesage from Le Carbet. Nine of these died on the *Suchet*, leaving 'about thirty' victims who reached hospital at Fort-de-France. In addition, Raphaël Pons, stoker on the *Roraïma* was rescued by Vaillant and Tribut. Five lived from Chavigny's pirogue near Le Prêcheur. On the inland edges of the nuée ardente, Edouard Lasserre, his farm manager and coachman; Madame Montferrier, Simon Taudilas and the three women with him, as well as the two ladies barricaded in the Laugier shop all survived, whereas people within a few metres of them died. The insane lady who emerged from Case Navire in Fort-de-France may or may not have been directly covered by the nuée. Thus, including Sylbaris and Compère-Léandre, a minimum of sixty-nine people

Montagne Pelée on the
afternoon of 30 August 1902.

The cemetery at
Le Marigot on 26 August
1902.

survived the nuée ardente. This figure does not, of course, include people such as the Dujon and Raybaud families, who were terrified – but not touched – by the nuée ardente. In fact, 151 people were admitted to hospital, amongst whom was an unknown number of victims of falling ash and flood damage. Of these 151 people, 111 recovered – and this total must represent the absolute maximum number of possible survivors. Thus a minimum of 69 and a maximum of 111 people withstood the great nuée ardente.

Epilogue

The death of 27,000 people was not the end of the matter – either for Montagne Pelée, or for the authorities. The volcano erupted small nuées ardentes practically every day between 16 May and 26 May and again on 6 June and 9 July. At 5.20 a.m. on 20 May, Montagne Pelée unleashed its second great nuée ardente. It was just as powerful as the first and covered much the same area. It completed the devastation of Saint-Pierre, but, by then, there were only perhaps a few looters left in the city to kill. That afternoon, the people of Morne Rouge were evacuated to Fort-de-France; 3,000 people left the capital for the far south of Martinique; and over 1,000 embarked for Guadeloupe.

In spite of the continued eruptions, Saint-Pierre attracted looters from all over the West Indies. Many balanced the unpredictable risks of death by nuée ardente against the prospects of legendary pickings. There were antiques, strong-boxes and safes under the ash and masonry – and jewellery to be wrenched from the dead. On 14 May alone, for instance, forty-five looters were arrested. The captured guilty were condemned to five years in jail. But it was impossible to guard all the city all the time, and the volcano threatened both guards and looters with masterly impartiality.

Dr Berté got permission to search for his own house on 30 May. All he found was a wall, 25cm high. In an awesome silence, he sat on the wall thinking 'All my family is buried under the very ground I am trampling upon.' He had gone to Saint-Pierre with the cremation squads, who had already been at work for several days, but only about 4,000 corpses were recovered and burnt. The rest decayed under the ruins and ash, and were sometimes exposed after torrential rains.

Alfred Lacroix, the government's scientific envoy, and his team, began their investigations on 23 June. They were photographed in their colonial splendour – white tropical kit and pith helmets – against the background of total devastation. But they stare out in complete incomprehension, as if they had suddenly been dropped into the Inferno. Not since AD 79 had a volcano so completely destroyed a city . . .

Meanwhile, there were 25,000 displaced persons in Martinique, including 15,000 in Fort-de-France alone. They were housed in every available public building, in many homes and in temporary huts. Victor Sévère, the young and able mayor of Fort-de-France, organized their daily rations of bread, salted

Officials on the steps of the ruined Chamber of Commerce in Saint-Pierre on 11 May 1902.

pork, cod and dried vegetables. But, of course, many gathered rations at different centres and sold them; many also came for the bounty from unharmed areas. The very idea of giving out free food also met with opposition. A Breton officer, for instance, declared that it was disgraceful to distribute quality white bread to 'these Negroes' when thousands of Bretons and soldiers would never be given any. The victims received 1.25 francs per person per day in cash, food and clothing. This was more than most of them had earned in their lives, for the average daily wage of a farmworker was less than 1.50 francs. It also fermented the jealousy of those who had lost nothing and therefore still had to work. By the end of August, 'good sense' – and a new Governor – prevailed. Allowances were reduced to a more fitting 70 centimes for men and 50 centimes for women, with a maximum of 1.60 francs per family. Grants were in cash only – to prevent profiteering. Not all the refugees, however, were poor landless labourers. The wealthier people received much larger sums, for the government acknowledged that the rich could not be expected to withstand being as poor as the poor for very long.

There were still too many refugees for comfort in Fort-de-France by the end of July, and one typhoid epidemic had already broken out. The evacuees were encouraged – practically forced – to return to their own villages. On 2 August, the interim Governor, Georges Lhuerre, decreed that the refugees had until 15 August to return to their homes. They were not forced to go back home, but those who refused would get no further help. Those who ignored the injunction were in effect, at liberty to starve. Thus it was that the refugees went back to Morne Rouge.

On 31 July, Alfred Lacroix left for Paris, believing that the worst of the eruption was over. However, after a month's rest, Montagne Pelée started erupting again with great gusto on 13 August. Those who had returned to Morne Rouge began to regret it. Jean-Baptiste Lemaire took up his new post as Governor of Martinique on 21 August, but, unlike Louis Mouttet, he had a low opinion of indigenous peoples. On 26 August, faced with the increasingly terrifying spectacle from Montagne Pelée, a delegation from Morne Rouge went to ask the new Governor to evacuate them from their obviously threatened homes. Governor Lemaire wasted no time. He told them to go back to Morne Rouge – or else their food allowance would be cut off completely. As the hapless delegation had no other resources, they had to comply and await the pleasure of the volcano. Not for long.

The next eruptive climax duly came at 8.45 p.m. on 30 August. There was an enormous explosion and a great red nuée ardente spread over double the area of any of its predecessors. It covered Saint-Pierre again, but also enveloped Morne Rouge for the first time. Most of the inhabitants of the village had been barricaded in their homes for several days. They heard a fearful noise. Several gendarmes saw the danger coming, mounted their horses and rode off in a desperate posse towards Fort-de-France. The nuée ardente caught three of them and burnt them to death.

The nuée arrived in three separate surges. Father J. Mary heard the first wave and left his home to open the church so that his parishioners could shelter and pray inside. The second and third waves caught him on his way to his church and he died of his burns on 1 September. The church, jail and many buildings were badly damaged and the whole village was blanketed in hot ash. Over 1,000 people died, and the new Governor was largely to blame. However, both he and his ally, Gaston Doumergue, the Colonial Secretary – and a future President of France – escaped censure because they proved to be skilfully economical with the truth. It is odd that they have escaped much criticism until very recently, whereas Governor Mouttet has often been unjustly condemned for the deaths in Saint-Pierre. The survivors abandoned Morne Rouge for over a year. That was the last lethal nuée ardente expelled in 1902, although many others rolled down the Rivière Blanche valley until the middle of 1903.

Little by little, the centre of attraction on the volcano changed from the nuées ardentes to the dome of fuming hot lava that pushed out of the volcanic chimney like molten glass. From its summit, an incandescent spine soon began to emerge like an enormous, ominous and yet spell-binding finger. It was given the singularly innocuous name of 'the Needle of Pelée'. Those who liked symbolism were not clear whether it was accusing the heavens or admonishing what was left of Saint-Pierre. On 31 May 1903, the dome rose 300m from the old Etang Sec and the spine protruded a further 272m above it. Gradually, however, explosions and weathering got the upper hand, the spine disintegrated and the dome finally stopped growing by 1904.

From early in 1903, boatloads of tourists began to visit the ruins of Saint-Pierre. At first, they had to get permission from Governor Lemaire, who kindly arranged that any bones exposed by erosion or looters were buried again so that the visitors would not be upset.

The government purchased or rented land to build refugee cabins, and provided seeds, stock, tools, boats and sewing-machines that would form the basis of the new society. Roads, cisterns, fountains, bridges and a dozen new schools were constructed. But the new settlements were ruled by the military, and civilians found their discipline both incomprehensible and irksome. By 1905, out of some 22,000 refugees, about 10,000 were living in the new settlements, but 11,300 had gone back to the northern zone. The resettlement was often chaotic. At first, charity organizations and many eminent persons, such as Kaiser Wilhelm II of Germany, King Edward VII of England, Pope Leo XIII and the US government, gained much prestige by sending well-publicized donations to the ravaged island. Unfortunately, the gifts stopped when several books and articles propagated lies about the survivors that have held currency for many decades. One of these lies was that the administration had forced the citizens to stay in Saint-Pierre to vote. Another lie, altogether more damaging, was that the indolent blacks were dancing and partying on the profits from the charities. In fact, they had nothing whatever to dance about. They were hungry, homesick, bereaved, browbeaten, poverty-stricken, terrified and helpless. But these calumnies would form a substantial chapter in themselves.

The first general election after the catastrophe in 1902 was held in Martinique (North) in May 1906, when Victor Sévère, the mayor of Fort-de-France, was elected. 'Normality' gradually returned to Martinique. People also began to come back to Saint-Pierre, clearing the ruins and building on the surviving foundations. There were 500 inhabitants in 1910 and nearly 2,000 in 1915. It became a municipality again in 1923, when Louis Percin was elected mayor. In 1927, twenty-five years after the catastrophe, Saint-Pierre had a population of 3,250. When Montagne Pelée erupted again in the autumn of 1929, Saint-Pierre was soon deserted. Eruptions continued irregularly until the end of 1932, but they were weaker than those of 1902 and never reached the little patched-up village that Saint-Pierre had become.

Saint-Pierre is now a sleepy place with a population of about 7,500. It has never recovered the pre-eminence it had before the catastrophe. The professional and commercial classes had been destroyed and the economic and cultural centre of gravity of Martinique shifted at last to Fort-de-France. The memory of Saint-Pierre became a romanticized symbol of tropical colonial *douceur de vivre*.

12

Parícutin, 1943

Native Americans saw this eruption from its very beginnings in a field in upland México, and then suffered a prolonged agony – first as lava encroached upon their homes, and then as they began new lives in new settlements. Grief was the main cause of death during this eruption.

A New Volcano in México

It began, they said, when the cross was broken. Then there was a plague of locusts. Then there were the earthquakes. Then the new volcano was born. Then the lava and ash buried the village. Then the people had to go and live in Caltzontzin. Parícutin was no more, and the volcano took its name.

*

A line of large volcanoes runs for 1,200km from east to west across the high plains and sierras of southern México. Repeated eruptions in the same spot for thousands of years have built them up well above the snow-line to form glistening cones like Popocatépetl. About 300km west of México City, however, in the state of Michoacán, the style of the volcanic activity has changed. The large volcanoes are extinct, and the eruptions have become much more scattered. Many new volcanoes formed at irregular intervals, each holding the stage only for a few years before lapsing into extinction. The volcanic cones are thus much smaller and less impressive than Popocatépetl, but they number more than 1,000. Intervals of tranquillity were long and common. Since the Spanish Conquistadors came to upland México in 1519, only two entirely new volcanoes have been born in Michoacán – Jorullo in 1759, and Parícutin, 80km away to the northwest, in 1943. Although the eruption of Parícutin was neither the most varied, nor the most violent, nor the most disastrous in human history, its biography is more comprehensive than of many of its more glamorous rivals. No brand-new volcano has ever been so closely watched and studied as Parícutin – from the very moment of its birth on 20 February 1943, until its death, nine years and two weeks later, on 4 March 1952. The eruption also provided valuable insights into the reactions of a traditionally oriented people to the threat – and then the reality – of displacement to new homes in different environments.

Parícutin.

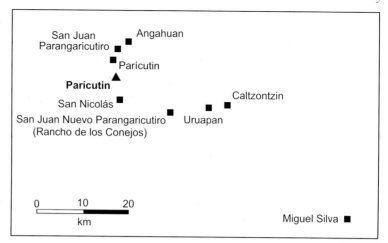

San Juan
Parangaricutiro   Angahuan

Parícutin

Parícutin

San Nicolás   Caltzontzin

San Juan Nuevo Parangaricutiro   Uruapan
(Rancho de los Conejos)

0   10   20
km

The area around
Parícutin.   Miguel Silva ■

The sharp-eyed witnesses of the start of the eruption were native American Tarascans, who were well acquainted with the vagaries of nature. The course of the eruption was studied by American and Mexican scientists, notably William Foshag and Jenaro González-Reyna, while Mary Nolan studied its effects on the displaced populations. In 1993, to celebrate the fiftieth anniversary of the start of the eruption, J. F. Luhr and Tom Simkin brought together the chief articles about the volcano in *Parícutin. The Volcano Born in a Mexican Cornfield*.

The eruption took place in the upper Itzicura valley, isolated in the mountains of Michoacán, some 2,300m above sea-level, and about 325km west of México City. Almost surrounded by the eroded remains of large volcanoes, the whole valley was also filled with smaller volcanic cones and lava-flows. The cones and the steep edges of the flows were forested; the weathered older flows and tracts of river alluvium gave even, fertile soils; but the newer flows were far too rugged to plough and formed tongues of *malpaís*, badlands. These volcanic features gave a terraced effect to the beautiful rural landscape where popular traditions had changed very little since the early days of the Spanish Conquest. The colonial monks had made the Tarascans settle in villages where they could teach them agriculture – and keep an eye on them at the same time. Each settlement was built on the typical Spanish Colonial grid-pattern, centred on the church in the main plaza, with simple white houses, a bar, a baker's, a butcher's and a general store or two. The people subsisted from the produce of their land, supplemented by wood-cutting for fuel and handicrafts and resin collection from the nearby forests for the turpentine distilleries in the regional centre, Uruapan. They tilled the soil with wooden ploughs, drawn by cattle or oxen, and grew maize on the best soils, with wheat, barley, beans or squashes on the slopes around them. Each family grew vegetables and fruit, and kept a donkey, a pig, and a few hens and rabbits; many also reared a few sheep for meat and wool; cattle, costly and prestigious, were less common. The

Tarascans lived together in their villages and hamlets and travelled daily to their plots of land. Nobody was wealthy; few ever even entertained aspirations that would separate them from the traditions of their ancestors. These social traditions were a 400-year-old hybrid of Tarascan and Spanish practices.

Like all native Americans, the Tarascans had a strong communion with nature. They believed that they interacted with the natural world; that they would prosper if they respected its harmonies; and that they would be warned by portents and symbols – and then punished – if they went astray. The Tarascans were deeply attached to the land, where they worked, lived, and had buried their ancestors. They were also fervent Catholics. They cherished, in particular, a venerable crucifix, *El Señor de los Milagros*, the Lord of the Miracles, which was the focus of pilgrimages to the church in San Juan Parangaricutiro. This was not the old colonial church, which had been abandoned, but a new, and still unfinished, church that the citizens had started to build some thirty years before.

In 1943, México had hardly emerged from a long, harsh struggle, verging on a civil war, between the government and the Catholic Church. It formed, for instance, the background to Graham Greene's *The Power and the Glory*. Then, when General Lázaro Cárdenas was President between 1934 and 1939, many large estates had been broken up, the government had taken control of vast areas, and one third of all the land in the country had been redistributed to new, peasant, owners. Thus, when the volcano erupted, traditional attitudes, land ownership, and religion were real and vital issues, even amongst the isolated communities of Michoacán. Any further upheaval, any other psychological pressure would be hard to bear ... In the event, far more of the uprooted peasants died of grief than were ever killed by the volcano.

The Portents, 1941–3

The eruption directly affected only a small area and a small population. The main township, or *municipio* in the valley was called San Juan Parangaricutiro, a hybrid of its Spanish and Tarascan names. It had a population of 1,895 and its revered crucifix was its sole claim to fame. Some 2km to the south, the hamlet of Parícutin, which sheltered 733 people, was reputed for its pears. There were constant disputes between San Juan Parangaricutiro and Parícutin about land ownership and plot boundaries, which were to plague the two communities long after the eruption ceased.

During one particularly furious quarrel in 1941, Nicolás Toral from Parícutin was killed – in fact, very close to the place where the volcano was to erupt. The church decided that enough was enough, and set up a large wooden cross on the mountainside overlooking the disputed area. The priest of Parícutin blessed the symbol of peace in front of a fervent throng. Some, however, mistakenly thought the cross marked the contentious boundary line. They took the symbol down and hid it. (In Parícutin they suspected a man called Padilla, who was cursed with a stammer and could well, therefore, be guilty.) The sacrilege filled the Parícutin council of elders with foreboding: misery and ruin would surely soon punish them. A little later, a woman of Parícutin, Justina Sánchez, dreamt that fire issued from the earth and burnt everything in Parícutin.

Divine retribution apparently continued. In February 1942, a plague of locusts covered the ground and blotted out the sun. Those who knew their Bible turned to Exodus 10, verses 14–16.

> And the locusts went up over all the land of Egypt . . . very grievous were they . . . For they covered the face of the whole earth, so that the land was darkened; and they did eat every herb of the land, and all the fruit of the trees . . . Then Pharaoh called for Moses and Aaron in haste; and he said: I have sinned against the Lord your God.

The government sent poison – which killed the cattle instead of the locusts. Then they sent petrol to burn the pests. But for every locust killed, dozens more seemed to arrive. In desperation, the people tried to frighten them off 'with bands of music, fireworks, drums, tin vessels . . . and thus the locusts were forced to retreat'. Noise was to have no effect when the volcano came.

In December 1942 the villagers harvested and stored their maize crop, as usual. In the New Year, the ground started to shake. (The first earthquake, on 7 January 1943, passed unnoticed at Parícutin, but was recorded on instruments in México City. Several others followed during that month.) The tremors began in earnest at noon on 5 February. The ground rumbled ominously just before each tremor. For two weeks, the rumbles and tremors beat out a gradually increasing rhythm, until the ground seemed to be rocking continuously. People no longer dared sleep in their houses and the larger earthquakes caused many to sink down to their knees and pray for salvation. Soon, even the newspapers in México City were reporting them.

Meanwhile, in spite of these portents, the farmers had started clearing their land again and had yoked up their oxen for the first ploughing before the new sowing season. It was not to yield much more than anguish . . .

Father José Caballero, priest at the parish church of San Juan Parangaricutiro, began to fear that the strengthening earthquakes might throw down the massive new church and destroy the venerated crucifix of the Lord of the Miracles. To be on the safe side, he took the statue out onto the main square. Later, the faithful were to criticize Father Caballero strongly for such a rash act, claiming that the church could have been saved if the Lord of the Miracles had stayed inside.

The increasing earthquakes were also worrying the *presidente municipal* of San Juan Parangaricutiro, Felipe Cuara-Amezcua. By mid-February, over 200 tremors were shaking the district every day. On 19 February there were 300. Unlike many people in the area at the time, he realized that the earthquakes might be caused by molten rock rising up towards the earth's surface. This

Dionisio Pulido.

molten rock could provide the lava-flows, ash and gases to form a volcano. He
noticed, too, that the earthquakes were concentrated near Cuiyúsuru. Was that
old volcano, Cerro Prieto, going to erupt again, he wondered? But what could
he, or anyone else in San Juan, do about it? On 20 February, the *presidente*
decided to ask the advice of his opposite number in the city of Uruapan, 25km
away. Before he could get a reply, Felipe Cuara-Amezcua's worst fears were
confirmed. The eruption began. Almost exactly where he had thought it
would happen.

About 2km southeast of Parícutin, there was a small valley, 2km long and
1.5km wide, that was drained – in the wet season only – by the Parícutin *arroyo*,
which skirted the east of the village and ran northwards to join the *arroyo principal* of San Juan Parangaricutiro. These *arroyos* were later to guide lava-flows
directly to those villages. The people of Parícutin owned many fertile plots of
land in this valley and they travelled out daily from their village during the
planting and growing seasons with their animals and farm implements. Dionisio Pulido owned the plot of land known as the Llano (plain) de Cuiyúsuru.
It contained a small knoll, with a pit in it, that was about 5m across and at
least 1.5m deep. Nobody took much notice of it. However, Severiana Murillo
recalled later on that, at the turn of the century, she used to play near the
hole which gave off a 'pleasant warmth'. Her father had warned her that it
might be dangerous, because underground noises could be heard there, as if

stones were falling down a deep shaft. This was why some thought it was an old Spanish mineshaft.

The Birth of Parícutin, Saturday, 20 February 1943

Happily, the Tarascans who saw the very first moments of the birth of Parícutin were very observant and were used to watching their environment closely. Their testimony is thus probably more valuable than the eye-witness accounts of all but the most acute of 'trained' observers.

As Dionisio Pulido made his way to his plot of land at Cuiyúsuru on that fine morning on 20 February 1943, he could never have imagined that he was soon to witness a very rare geological event that would see his testimony and his photograph published in learned periodicals. He and his helper, the deaf-mute Demetrio Toral, set about clearing branches from the fields for the spring maize sowing, and his wife Paula and small son were watching over the grazing sheep. When they met for a chat about four o'clock that afternoon, Paula Pulido confessed that she had been worried by the thundering noises coming from below ground. Dionisio then himself heard a rumble like thunder, although the sky was as clear and calm as always in February. But Dionisio had work to do and, just before 4.30 p.m., he moved about 100m away to burn the pile of branches he had collected. By this time, Demetrio Toral was already ploughing the field with a team of oxen. Paula Pulido returned to watch over the sheep from the welcome shade of an oak tree. What a beautiful afternoon it was!

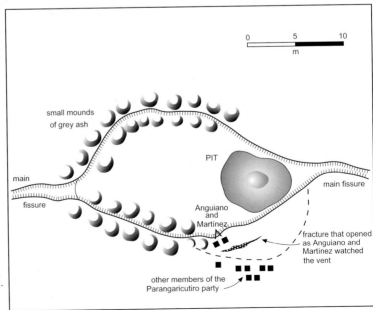

Parícutin at 6 p.m. on 20 February 1943.

Paula Pulido saw it all start. About 1km away to the west, she noticed a pretty dust-devil coming towards her in a swirling column. Then she saw that a crevice, about 5cm wide and 30cm deep, was opening in the soil behind it. Soon, it formed a hole that started to smoke. Her husband saw the crack extend swiftly eastwards until it was about 50m long.

I noticed that a little hole . . . on one of the knolls on my land had opened [up], and I noticed that this fissure, as I followed it with my eye, was long and passed from where I stood, through the hole, and stretched back [westwards] to Cerro de Canicjuata . . . 'Here is something strange', I thought . . . and I searched the ground for marks to see if it had opened during the night or not, but I couldn't find any.

But Dionisio went on setting fire to his dead branches. Suddenly,

I heard some thunder, the trees trembled, and I turned to speak to Paula . . . Then I saw how the ground swelled up [about] 2m or 2.5m in the hole, and a kind of smoke, or fire dust – grey like ashes – began to rise from a part of the crack I had not seen before. [Because it had just formed?] Immediately, more smoke began to rise up with a loud and continuous hiss or whistle, and there was a smell of sulphur.

About 100m away, Paula Pulido saw the grey cloud escaping and she was terrified when the pine trees caught fire, about 30m from the hole. She called out to warn her husband.

Then the ground rose in the form of a confused cake above the open fissure, and then disappeared, but I cannot say whether it blew out or fell back – I believe it swallowed itself. I was sure the earth was on fire.

Paula Pulido wasted no more time. Panic-stricken, she took to her heels and fled to Parícutin.

Meanwhile, Aurora Cuara was returning to San Juan Parangaricutiro from the family plot at San Nicolás. She saw Dionisio Pulido piling up his branches and Demetrio Toral, ploughing. As the ploughman turned to start a new furrow, the ground cracked open from the west. A wall of earth sprang up from it, about 10m long and 2m wide, and perhaps 1m high. Grey smoke, or very fine dust, and 'sparks' spurted from the middle of the furrow that Demetrio Toral had just ploughed. She saw fear get the better of Dionisio Pulido, and ran off to Parícutin herself. The farmer confessed later:

I then became greatly frightened and tried to help unyoke one of the ox teams. I was so stunned I hardly knew what to do . . . or what to think . . . and I couldn't find my wife, or my son, or my animals. At last I came to my senses and I remembered the sacred Lord of the Miracles. I shouted out 'Blessed Lord of the Miracles, you brought me into this world – now save me!' . . . and I looked at the fissure where the smoke was rising and my fear disappeared for the first time. I ran to see if I could save my family, my companions and my oxen, but I could not see them and I thought that they must have taken the oxen to the spring for water. I saw that there was no water in the spring . . . and I thought the water had gone because of the fissure. I was very frightened, and I mounted my mare and galloped to Parícutin where I found my wife and son and friends waiting for me. They were afraid that I was dead and that they would never see me again.

Somehow, the yoked oxen and his animals had also turned up at the house . . . The farmer alerted the head man of Parícutin and, together, they rode to San Juan Parangaricutiro to warn the *presidente*, Felipe Cuara-Amezcua.

Tales of the crack in the ground spread like wildfire through San Juan. An enterprising teenager, Luís Mora-García, went to the outskirts of the town and took two photographs of the smoke escaping gently from the hole about 4.5km away to the south – one at 5 p.m. and the other, showing much more smoke, at 6 p.m. They were the first photographs ever taken of the start of a brand new volcano. By 5.30 p.m., the thin column of fumes rising lazily into the evening sky confirmed the news to those who had assembled in the square in front of the parish church in San Juan. The priest blessed and dispatched a posse of about a dozen men to see what was afoot. Two 22-year-olds, Jesús Anguiano and Jesús Martinez, were the first to reach Cuiyúsuru, at 6 p.m. The fissure had developed into a trench. The hole at one end of it was belching smoke and throwing out stones like glowing marbles and oranges. An area about 20m long and 12m wide had subsided and mounds of fine hot grey ash, about 50cm high, had formed around its edges. Jesús Anguiano collected some of the dust in his handkerchief as a souvenir.

The ground was 'jumping up and down, not with the swaying motion we felt in Parangaricutiro'. The pair crept to within about 2m or 3m of the hole. It was erupting choking fumes, and throwing dust, sparks and hot stones nearly 5m into the air. The 'sand' in the bottom of the hole seemed to be bubbling, boiling and rumbling like boulders being dragged along by a stream in flood. Jesús Anguiano collected a couple of the stones. They were very hot. Suddenly, one of their companions, Luís Ortíz Solorio, shouted a warning. They jumped back. Just in time – the lip of the hole where they had been standing collapsed into the abyss. The smoking column thickened, the hole widened to 2m across, and the adventurous pair shook in terror – and relief – that they had just missed being swallowed up.

The posse returned post-haste to report to the anxious citizens of San Juan Parangaricutiro. Jesús Anguiano presented his souvenirs to the priest. The stones were still so hot that they had to be put in a dish. Father Caballero exorcized the relics and begged the Almighty to stop the terrible apparition. In vain. He consulted a book on Vesuvius. Then they knew for sure that they had seen a volcano.

A villager watches Parícutin, on 22 March 1944.

Nobody in the town needed any further persuasion after nightfall. Darkness brought out the glow from the red-hot rocks; and the eruption itself began to roar much more powerfully. Molten rock started to spit out. Celedonio Gutiérrez was fascinated. He noted that 'tongues of flame, like fire, rose 800m into the air . . . and released showers of golden rain . . . lightning was flashing through a dense, black cloud'. He decided to keep a diary describing the events. Little can he have realized on that Saturday evening that his observations would cover nine years and that he would end up as a keeper of a volcano museum.

Volcán de Parícutin, Sunday, 21 February 1943

The young volcano was not yet threatening the whole district, however. At 8 a.m. on Sunday morning, Dionisio Pulido went back to Cuiyúsuru. A new cone, about 10m high, now decorated his plot. At 11 a.m., Aurora Cuara walked by on her way to see if her husband was still safe at San Nicolás. She saw a hill of stones, hurling rocks into the air, with molten lava oozing from its base. By noon, the eruptions had piled up a cone of ash, cinders and blocks, nearly 30m high.

Parícutin on 21 February 1943.

Meanwhile, the people had suffered what seemed to be an even more pressing threat – a big earthquake shook their homes. Most of them fled to the apparent safety of the next village. Those from Parícutin fled to San Juan; those from San Juan to Angahuan or Uruapan; and those from Angahuan fled to the hills.

The local authorities did not take long to react. At 10 a.m. on 21 February, the *presidente*, Felipe Cuara-Amezcua, called a meeting of the municipal council of San Juan Parangaricutiro and they granted him special emergency powers to deal with the crisis. He acted at once. He immediately informed the Mexican President, General Manuel Avila Carnacho, the Defence Minister and former President, General Lázaro Cárdenas, the Michoacán State Governor, General Felix Ireta Vivieros, as well as the Ministry of Agriculture and the *presidente* of the nearby city of Uruapan. The meeting even discussed naming the object of their fears – 'know thine enemy'. It was unanimously agreed to call it the 'Volcán de Parícutin'.

Celedonio Gutiérrez described how fine ash was thrown out all afternoon, and white vapours billowed skywards, as if a sheet was being shaken in the air. The explosions were noisier than any cannonade, and their main pulsations sent volcanic bombs and coarse ash hurtling more than 300m from the hole. As night fell, the day-old volcano was already between 30m and 50m high.

Monday, 22 February 1943

During the night, at 3.21 a.m., a large earthquake rocked most of the state of Michoacán for nearly eight minutes. To Celedonio Gutiérrez, it seemed 'the ultimate agony . . . Only . . . God, in his great power . . . thought of us. It was He who saved us.' In the afternoon, Celedonio Gutiérrez went to inspect the volcano. He would never forget seeing the cinders cascading onto the fields where he used to watch over his grandfather's cattle. Incessant explosions were shooting ash, cinders and bombs all around the growing volcano, and a plume of ash, steam and sulphurous fumes was rising about 1,500m into the air. Sometimes the volcano chugged like a steam engine starting out from a station. Red-hot molten lava was bubbling and spurting in fountains from three holes in the bottom of the crater. The lava was escaping from the gap on the east side of the cone and oozing over the plain called Quitzocho at a rate of about 5–10m an hour.

However, the most important event of the day in Parícutin village was the arrival of the venerable Ezequiel Ordóñez. He was 75 and the most famous and experienced geologist in México. As he wrote later: 'I was soon convinced that I was witnessing a sight that few humans have ever seen – the initial stages of the growth of a new volcano.' His great merit was his ability to communicate with the villagers. He calmed their fears and advised them to return to their homes. Most of them had no idea that they were even living in a volcanic area. Ezequiel Ordóñez explained that Parícutin was surrounded by hundreds of volcanic cones formed by similar eruptions in the past. He pointed out, too, that the lava-flows first cooled to form the rugged, useless *malpaís*, but eventually they weathered to form the fertile soils in their own fields. Such teaching was worth a dozen technical research papers – although Ezequiel Ordóñez also wrote ten scientific articles on the eruption before he died on 8 February 1950.

Spring and Summer 1943

March 1943 came in like a lion. The eruption grew more powerful, blasting out cinders and big bombs of lava that soared almost a kilometre into the air, and sometimes landed a kilometre away. The blasts made a fearful noise and rattled the windows in San Juan Parangaricutiro. The cone was growing so fast that it was already nearly 140m high; and the fuming lava-flow was still creeping over Quitzocho.

Then, on 18 March, the mood of the volcano changed. The ground shook menacingly. A much broader, turbulent column of ash, gas and steam, billowing like dark-grey cauliflowers, roared over 6km skywards. There were far fewer bombs, but much more ash. The ash enshrouded the half-abandoned village of Parícutin and its fields and swished down through the forests. 'Figures passing but a few yards away appeared eerie and ghost-like in the ashy haze.' The people were terrified. For the first time, a threatening black veil spread beyond the immediate neighbourhood of the volcano. Ash reached Uruapan, 25km away, and brought traffic to a halt. The citizens feverishly swept it from their rooftops, for fear that they would collapse under its weight. It dimmed the sun at Toluca, 265km away, and even reached México City, 320km away, from time to time.

The ash showered down incessantly for twelve weeks. When the wet season started in June, the ash changed to muddy rain, and the black pall kept the weather chilly. On 9 June, the cone was 198m high. Suddenly, at three o'clock that afternoon, the volcano stopped erupting – but only to gear itself up for another change of mood. Within a couple of hours, it had started to blast out bombs again in long bursts, that were separated by short, ominous silences. This bombastic mood lasted until 17 October.

As the resident geologists, William Foshag and Jenaro González-Reyna, remarked:

> At night, the volcano offered a magnificent sight – a bright, incandescent eruptive column showered bombs upon the cone; and two brilliant rivers of orange lava cascaded . . . to the base of the cone and flowed to the lava field in the valley, where myriad lights looked like a city viewed from a distant hill.

At times, the show was so spectacular that onlookers could not help bursting into applause. It was a meagre consolation for Parícutin.

Villagers watch the blanket of ash and rugged lava-flows from Parícutin in March 1944.

The Evacuation of Parícutin Village, June 1943

On 12 June a threatening tongue of lava started to flow down the Parícutin *arroyo*, the gully leading directly to the village. The flow was advancing, at about 25m an hour, in bulging lobes like bunches of enormous grapes, 4m high. Next day the *presidente* of San Juan, Felipe Cuara-Amezcua, and the resident geologists agreed that it would be best to evacuate Parícutin, although the village seemed to be in no immediate danger.

In any case, the government had acted well in advance of an emergency, and was not taken unawares. Within a week of the start of the eruption in February, the authorities had started searching for vacant land where any victims could be resettled. In early May they bought land at Caltzontzin near Uruapan, about 30km east of the Parícutin. Relief agencies gave $US165,000 worth of food to forestall a famine, and the Red Cross set up a station in San Juan in May. A few villagers made a little money selling volcanic rocks, or refreshments to visitors – or acted as their guides.

But the rural economy was faltering. Ash covered everything. The cattle and sheep could not reach the grass below its thickening blanket. The pines were dying and no longer yielding resin to sell for turpentine. Birds, bees and rabbits had vanished. Springs and streams had dried up. Worst of all, the ash had piled up faster than the crops could grow; they had perished and could not be replaced. There would be no harvest in 1943. How would everyone survive? Delaying evacuation would only prolong the pain to no avail. This safety-first policy was economically and politically sensible, although the eruption presented no direct threat to human life farther than one kilometre from the volcano. But many villagers were already tired of being drenched in wet ash. Several families with transferable assets had already left the district. The young people, in particular, saw no point in staying on in such conditions, especially since the government was offering help and new accommodation.

The older Tarascans saw things differently. Such was their attachment to their land, they declared that, 'they preferred to die covered by lava rather than abandon their homes'. In the event they were persuaded – some say, forced – to leave the village of their ancestors, and all the places where they had communed with the natural world for centuries.

Once the decision to evacuate had been taken on 13 June, the authorities acted speedily. The first government lorries arrived to take people from Parícutin the next day. The villagers quickly took as much as they could from their houses, for the lava had crept from the *arroyo* to within 20m of their homes. Some of the villagers stood a cross in front of the house nearest to the advancing flow. In fact, the lava-flow was starting to slow down, and it only began to cover the houses in Parícutin fifteen months later, on 27 September 1944. But, by then, the village had long been abandoned – for the evacuation to Caltzontzin had been completed by 10 July 1943.

The government was quick to reward the villagers for co-operating in their evacuation. In Caltzontzin, they built them new houses in the old style, on the traditional gridiron pattern, and assigned them plots of fertile land ready for cultivation. They even gave the evacuees shoes . . . Nevertheless, the authorities still ran into social and psychological problems amongst the villagers. For many, the culture shock was almost too great to bear. They felt uprooted. They did not like their new houses. Caltzontzin was 750m lower than Parícutin and different climatic conditions forced the villagers to change their centuries-old rural practices. And they had hardly ever worn shoes.

Why on earth did the government not christen the new village Parícutin Nuevo, which might have kept some semblance of traditional continuity? It can scarcely have helped that Caltzontzin had been the nickname given to the last Tarascan chief who had been forced to bow to the Spanish Conquistadors in 1522. What was more, Caltzontzin means 'broken sandal' – which hardly made it a striking symbol of rebirth.

The Evacuation of San Juan Parangaricutiro, 1943–4

The resettlement of the citizens of San Juan Parangaricutiro started more hesitantly, and lasted for much longer than in the village of Parícutin. They lived farther from the evident danger – and they insisted on choosing their new home. Of course, they did not want to 'uproot their hearts' and go to another place, far away. Ex-President General Lázaro Cárdenas, the architect of the recent land-reform programme, himself came to encourage the citizens to leave their town. With its violent eruptions at the end of July 1943, the volcano, too, seemed to be adding its voice to the persuasive chorus. But in August the volcano relented, and calmed down visibly. The citizens of San Juan vowed to hang on to their homes at least until 14 September – the feast of the Lord of the Miracles – the most important day in their calendar. It might be the last time that they could celebrate the feast in their home town. They were right. Thousands of pilgrims flocked to San Juan Parangaricutiro for the event. 'Men and women, with tears in their eyes, kissed the divine feet of Our Lord of the Miracles.' But, in fact, the revered statue did not have to leave the church just yet . . .

On 6 October, the community leaders of San Juan Parangaricutiro chose the site of their new town, at Miguel Silva, 65km southeast of the new volcano. It was on a former hacienda, expropriated in 1938 during the government land reforms.

On 17 October 1943, cinders and lava-flows started gushing from the base of the main cone and formed a smaller cone that was called Sapichu, 'the little one'. For ten weeks, the main volcano stayed quiet. Several observers, including Celedonio Gutiérrez, took their chance to climb up to the summit and peer into the 100m-deep crater. The fumes smelt of hydrochloric acid. When Sapichu stopped erupting on 8 January 1944, two other little chimneys burst into activity at the opposite side of the main cone. They gave off molten lava that often spurted out in fountains 60m high, before flowing northwards in a black and hissing mass.

In the early months of 1944, however, the people of San Juan Parangaricutiro had problems of their own, and had little time for these volcanic niceties. The settlement that they had chosen at Miguel Silva was proving to be a big mistake. During the winter, about 1,200 people and their possessions had arrived on government lorries from San Juan and the neighbouring village of Zirosto. But they soon discovered that only about 350 hectares of the land offered to them could be cultivated. Miguel Silva lay at an altitude of 1,500m, some 750m lower than San Juan, and the seeds that the refugees had brought with them did not flourish, even when they could find a plot to plant them in. The local water was so bad that many refugees fell sick. Some caught malaria. In such conditions, the older people had no will to live; and 10 per cent of all the settlers died within a year. The survivors also faced violent local opposition. During the winter of 1944, for instance, the local farmers killed some of the refugee leaders, and much of their livestock – and they even threatened the new priest, who was promptly 'recalled to another post'. (In such circumstances, it is rather surprising that as many as 300 refugees were still clinging to the settlement at Miguel Silva in October 1944.)

As a result of these serious problems, the men of San Juan Parangaricutiro chose another site for their new settlement in March 1944. It was far more suitable, because it lay in a similar agricultural environment, only 380m lower down in altitude and only 20km from their home town. The site was called the Rancho de los Conejos, 'the hamlet of the rabbits', which later gave rise to many jokes, but not, at least, to aggression such as they had suffered at Miguel Silva.

The new site had been chosen just in time, for events in San Juan Parangaricutiro had taken a turn for the worse. Throughout late winter, the lavas issuing from the foot of the volcano had been slowly making their way northwards. But, in March 1944, the citizens vowed to stay in their home town until the lava-flow reached the cemetery. Symbolically, they would then be cut off from their past. Many people still cherished the hope that the Lord of the Miracles would save San Juan. However, towards the end of April, the lava-flow began to advance more quickly down the *arroyo* towards the town at a speed of about 5m an hour. The road to Uruapan was cut. The water supply was in danger. Although the flow did not endanger the lives of the people, it was an obvious threat to their homes.

During the first week of May 1944 the lavas slowed down almost to a halt, but still began to edge into the cemetery. Whole families assembled at the lava-front, kneeling in prayer on the graves of their ancestors, begging for respite enough to salvage all their goods from their homes and to empty the church.

On 8 May the Bishop of Zamora came and celebrated mass and confirmed the children. On 9 May, the Bishop removed the Lord of the Miracles from the church and took it out in a procession of churchmen and villagers to encourage the people to evacuate the town. The priest, Father José Caballero, was not pleased to see the statue depart. Indeed, some of those who still believed that the statue could save the town threw themselves in its path. Eventually 'realists' persuaded them to join the procession that formed behind the Bishop as he walked away from the lava-front towards the village of Angahuan. The next day, the procession continued on to Uruapan. The faithful flocked to kiss the revered statue and give food and water to those following it. It seemed that the whole of Uruapan had turned out. The town was decorated. Some people let off fireworks. It was just like the fiesta.

On 11 May, the procession reached the site of the new settlement at Rancho de los Conejos. But, in spite of the fanfares, the early days were harsh. At first, the people had to live in tents, but they quickly built a chapel for the Lord of the Miracles. They had no houses, no land, no school, no piped water and, of course, no electricity.

Not all the citizens of the old town had followed the sacred statue to its new destination, for many were determined to hang on to their homes until the last possible moment. Many stayed on until the lavas covered the

The unfinished church of San Juan Parangaricutiro, emerging from the lavas of Parícutin.

very last corner of their own land. Then, they sadly piled their movable possessions onto the lorries provided by the government, and left their age-old home.

On 7 July 1944, only one street in San Juan was still free of the lava. The flow was about to invade the church. Everything that could be saved was saved: the beams, the cupboards, the flower stands, the confessional boxes, the pulpit – and even the baptismal font carved in stone. The priest, Father José Caballero, was still claiming that the church would have been saved if only they had not taken the Lord of the Miracles away. By mid-July the last – and some of the oldest – inhabitants had left the old San Juan for the new. Eventually, the government gave the citizens housing lots of the same size and in the same relative positions as those they had had in San Juan and the 'hamlet of the rabbits' officially became San Juan Nuevo Parangaricutiro on 9 July 1944. The lava-flows had stretched 2km beyond San Juan Parangaricutiro, and had covered most of the town before they slowed to a halt in mid-August. But the two church towers – one still unfinished – stuck out defiantly, if symbolically, above the black, rugged and all-embracing mass.

On 27 September, more lava overwhelmed nearly all the ash-covered remnants of Parícutin. On 8 December 1944, another pulsation of lava had the impertinence to advance upon the cabins of the scientific observers, which had to be quickly dismantled and re-sited, 50m higher. (These new positions seemed safe, but the cabins had to be moved again in December 1946 when yet more lava threatened. Volcanology is an inexact science.) A similar pulsation of lava on 28 January 1946 finally buried the very last vestiges of the village of Parícutin. Yet another surge buried the little cone of Sapichu in December 1947.

In the meantime, the volcano continued erupting at a more sedate pace than in the fury of its youth. By its second birthday, on 20 February 1945, it had done most of its damage. It had already expelled two-thirds of its output of ash and cinders and its lava-flows had virtually reached their maximum extent. Later flows merely piled up over earlier lavas. At length, the *Volcán de Parícutin* stopped erupting, 'not with a bang, but a whimper', at 9.15 on the morning of 4 March 1952.

Renewal?

In all, very nearly 25km^2 were covered by lava-flows and some 300km^2 were blanketed by at least 15cm of ash, which was deep enough to damage most of the vegetation. The effects of the eruption were most serious within 5km of the volcano, but they were also variable, and not always disastrous. The ashfalls did most of their damage during the first eight months of the eruption, while most of the devastation from the lavas occurred in both 1943 and 1944.

Heavy ashfalls in the summer of 1943 caused most of the casualties amongst the animals and insects near the volcano. Swirling ash battered the insects and birds, clogged the lungs of the mammals and buried their food supply. And so they died. About 4,500 cattle, 550 horses and unknown numbers of sheep, goats and rabbits quickly succumbed to ground-down teeth, lungs filled with mucus and ash, and starvation. Leaves and blossoms were stripped from the fruit trees. Where the ash lay 15cm or more deep, the land was virtually useless for over a decade for crops such as maize or beans, although the fruit trees fared better. A few farmers invested in steel ploughs that dug furrows deep enough to reach the old soil below the ash, but most were too poor to buy such an implement and had to wait until the rain managed to wash the ash away. The economy of the area close to the volcano was ruined long before the lavas buried Parícutin and San Juan Parangaricutiro.

But on the fringes of the ruined area, where the ash was sprinkled less than about 3cm thick, it acted as a mulch that retained moisture in the soil. Wheat and barley gave unusually high yields. Similarly, the ash had eliminated a fruit-fly pest so that, wherever the blossoms had survived, the fruit trees cropped magnificently – until the pest found its way back into the area. The sprinkling of ash also nourished the grazing-lands, so that more cattle than ever before eventually flourished upon them. With government encouragement, the farmers later planted more maize and fruit trees, such as avocados, on the steeper slopes that they had neglected before the eruption. On the other hand, the land swamped by the lava-flows will only become naturally fertile after many centuries of weathering have reduced the rugged rocks to fine soil.

The eruption directly caused only three deaths – which occurred in an unexpected way when lightning struck down from the erupting column. The displacements caused by the eruption affected a relatively small number of people in a relatively small area; and the lavas destroyed only two settlements, although ash damaged several others nearby. Probably fewer than 6,000 people were involved in the evacuations, which were both orderly and well organized by the authorities.

But the resettlement was a major physical, psychological and cultural upheaval for the evacuees, for which neither the volcano nor the government could fairly be blamed. When the citizens of San Juan Parangaricutiro made their first unhappy settlement at Miguel Silva, more than 100 settlers died as a result of polluted water, hostile neighbours, and the loss of the will to live. In the calmer resettlements in San Juan Nuevo and Caltzontzin, uprooted villagers also died of grief in new houses that they could never call homes. Those in the new settlements were not united by misfortune. Disputes over land ownership continued as before. Crops and livestock were destroyed, houses were burnt, gunmen were hired, and people were killed or injured – even as recently as 1990. But such disputes were more or less endemic, and would probably have gone on just as passionately whether the eruption had happened or not.

Yet time did soften the blows caused by the upheaval. Although fewer and fewer people still spoke Tarascan, many of the younger generation benefited greatly from much-improved education. They earned professional qualifications that would have been unimaginable in the old settlements. But new and old mixed ambiguously for a long time. In 1967, the new priest in Caltzontzin had raised money to build a new church, but the young people preferred a basketball court, which was duly finished in 1971. The team proudly displayed PARÍCUTIN on their shirts. They built the church later.

Fifty years after its foundation, the population of Caltzontzin had increased from about 700 to over 2,000. It has become a rather dusty suburb of Uruapan and the government has built a state prison in the town, which most of its citizens claim has not improved its image. The population of San Juan Nuevo has risen from less than 2,000 to over 13,000, and a fifth of the population make a living from small industries. Very few people can now recall the exciting days when the volcano was born. Dionisio Pulido himself died in Caltzontzin in 1949, and the *Volcán de Parícutin* now rises 424m above his old fields at Cuiyúsuru. It is probably extinct.

13

Mount St Helens, 1980

The eruption of Mount St Helens brought yet another form of volcanic devastation to the fore when the bulging mountainside collapsed and laid bare the molten rock inside. Although the volcano had been closely monitored for weeks, the intensity of the eruption surprised the experts and would have claimed many more victims if it had not happened in a sparsely populated recreation area.

An Ethereal Beauty

It was the British explorer, George Vancouver, who first named Mount St Helens when he was sailing in HMS *Discovery* along the Pacific coast of North America in 1792. He honoured the British diplomat, Alleyne Fitzherbert, the first Lord St Helens, who had helped him obtain permission from the Spanish authorities to explore beyond the wild and neglected northwestern fringes of their American Empire. Thereafter, for almost 200 years, most of those who knew the Pacific northwest of the USA would probably have agreed that Mount St Helens was the most serenely beautiful volcano in the whole of the Cascade Range. In 1980, Mount St Helens revealed the darker side of her nature, and, afterwards, there was no doubt at all about which volcano was the ugliest. Mount St Helens was also, by far, the most famous.

*

Mount St Helens rises in Washington State, 80km north of Portland, Oregon. The thick coniferous forests and a scattering of lakes around its base made it an ideal haunt for those who liked the quiet solitude that is a feature of much of the Cascade Range. There were camping grounds, cabins and second homes, especially near Spirit Lake at the foot of the northern flanks of the volcano. It was nature at its best.

The native Americans, who knew the area long before George Vancouver, were apparently well aware of earlier eruptions of Mount St Helens. They called the mountain Loo-Wit (Keeper of the Fire), Lawelatla (One from whom the Smoke Comes), or Tah-One-Lat-Clah (Fire Mountain). The native Americans also incorporated these eruptions into one of their legends. One day, the Spirit God turned an ugly old woman, called Tah-One-Lat-Clah, into a beautiful virgin. Two great warriors, Pahto and Wyeast, immediately vied for her hand. As is the way with virgins in legends, she could not decide which of them she loved. The impatient rival suitors soon came to blows, hurling fire,

Mount St Helens and Spirit Lake after the eruption of 18 May 1980.

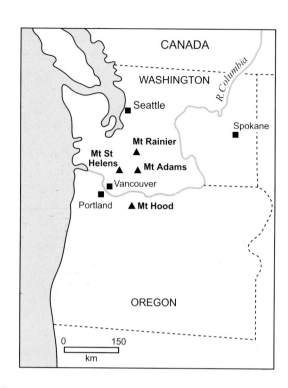

The location of Mount St Helens.

The eruption of Mount St Helens, 18 May 1980.

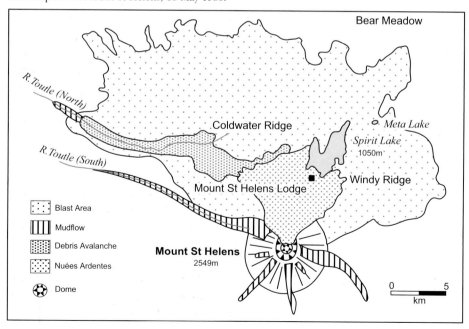

Mount St Helens before the eruptions in 1980.

lightning and hot rocks at each other. The sun was blacked out and the earth shook. The terrified people begged the Spirit God to help them, but he was so angry with the behaviour of the protagonists that he turned all three of them into mountains. Wyeast became Mount Hood; Pahto became Mount Adams; and Tah-One-Lat-Clah became Mount St Helens. The original transformation of Tah-One-Lat-Clah from an ugly woman into a beautiful virgin may itself represent a change in the appearance of the volcano. The ugly woman would be the mountain scarred by violent eruptions. Little by little, smaller eruptions would have filled up the crater, and eventually formed a sleek and beautiful summit. This process has already started again at Mount St Helens, and it will no doubt complete a similar change again within the next few hundred years.

The ethereal beauty of Mount St Helens masked a more violent eruptive past than that of any of its Cascade companions. This violence, however, was not evident from the events of the last two centuries. Literate observers had only recorded small eruptions in 1831, 1836, and again at intervals between 1842 and 1857. A rather larger eruption had probably taken place about 1800, just before the first European settlers came to the area. Many of the more recent eruptions took place on the north side of the volcano, and perhaps helped to weaken it when the more powerful explosions occurred in 1980.

Scientists have since revealed the mountain's real secret past. When D. R. Crandell and D. R. Mullineaux of the United States Geological Survey investigated its history, they found that it had erupted more than any volcano in the Cascade Range and was the youngest and most vigorous amongst them. The eruptions had built up the bulk of the cone to a height of 2,950m in the past 2,500 years, which is a fast rate of construction for a large volcano. The geologists calculated that small eruptions would occur on average every 100 years and a large outburst, producing perhaps 1km^3 of fragments, would occur once every 3–4,000 years. Now, it so happened that the last small eruption before 1980 had taken place in 1857, and the last major outburst had occurred about 4,000 years ago. Thus, in 1975, geologists forecast that Mount St Helens could well erupt before the end of the century. This was the most accurate eruption forecast made until that time. But events proved to be more complicated than expected. When the catastrophe happened, both the intensity and the very type of the eruption were completely unexpected; and the geologist monitoring the volcano that day lost his life.

Many aspects of the greatest volcanic eruption recorded in the forty-eight coterminous United States were recounted in two professional papers of the United States Geological Survey, on which this chapter is partly based. B. L. Foxworthy and M. Hill edited *Volcanic Eruptions of 1980 at Mount St Helens. The First Hundred Days*; and P. W. Lipman and D. R. Mullineaux edited the monumental volume, *The 1980 Eruptions of Mount St Helens, Washington*.

Spring 1980

Rising molten rock first revealed its presence beneath Mount St Helens at 3.37 p.m. on 20 March 1980 when it caused a moderate earthquake, centred just below the volcano. Almost incessant tremors and some more powerful shocks then immediately began to affect the mountain. On 25 March the volcano was closed to climbers, and the following day an emergency co-ordination centre was established at Vancouver, Washington. These safety measures did not please everybody. Some people living in the area simply refused to accept that their peaceful mountain could possibly threaten them. One disgruntled resident even claimed that the warnings were only a devious plot by the US Forestry Service to prevent the further development of the recreation area around Spirit Lake.

Mount St Helens produced its first eruption for 123 years at 12.36 p.m. on 27 March 1980. A little crater formed on the ice-covered summit and black ash exploded 3km into the air. The eruption started when waters filtered down into the volcano and were changed into steam on meeting the rocks heated by the molten materials rising from below. The resulting explosions shattered some of the rocks of the mountain near the volcanic chimney and ejected the fragments as fine, but cold, ash. Molten fragments would not be expelled for nearly two months yet – and, then, all the world would know.

The state authorities acted without delay. Hundreds of residents and forestry loggers cutting timber were evacuated from the vicinity of the mountain, and people living within a 24km radius of the summit were advised to leave. The first of many road blocks were placed around the restricted zone. As the eruptions continued, the experts of the United States Geological Survey and local universities were marshalled to witness and monitor the new spectacle. Mount St Helens kept her observers busy. The eruptions were not very large, but enough to generate a billowing plume above the crater and blacken the upper slopes of the volcano that usually glistened with snow and ice in springtime. Ash and the snow competed for domination of the slopes. The ash won. But this contest was only a side-show. The significant moves were elsewhere. Molten rock began to penetrate into the body of the volcanic cone, and started invading its northern sector in particular. On 27 March, the upper northern flanks of the cone began to crack and slowly swell outwards.

On Sunday, 30 March, sightseers flocked to the area, and journalists began their long quest to find out what was going to happen next. David Johnston, one of the geologists now monitoring the volcano, declared that it was like a lit fuse attached to some dynamite, 'but you don't know how long the fuse is'. That Sunday, there were no fewer than ninety-three explosive outbursts, and seventy aircraft were counted flying around the mountain. So many people swarmed into the area by car that the roads up to the mountain 'looked like downtown Seattle in the rush hour'. A publicity firm also put the volcano to good use: a helicopter landed on the rim of the new crater to film a beer commercial.

On 3 April the Governor of Washington State, Dixy Lee Ray, declared a state of emergency and issued leaflets about what to do in an ashfall. Nevertheless, forestry loggers – successfully – begged to be allowed to return to their livelihood in the restricted zone. The geologists set up an observation site at Coldwater ridge, about 13km from the crater. The volcano erupted frequently during the early days of April, often sending columns of ash and steam as much as 3km into the air. More sightseers than ever flocked to Mount St Helens on Sunday, 13 April, and many defied the access restrictions to get a closer view of some of the eighteen eruptions. So much airborne monitoring was going on by now that aircraft were scarce, and even important visitors had to wait a long time for their 'Mount St Helens experience'.

The main preoccupation of the many visiting journalists was to find a suitably clairvoyant scientist, who would forecast what was most likely to happen next. The main concern of the experts was the bulge that was still growing on the northern flank of Mount St Helens. On 17 April, the scientists stressed for the first time that a landslide was threatening the northern flank of the volcano. Meanwhile, the eruptions began to wane. The volcano put on a disappointing show for the Sunday visitors on 20 April. But a carnival atmosphere still prevailed amongst the great throng of tourists, and they consoled themselves with the host of souvenirs that were on sale – ranging from plastic bags full of volcanic ash to T-shirts and coffee mugs.

Perhaps all this commercial interference upset Mount St Helens because it stopped erupting altogether for the two weeks between 22 April and 7 May. But the molten rock was still rising: the earthquakes and the bulging continued unabated. By 27 April, the bulge measured 2.5km across and was already protruding at least 80m, and it went on swelling by a metre or more a day. The northern slopes of Mount St Helens seemed likely to become very unstable. The experts feared that a big earthquake might cause an avalanche of ice, or even of rock. As a result, on Wednesday, 30 April, Governor Ray set up two restricted zones. The Red Zone, ranging from 5km to 13km around the volcano, was prohibited to all except scientists and appropriate officials. In the Blue Zone around it, logging could continue and property owners could get permission to visit their homes for the day. The chief volcanologi-cal observation post was moved to a new site, Coldwater II, which was only 9km from the volcano. By now, a wonderful array of equipment was register-ing every quake, fume, explosion and caprice of the volcano. But Mount St Helens had still not emitted any molten materials.

During the two weeks of apparent calm, the access restrictions seemed more and more irksome to many of those who wanted to enter the forbidden ter-ritory. Many people found the official pessimism hard to credit; Spirit Lake, for instance, seemed far too far away from the crater to be in any danger. Some property owners even refused to pay their taxes in protest. The hero of the hour was Harry Truman – no relation of the former President – who had refused categorically to leave his Mount St Helens Lodge at Spirit Lake. He was 83, had sixteen cats, and liked Bourbon and Coke. He expressed the homespun views of the true pioneer. He wasn't going to bow down to nature or to government interference and said so, frequently, on television. He'd take his chance with the volcano. 'This damn mountain won't ever do me any harm. In any case, if it explodes, well then, I'll go up with it, because it's part of me.' What scientist could compete with such popular appeal? In any case, the geologists and the journalists were not always on the same wavelength. The geologists offered poor copy and the journalists quickly lost patience with their cautious, and often complicated, statements. Harry Truman provided much better sound-bites. On 7 May, the mountain was shuddering so much that Harry Truman had to confess that he had felt seasick in bed. He had had to bring his bed downstairs, where it had pitched about less. That was the way to treat volcanoes! For many, Harry Truman became just as big an authority as the scientists; and a hero and a 'real character' into the bargain.

The scientists did manage to get a word in sometimes. Jack Hyde, geologist at Tacoma Community College, knew Mount St Helens well. He confessed to the *Tacoma News Tribune* on 5 May, 'I have a gut feeling . . . that, as the bulge continues to grow, something dramatic is going to happen soon.' He also believed that the geologists, who were monitoring the volcano at Coldwater, facing its north slopes, had chosen a very dangerous spot. It was as if they were 'looking down the barrel of a loaded gun'.

On 7 May Mount St Helens resumed its efforts and expelled columns of steam and ash. But events had now lost their former novelty. Familiarity had bred a certain contempt. 'Inflation and that damn volcano – it's a wonder we don't have ulcers,' a local resident complained. People just wished the mountain would 'get it all over with'. It became harder and harder to prevent people from entering the restricted zone illegally, but the swelling north flank was worrying its observers more and more because a gigantic landslide seemed increasingly likely. By mid-May the bulge had swelled 150m outwards and was severely disturbing the Forsyth glacier on the northern flanks of the mountain. Although swellings had sometimes been detected by accurate instruments on other volcanoes, few experts had ever seen such an obvious bulge before – and it was now clearly visible to the naked eye.

On Sunday, 11 May, Stephen Harris, author of *Fire Mountains of the West*, a popular book on the volcanoes of the Cascade Range, flew around Mount St Helens in a light plane. He saw that 'the bulge had grown to enormous proportions . . . Fellow passengers agreed that it seemed impossible for the oversteepened north flank to swell much farther without collapsing.' But it is doubtful whether any of the experts could have fully realized all the awesome implications of such a collapse. On 12 May, Mount St Helens suffered a larger than usual earthquake, which shook a small rock avalanche one kilometre down its northern slopes. Unfortunately, its significance was not fully appreciated at the time. In any case, the volcano had not expelled very much ash so far. On Wednesday, 14 May, Mount St Helens erupted very little. On Thursday, it erupted nothing at all. On Friday, it erupted nothing at all. And on Saturday, it erupted nothing at all. Earthquake activity was now at its lowest for a month. The rate of bulging on its northern flanks was not increasing. Could the lull continue? Did it mean that the eruption was coming to a rather tame ending? Or was it the calm before the storm? The answers were not long in coming.

On Friday, 16 May, Harry Truman gave another press conference and concluded his remarks by adjusting his cap and saying 'OK you guys, see you at the church.' He was not to keep his word. On 15 and 16 May, the authorities allowed Scout and YMCA workers into the zone to collect valuable equipment from their camps. The owners of homes within the zone also demanded access, and threatened to storm the barricades if the Governor refused. She gave in. About thirty carloads of satisfied proprietors went in a police convoy to salvage their more precious possessions on Saturday, 17 May. They were due to return for more at ten the next morning. A sheriff remarked that they were playing Russian roulette with the volcano. In the event, they won. When the balloon eventually went up, Mount St Helens produced its largest eruption for many thousands of years.

A Beautiful Morning, Sunday, 18 May 1980

Sunday 18 May was ideal for photography. It was a very promising day indeed for volcano watching, the newest of Washington's recreations. David Johnston was on duty at the Coldwater II observation post. He had exchanged turns with Harry Glicken, who had to go on a geological field trip. (Harry Glicken was to die during an eruption on Unzen, in Japan, on 3 June 1991.) Two geologists were due to join David Johnston at Coldwater II, but they were going to be late because their helicopter was not available, and it would take them two hours to make the journey by car from Vancouver, Washington.

Suddenly, at 8.32 a.m. on Sunday 18 May 1980, everything happened in thirty seconds. There was an earthquake, which shook loose the upper northern flanks of the volcano, which avalanched downhill, which released the pressure on the molten rock that had risen within the cone, which blasted out in a huge explosion, which unleashed a vast eruption that lasted for nine hours. The earthquake destabilized the bulging northern flanks of the volcano, which shuddered, and then collapsed like a landslide in a huge rock debris avalanche. About 3km^3 of rock, snow, ice, soil and trees from Mount St Helens hurled down to its feet at a speed of 250km an hour. This debris avalanche buried Harry Truman, his cats and his lodge in an instant, entered Spirit Lake, covered its floor with 60m of debris, sent a great wave splashing northwards over the 400m-high ridge nearby, and then swamped 22km of the valley of the North Fork of the River Toutle.

As the debris from its northern flanks avalanched down towards Spirit Lake, the wrecked volcano could no longer hold the pent-up molten rock and gases within it. The release of the confining pressure unleashed a huge explosion. A gigantic cloud of shattered fragments of molten lava at temperatures of about 300°C blasted outwards and downwards at speeds of between 300km and 500km an hour. Hugging the ground, and often seeming to bounce from ridge to ridge, the blast cloud soon overtook the debris avalanche and surged far beyond it, devastating 600km^2 within two minutes. After the first impetus given to the cloud by the blast from the volcano itself, its main subsequent driving forces were gravity and expanding steam and gases, generating hurricane-speed winds armed with fine fragments. These winds may have exceeded 1,000km an hour in places. The blast laid low the great forest as if a giant hand had swept across the land. Even the soil was completely scraped away to the bare rock in some of the more exposed places.

At that very moment, two geologists, Keith and Dorothy Stoffel, were flying over the crest of the volcano in a chartered plane.

> The nature of the movement was eerie . . . The entire mass began to ripple and churn up . . . Then the entire north side of the summit began sliding north . . . we were watching this landslide of unbelievable proportions slide down . . . the mountain toward Spirit Lake . . . Before we could snap off more than a few pictures, a huge explosion blasted out . . . We neither felt nor heard a thing,

even though we were [flying] just east of the summit at the time . . . the initial cloud appeared to mushroom laterally to the north and plunge down . . . The realization of the enormous size of the eruption hit us, and we focused our attention on getting out of there. The pilot opened full throttle and dove quickly to gain speed. He estimated that we were going 200 knots. The cloud behind us was mushrooming to unbelievable dimensions and appeared to be catching up with us. Since the clouds were billowing primarily in a northerly direction, we turned south . . . [and] . . . landed at Portland airport [just after 9 a.m.].

At Coldwater II, David Johnston just had time to radio to base 'Vancouver! Vancouver! This is it.' Then he died. On the ridge at the edge of the Red Zone, 3km to the north, volunteer volcano watcher Gerald Martin calmly described on his radio the start of the eruption and the terrible advance of the blast cloud of hot ash. 'The camper [van] and car over to the south of me are covered [David Johnston's]. It is going to get me too.' And it did. Gerald Martin died a few seconds after David Johnston. By that moment, more than 100m of the debris avalanche had already buried Harry Truman at Mount St Helens Lodge.

At Bear Meadow, 17km from the volcano, and just beyond the edge of the restricted zone, Gary Rosenquist and Keith Ronnholm took a remarkable series of pictures of the rapidly unfolding events. They are surely the most dramatic photographs of a volcanic eruption ever taken. Expert analysis has also made them the most informative. Gary Rosenquist took twenty-two photographs in about twenty seconds before awakening neighbouring campers who had slept through the most dramatic volcanic episode of the twentieth century; he then drove off as fast as he dared. Keith Ronnholm almost lingered too long. He stopped to take a last photograph as he fled, and the weakening leading edge of the blast overtook him. In the darkness of the swirling ash, he only managed to reach safety by following a forestry logging truck, whose driver was himself being guided by men on foot feeling out the road ahead. Near the northwestern fringe of the blasted area, others survived by driving down the North Toutle valley road at speeds of 160km an hour.

Some people were luckier than others. The blast cloud overtook one group as they drove away, burnt, and then enveloped them in the darkness. Lava fragments the size of golf balls sandblasted and pock-marked their vehicle, but they lived to tell the tale. Near Meta Lake, on the other hand, the blast cloud killed a whole family. Their car was stripped of its paint and its plastic trim melted, but the tyres did not burst. It is now a prime exhibit on the way to Mount St Helens. Four forestry loggers were working near the northwestern edge of the devastated zone when 'a crashing, crunching, and grinding sound' rushed upon them through the trees. It became totally dark and almost impossible to breathe in the searing heat that they had to endure for two minutes. When they could see around them again, they real-

The start of the eruption of Mount St Helens, seen from Mount Adams.

ized that the whole forest had been knocked down and covered with 30cm of ash. They were so badly burnt that only one of the four survived. In the far north of the devastated area, hot ash inundated another group. As one of them said, 'it was like someone pouring a bag of it over your head'. They had to scoop it out of their mouths with their fingers, and 'became cold, sleepy and nauseous'. Some described the very first ashfalls as cool and wet, probably because the fragments came from a mixture of ash and melted snow and ice. Such also was the more potent mixture of the mudflows that were soon to form.

Finally, as if to demonstrate the complete irrationality of some human behaviour – even in the face of such an obvious menace – one couple acted in a way that would have caused criticism in a lunatic asylum. They tried to drive *towards* the erupting volcano – and were lucky that a helicopter rescued them when the eruption began to wane that evening.

Less than half a minute after the hot blast had left its damaged crest, Mount St Helens unleashed a huge column of ash, steam and pumice that soared high into the stratosphere. It rose to a height of 25km in fifteen minutes, and continued to discharge like an enormous steam engine for nine hours on 18 May. The column soon developed a mushroom shape and spread 70km across. The upper winds winnowed out the finer materials towards the east, which caused twilight and ashfalls over eastern Washington and northern Idaho within a few hours. Luckily, at 9.45 a.m. on 18 May

The eruption of Mount St Helens a few seconds after it began.

twenty of the thirty-two helicopters of the National Guard in Yakima had managed to take off to safety before the ash could damage them. They were thus able to provide vital help in the subsequent rescue operations around the volcano. The ash reached Spokane, 430km away, at noon, and spoiled the Lilac Festival scheduled for that day. In all, measurable ashfalls covered an area of 60,000km². The ash was often very fine, like flour, talcum powder or dust. It penetrated everywhere. It clogged lungs and car engines alike; and the cars that remained mobile then often skidded on the slippery ash-coated road surfaces. The fine dust that stayed aloft passed over New York in three days and completed its first trip round the world in two weeks.

Meanwhile, perhaps just after noon, denser nuées ardentes started spurting from Mount St Helens. Time after time, they swept 8km down the northern slopes of the mountain, at speeds of 300km an hour and temperatures of 400°C. They surged into Spirit Lake and boiled the surface water. The masses of steam, trapped under the hot ash of the nuée ardente, then exploded out great craters and hurled steaming ash 1,500m into the air. Scientists only deduced this several weeks later. Nobody, of course, was alive to see the action in close-up, because the northern flank of the mountain was bereft of all living things. At length, at about 5.30 p.m., both the nuées ardentes and the enormous column belching from the shattered summit of the volcano lost their power, and the eruption quickly waned.

Mount St Helens had played a further card by then – mudflows. They formed as soon as the hot volcanic fragments melted the masses of ice around the summit. Most of the drainage just north of the volcano was directed into two branches of the River Toutle, and eventually joined the River Columbia. One mudflow invaded the South Fork of the River Toutle soon after 9.00 a.m., whereas the second, in the North Fork – which springs from Spirit Lake – did not develop until after 1.30 p.m. There would have been a major disaster below the confluence of the two forks of the River Toutle if these mudflows had formed together. The North Fork mudflow was particularly damaging because it was fed not only by hot ash and melting ice, but also by the debris avalanche and some of the displaced waters of Spirit Lake. This mudflow travelled relatively slowly and had the consistency of concrete. It was also quite warm, with a temperature of about 32°C. It made its own spectacular contribution to the television news that evening. It had shattered and picked up a selection of the features of the North Toutle valley – trees and millions of logs were most prominent, but there were also steel girders from broken bridges, twisted forestry vehicles, cars, and sometimes whole wooden houses. It thrust its weird trophies up against the bridge taking the Interstate-5 across the River Toutle. This important main road link on the American west coast only just held out. The mud then quickly made its way into the River Columbia, where it blocked waterborne traffic and closed the river ports for days.

A bus swamped by the mudflow in the north fork of the River Toutle.

The tall coniferous forest destroyed by the blast from Mount St Helens.

Evening, 18 May

When 18 May drew to a close, Mount St Helens had lost 400m from its crest. It was now only 2,450m high. The beautiful ice-capped summit had gone. In its place gaped a hideous, fuming, horseshoe-shaped hole that measured 3.2km long, 1.6km across and 700m in depth. That day, Mount St Helens had released energy equal to the explosion of 27,000 of the atomic bombs dropped on Hiroshima – amounting to nearly one for every second of the nine-hour eruption. About $3km^3$ of rock had avalanched from its northern flanks and about $1km^3$ of shattered, hot materials had erupted from the depths. This array of power killed around 57 people. The outburst claimed such a relatively small number of victims partly because the permanent population was sparse in this remote region devoted essentially to recreation and forestry, but also because of the – sometimes unwelcome – restrictions on access to the threatened area.

Helicopters combed the devastated zones as soon as they could, and rescued over 100 stranded people. A number of bodies were also recovered in the succeeding days, but some victims, such as David Johnston and Harry Truman, were never found. Autopsies showed that most had died of suffocation from inhaling the hot ash, although a few had died from their burns. An Inner Zone of total annihilation was surrounded by a Blowdown Zone, where everything above ground level was destroyed; and it was bordered, in turn, by a Singed

Regeneration at Meta Lake in 1986.

Zone, where most animals were killed and trees were severely charred. Untold numbers of deer, elk and bears as well as smaller animals and great flocks of birds had vanished. A superb coniferous forest of fir, spruce, hemlock and thuya (western red cedar), had been charred and shredded, stripped of every leaf and branch, uprooted, and cast down like giant matchsticks. Some of their leaves even found their way onto the summits of Mount Rainier and Mount Adams.

Aftermath

Mount St Helens erupted violently again on 25 May, 12 June, 22 July, 7 August, and between 16 and 18 October 1980. Each time the volcano produced nuées ardentes and a high column of ash and steam. But there were no more great blasts – the chimney was now open for the molten rocks to reach the surface. During the summer, two successive domes of sticky, viscous lava oozed out from the volcanic chimney and solidified at the exit like corks. Large subsequent explosions destroyed them, but a third dome that formed after the outburst in October survived. It grew by a succession of small eruptions at intervals during the next decade, and was so diligently studied that scientists could almost predict its every move.

The total cost of the damage was estimated at about $US1,000 million. The great eruption destroyed 250 homes, seven bridges, and some 300km of roads; abraded cars and temporarily damaged crops as well as devastating great forests. President Carter visited the area and declared that 'the moon looks like a golf course compared to what we have here'. But losses could have been far, far, greater in a more thickly populated area and in a less well organized country. On the credit side, too, soil fertility increased that summer in eastern Washington. Residents of the Pacific North-West sent ash by post to their friends, although the Post Office complained that it often escaped from the envelopes and threatened to damage the postal sorting machinery. Indeed, the increase in tourism ever since the eruption has helped offset some of the region's economic difficulties. Mount St Helens has been designated a National Monument. There are visitors' centres selling beverages, gifts and the famous pictures of the eruption – as well as a whole range of books about the natural world. Few volcanoes have done as much to stimulate awareness of the environment as Mount St Helens.

For most of the 1980s, the devastated area looked so gaunt that it seemed impossible to imagine that the old flora and fauna could ever return. Nature, though, is clearly not so easily impressed by mere eruptions – after all, this was not even the biggest volcanic outburst of the twentieth century. Revival began almost at once. Avalanche lilies, whose delicate air masks a formidable resilience, were blooming in new ash only 16km from the crater on 8 June 1980. Towards the edges of the blasted zone, snow had remained on the northern sides of many ridges, which were in the lee of the main direction of the blast. The heat therefore passed quickly over them, often leaving the life forms below untouched. It was as if they were in a kind of Baked Alaska. For example at Meta Lake, 13km from the crater, the snows soon melted to reveal flourishing saplings and seedlings, as well as fish and frogs cavorting happily in the waters. Gophers, beavers and mice, who had been underground at the critical moment, also lived to stimulate the regeneration. Birds, deer and other large animals soon began to investigate the new environment. Later in the summer, the dreary landscapes around these islands of life were set alight by huge colonies of rosebay willow-herb (*Epilobium angustifolium*), that the Americans know by the more appropriate name of fireweed. It is estimated that it will take about 150 to 200 years before the forests return to their old vigour. But many new seedlings have taken root already: willows have colonized the damper zones, and the higher slopes are a mass of lupin (*Lupinus latifolius*) and penstemon (*Penstemon cardwellii*). Large tracts have been set aside so that exactly how nature operates under such conditions can be studied. An explanatory trail has been constructed at Meta Lake to illustrate the remarkable recolonization since 1980. The regeneration of the landscape – and the volcano that might threaten it again – have been monitored and analysed ever since by the most sophisticated techniques known to science. The work has given whole new insights into some volcanic processes that hitherto had been little known. Mount St Helens has been in intensive care ever since the great eruption and has truly become the darling of the volcanic world. Which volcano will dethrone her?

14

Nevado del Ruiz, 1985

The eruption of Nevado del Ruiz gave a year's warning and was quite small for its type when it came. But it melted part of the summit ice-cap and formed a mudflow that devastated a town in the lowlands, 60km from the crater. One of the greatest tragedies of the century might have been avoided with more skilfully organised evacuations.

The glistening ice-capped volcanoes of the South American Andes are remote, aloof, silent, majestic, and almost unreal. Their terrible reality became only too obvious on 13 November 1985, when Nevado del Ruiz caused the greatest volcanic catastrophe since Montagne Pelée destroyed Saint-Pierre in 1902. Altogether about 23,000 people died. But the eruption killed nobody directly. The victims were claimed neither by lava-flows, nor by incandescent clouds of ash and toxic gas, but by mudflows which formed when the molten rock melted part of the ice-cap. And it was said that even these deaths could have been avoided.

Most of the fatalities were caused when these mudflows overwhelmed the little town of Armero. It was situated on the plains bordering the River Magdalena, nearly 5,000m below, and about 60km from, the crater. At the time, few had heard either of Armero or Nevado del Ruiz. The television pictures of the disaster revealed to the world that both the volcano and its victims were in the South American republic of Colombia. In fact, the eruption was small and not particularly violent for an Andean volcano, but it caused damage estimated at $US1,000 million.

The eruption of Nevado del Ruiz became the subject of two special numbers of the *Journal of Volcanology and Geothermal Research* in 1990. In that journal, Minard Hall and Barry Voight, in particular, laid bare the efforts – and mistakes – that were made as the emergency developed, but they also pointed the way towards preventing such catastrophes in the future.

Forecasting the exact moment when molten rock will erupt from a volcano is a very tricky job. It was vital at Nevado del Ruiz, because this was when the dangerous mudflows would probably form. The experts would have the hard task of being right, clear and persuasive. The administrators would then have the equally difficult job of deciding if, and when, to evacuate the threatened people. The people might be unwilling to leave the apparent safety of their homes – and they might also be totally confused by conflicting, or incomprehensible, reports and rumours. Capable, trained officials need to demonstrate that the dangers are real, and, if necessary, evacuate the people to prepared

The summit of Nevado del Ruiz.

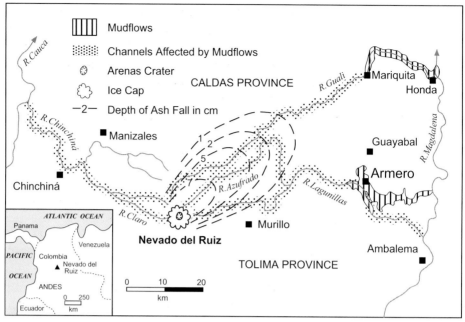

The eruption of Nevado del Ruiz.

and clearly marked places of refuge. The timing of any evacuation is crucial: too early causes unrest; too late causes deaths. But it is no good at all telling people to run away at the last moment. And all these measures cost money that rarely seems to be available – after all, a volcanic emergency is not a war . . . Such points would seem obvious to anyone sitting comfortably far away from a crisis. Those directly involved do not usually see the problems in exactly the same way. Errors of judgment have been made time and again, even during the twentieth century. Nevado del Ruiz was to provide another notable example. There is always a long chain of events, opinions and value-judgments stretching from a likely volcanic eruption to the true perception of the grave danger that it presents. The chain is full of weak links. Many of these links failed in Colombia in 1985. Yet the eruption of molten rock was not a surprise, and neither were its effects. Except, of course, to most of its victims.

That a volcano like Nevado del Ruiz was erupting at all should have made everybody's hair stand on end in every valley draining from the mountain. The threat lies even in its name – for *Nevado* itself means 'snow-capped'. Old snow compacts into ice, which presents special problems on volcanoes. When fragments of molten rock erupt, they quickly melt a lot of ice and generate powerful torrents, which can pick up soil and loose rock. The torrents soon change into unstoppable mudflows that can travel as fast as a racehorse. The steeper the slopes, the faster they can move. When they sweep down into steep mountain valleys, they bring damage and death. Mudflows from Ruiz had already done just this in 1595 and 1845. The problem during any eruption on Nevado del Ruiz was twofold: *when* exactly, and *where* exactly would they flow?

Tragically, the fatal moments on Nevado del Ruiz could not have been predicted with great accuracy. The volcano did not even seem to be building up to a crescendo when experts inspected the crater on 12 November, the very day before the disaster came. Yet months of sporadic earthquakes centred under the volcano, as well as explosions of steam that shattered old volcanic rock into cold ash and scattered it well beyond the crater, both showed that molten rock was rising dangerously towards the summit. Nevertheless, *where* the eruption was happening was much more significant...

Nevado del Ruiz is a bulky volcano, which rises to a height of 5,389m. Its main crater, Arenas, lies near the northeastern edge of its ice-cap, so any volcanic materials that Ruiz erupts are most likely to invade the valleys radiating northeastwards from the summit. These dangerous areas could have been pinpointed at a glance on 'hazard maps'. But, at the end of November 1984, no such maps had been prepared. Work on a hazard map did not start until in September 1985 – no less than six months after a visiting scientist had recommended it.

In 1985, all the ingredients of a catastrophe were assembled at Nevado del Ruiz. They are *still* there. When the next eruption happens, the valleys of the Gualí, Azufrado and Lagunillas rivers will continue to guide any future mudflows swiftly down the northeastern flanks of the volcano to the populous plains below. The only difference now is that intricate warning systems have been set up. But an eruption still could not be stopped, although its dangers might possibly be avoided.

Precedents, 1595 and 1845

It had all happened before, but with fewer casualties. Father Pedro Simón recounted tales of the eruption that had occurred at 11 a.m. on 12 March 1595, some nine years before he had arrived in what was then the Spanish colony of New Granada. There were four big bangs. Nevado del Ruiz then threw out lumps of pumice, like 'erratic stars . . . sparkling red like iron from the forge', that were 'the size of dove's or ostrich eggs'. Some fell on the Spaniards and on their horses, which upset them no end. Mudflows swept down the valleys of the River Gualí and the River Lagunillas as far as the River Magdalena. The rivers carried so much ash that they looked 'more like a thick soup of ash than water'. The land was so devastated that it produced nothing but stunted weeds for many years afterwards. The mudflow killed 636 people, mostly members of the Gualí tribe.

The naturalist, Joaquín Acosta, reported the second disaster to the Académie des Sciences in Paris in 1846. At 7 a.m. on 19 February 1845, the earth rumbled and then trembled. Soon an immense mudflow flooded into the upper valley of the River Lagunillas, burying and sweeping away trees, houses, people and animals. 'The whole population of the upper valley perished. Lower downstream, several people escaped by fleeing upslope. Others were less fortunate and were stranded on knolls, where it was impossible to help them and snatch them from the jaws of death.' The mudflow rushed out of the canyon of the River Lagunillas and spread across the plain in a mass of stinking mud, broken trees, sand, stones and huge blocks of ice in a mantle 5m deep. It destroyed Ambalema on the River Magdalena, and claimed most of its 1,000 victims in the town. Armero did not then exist. It developed later – on this very mudflow – and just opposite where the River Lagunillas entered the plain. The builders of Armero chose one of the most dangerous spots in the whole area. He who builds his house on an old mudflow is likely to be buried by the next . . .

Fifty-one Weeks of Hesitation

A cynic might claim that Nevado del Ruiz gave the people of Armero plenty of warning. But, for fifty-one weeks, the volcano did not spell out that warning clearly enough. Minor earthquakes were felt near the crest of the mountain on 22 November 1984, and many more tremors accompanied the first small explosion on 22 December. But the volcano seemed far too remote to present any real threat to the towns around the mountain; sometimes it shook the ground; sometimes the rising molten rock heated the groundwater to steam and exploded ashy rock fragments 200m into the air. Just enough to keep the nervous on their toes.

So, what else was Ruiz going to do? Nobody knew. Hardly anyone in Colombia was in a position to find out. It was just as well, therefore, that the volcano seemed to be in no particular hurry. Unfortunately, very few scientists had studied Ruiz, but enough was known about it to indicate that it could erupt violently, and that it could also produce lethal mudflows. But Colombia had no equipment to monitor its volcanoes and few geologists trained to use it. Skilled help, therefore, had to come from other countries. When help came, it varied in quality. Some equipment was poor. Experts and non-experts alike gave conflicting advice. Many local committees met regularly, but the national government concentrated on what seemed more pressing problems instead of giving a firm lead. Nevado del Ruiz rises between the provinces of Caldas in the west and Tolima in the east. The administrators of Caldas Province, however, paid more attention to the threat from the eruption than did those of Tolima Province. Armero was in Tolima.

The initial stirrings of Nevado del Ruiz produced more curiosity than fear amongst the surrounding population. The volcano erupted throughout the first eight months of 1985; but these were not the strongest eruptions in the world in that period. In late January 1985, a local scientific commission was formed to monitor events from Manizales, capital of Caldas Province and a city of 350,000 people. But they had few practical means of fulfilling their aims, although they soon contacted the National Bureau of Geology and Mines (INGEOMINAS). Accounts of the volcanic events finally reached the press in the Manizales newspaper, *La Patria*, on 21 and 22 February. The scientific commission and some journalists visited the crater at least twice before the end of February. Their report, with photographs of activity, appeared in *La Patria* on 3 March. They suggested that a survey of the likely risks from the eruption should be undertaken. At the request of the Colombian Civil Defence authorities and INGEOMINAS, a scientist from the UN disaster relief organization (UNDRO) also inspected the crater, on 9 March. He recommended that the crater should be examined almost daily; that the temperatures of the escaping gases should be measured regularly; that alarm systems should be set up to warn the people of threatening events; that seismographs to record earthquakes should be bought and installed on the mountain; and that a hazard map of the areas at risk from a larger eruption should be made. He stressed that these recommendations should be put into operation at once. They were not.

On the contrary, after a team from INGEOMINAS had visited the crater, they concluded in late March that its activity was 'normal' and did not represent an 'imminent danger'. Alas, both terms were virtually meaningless in this volcanic context. However, they did say that the volcano ought to be monitored. A conference on volcanic risks at the National University in Manizales on 20 March urged the government to inform and protect the people under threat, and to prepare an evacuation plan for them. At this stage, however, Ruiz was worrying those in Manizales – and the few foreign experts who had visited the volcano – much more than the authorities in the capital, Bogotá, which was only 150km from the volcano, but seemed a world away. But the local authorities had no money to do much about it. At least the Civil Defence in Manizales had prepared a disaster plan. At the request of UNESCO, the Ecuadorian geologist, Minard Hall, visited Manizales in May 1985. It was only when he was interviewed in *La Patria* on 7 May that the seriousness of the situation was first mooted in the press – five months after the eruption had begun.

In his report on 15 May, the Ecuadorian geologist agreed with the proposals that the UNDRO scientist had first made on 9 March. He also stressed that the volcano was still not being monitored, although mudflows were likely to threaten the cities around it. On 30 May, INGEOMINAS made the first official Colombian request for expert technical help from abroad – from the USA. However, the US Geological Survey regretted that it could not send any scientists because they were busy with eruptions in Hawaii and at Mount St Helens. They sent three instruments instead. Meanwhile, international protocol *oblige*, UNESCO was only waiting for the necessary formal request from the Colombian government before dispatching experts to Bogotá. In fact, UNESCO had already written offering a multinational team of volcano experts, suitable equipment, and opportunities for training Colombian scientists in the wiles of erupting volcanoes. Their letter was unaccountably lost in the entrails of the Colombian bureaucracy for the next two months until it emerged with another letter sent to the Governor of Caldas Province from the Ministry of Education on 21 August.

When the Manizales Scientific Commission inspected the crater again on 8 July, they saw that steam was starting to melt some of the ice. Because the molten rock was clearly nearing the summit, the threat from Ruiz was obviously increasing. A Volcano Risk Committee was formed in the city, composed of the older commission, scientists from the chief universities, and representatives of commercial and financial interests. Caldas Province granted money to help monitor the volcano. On 10 July the mayor of Manizales and the Governor of Caldas Province asked the Swiss Disaster Relief Corps for help. They sent out an earthquake expert, who arrived with his equipment in Manizales on 8 August. On 15 July, INGEOMINAS installed four seismographs on the volcano to monitor earthquakes and thus to help plot the rise of the molten rock into the body of the volcano. But these seismographs were not well-placed, in poor condition, and did not work properly. On 5 August 1985, INGEOMINAS asked UNESCO for money to map the areas that were most at risk. In late August, the Volcano Risk Committee in Manizales placed about five seismographs in better positions so that the tremors could, at last, be recorded efficiently.

One of the major organizational defects at this stage of the emergency was that INGEOMINAS and the Volcano Risk Committee in Manizales were not sharing their information. Progress was therefore slower than it could have been. In early September, too, the visiting Swiss scientist was disturbed to discover that earthquakes had started to occur more often, but the INGEOMINAS earthquake records were merely being sent directly to Bogotá without being analysed.

On 11 September, even more earthquakes heralded a vigorous blast of steam from the crater at 1.30 p.m. The eruption lasted for seven hours, coating the summit with a centimetre of fragments and showering ash onto Manizales. The steam melted some of the ice-cap and at 6.30 p.m. formed a mudflow that soon sped 27km down the River Azufrado valley. This was a dress rehearsal for the première on 13 November. Ruiz had given a very explicit warning about what was in store. The Volcano Risk Committee in Manizales put the citizens 'on alert', but no one was evacuated, because that area had only had a shower of ash.

This eruption nevertheless sharpened a few ideas about the threats from Ruiz. The first joint meeting of the Red Cross and Civil Defence committees of Caldas and Tolima took place on 13 September. On 14 September, in the Bogotá newspaper, *El Espectador*, the authorities of Caldas Province warned that the valleys of the Rivers Claro, Azufrado, Lagunillas and Gualí would be most at risk if a bigger eruption were to occur. Nevertheless, the headline in *La Patria* on 13 September proclaimed that RUIZ ACTIVITY IS NOT DANGEROUS, meaning, of course, for Manizales – which turned out to be true. The Governor of Caldas himself inspected Nevado del Ruiz on 15 September. He was impressed enough to organize a meeting of officials from all the threatened provinces. They called for help both from the national government and from international agencies. Unfortunately, they also decided that each province should organize its own emergency plan, which had the unhappy effect of handicapping inter-regional co-ordination. However, the national government at last formed a National Committee of Directors of Civil Defence and Emergency Plans to devise a response to any further eruptions – along the lines suggested six months before by the UN Disaster Relief Organization's report.

People did not know what to think. Public perceptions of the emergency, as represented and influenced by the press, were still conflicting and changing. On 18 September, a colour photograph on the front page of the Bogotá newspaper, *El Tiempo*, brought Armero to national notice for the first time during the crisis. In 1984 a landslide had partially dammed up the River Lagunillas at Cirpe, 12km upstream from Armero. The newspaper reported that the mayor of Armero feared that an eruption might break the dam and unleash vast volumes of water onto the town. In the same edition, the President of the Red Cross in Tolima Province declared that Armero 'might disappear' if a major eruption were to form a big mudflow. (Nothing was ever done about this dam.)

The mayor of Armero, Ramón Antonio Rodríguez, however, was determined to try and save his town. He formed an eight-man emergency committee to ask President Betancour for help. The dam, they said, was 'a time bomb' threatening Armero. Not everyone shared such views. INGEOMINAS, for instance, declared that the dam was in no danger of failure 'under normal river conditions'. They completely ignored the fact that a large mudflow would hardly represent 'normal conditions'. But the authorities in Tolima Province were now starting to show as much interest in Nevado del Ruiz as their counterparts in Caldas Province. Not before time.

On 20 September a group of scientists met at the Hotel Termales in Manizales to start working on the hazard map first recommended on 9 March. The mappers now made the danger from mudflows their prime concern. Unfortunately mudflows did not appear to worry the US geologist who had written his thesis on Ruiz. In a public lecture in Manizales on 23 September, he said that another eruption would only affect an area within a radius of about 10km of the summit. *El Espectador*, in Bogotá, reported these glad tidings on 28 September. Nevado del Ruiz riposted by exploding clouds of ash more than 20km from the crater during the last week of the month. It was true that Manizales itself stood in no great danger, because it lay away from the paths of any likely mudflows. But the mantle of safety was – inadvertently, and disastrously – also extended over the valleys draining northeastwards from the crater to Tolima Province. They were in very great danger indeed.

In the Colombian Parliament on 24 September, a member representing Caldas Province complained about the inactivity of the government. An appropriate minister gave the 'reassuring' promise that a plan of action should be available before the end of October. At the end of September, a New Zealand scientist found that Ruiz was giving off so much sulphur dioxide – from the rising molten rock – that a bigger eruption seemed likely to happen quite soon.

On 30 September, local scientists monitoring the volcano told the authorities in Tolima Province that people with radios should be stationed in the valleys draining Nevado del Ruiz to warn of any impending disaster. But, once again, a contrary view did not take long to emerge. The director of the Geophysical Institute of the Andes declared in *Magazin 8 Dias* at the end of September that 'nothing [was] happening on the volcano that threatens the inhabitants of the region'. As if to support the director, Nevado del Ruiz almost stopped its constant trembling during October, although a plume of steam still rose 2km from its crater. In *La Patria* on 4 October, the Chamber of Commerce in Manizales criticized the press for irresponsible reporting 'that will cause economic losses in the region'. Next day, a well-known doctor in Manizales declared that radio announcers had greatly exaggerated the dangers from an eruption. The Archbishop of Manizales also blamed the media for spreading 'volcanic terrorism'. On 7 October, *La Patria* wrote that a volcanic risk map would lower property prices. Such was the bogus expertise trumpeted in the media.

The first edition of this hazard map finally saw the light of day on 7 October at a press conference attended by all the important actors in the emergency, except the Governor of Tolima Province. But only ten copies of the map and its accompanying explanation were distributed. It was published, however, in the newspapers the following day, but with errors in the key and in the distribution of the likely dangers. Thus the hazard map, as published in the press, was as much a liability as an asset. However, *La Patria* did observe that the citizens of towns such as Armero would have about two hours to evacuate their homes once any mudflows began. Nobody, however, seems to have had the slightest idea about where the people would go, or who would give the necessary orders, or who would pay.

It was also on 7 October that INGEOMINAS first released their interpretations of the earthquake data that they had been collecting since 20 July. Thereafter, the data were interpreted – as collected – in Manizales. But the seismographs were not linked to base by radio and the information still had to be retrieved painstakingly every day from the volcano.

Nevertheless, by the first week in October, the authorities seem to have recognized that Ruiz presented a real, and potentially dangerous, threat. Various plans were being evolved, but whether they were tight enough to save lives was an entirely different matter. It was a sign of the times that, after months of scepticism, INGEOMINAS finally declared in *El Espectador* on 8 October that a larger eruption would melt some of the summit ice-cap and make mudflows inevitable: 'There is a 100 per cent probability of mudflows . . . with great danger for Armero . . . Ambalema, and the lower part of the River Chinchiná'. But how many readers realized that '100 per cent probability' meant 'certain'? The language of communication was wrong: not even many gamblers know much about probability. Some government officials dismissed this report as 'too alarming'. In any case, the authorities did not want to start any evacuations until the experts had assured them that they were essential. Then, of course, when that essential moment did arrive, the consequences developed too quickly for the people to be evacuated to safety.

Doubts of a different kind prevailed in the little towns around Ruiz. Interviewed in the magazine *Consigna* on 15 October, the mayor of Armero said that his local Emergency Committee had neither the financial resources, nor the necessary information, to do anything if a catastrophe occurred. The people, he said, did not know whether to leave their homes, or to stay put. 'They have lost all confidence in the truth of the information served up to them, and have commended their fate to God.'

Meanwhile, Civil Defence organizations were assessing the risks in the valleys draining from Nevado del Ruiz. Nevertheless, at the end of October, they had not yet assessed the River Azufrado valley, which, on all available evidence, should have been their very first task. The Civil Defence and the Red Cross in Caldas and Tolima Provinces had also sent radios to villages, started volcano awareness programmes in schools, and explained to local officials how they might counteract the emergency – including evacuation from areas near rivers. They tried to build up public perceptions of the dangers in order to prevent future panic. But, with hindsight, perhaps a little more public anxiety might have made the National Government take the crisis more seriously.

When an Italian team of experts arrived in Manizales on 16 October, they realized that the monitoring programme was inadequate, that even quicker means of relaying warnings had to be devised, and that every threatened town should have a designated refuge – for the simple reason that the people need to know where to run. On 31 October, the Italians also told the Colombian government that the gases fuming from the crater were escaping from the molten rock which had probably already risen into the body of the volcano. Thus a larger, and more dangerous, eruption was on the cards.

On 29 October, INGEOMINAS officials reported to the Emergency Committee in Tolima Province that they had visited twelve threatened settlements to examine their contingency plans and to advise them on the volcanic risks and what to do about them. A meeting of the mayors of the towns threatened by Ruiz was arranged for 13 November in the provincial capital, Ibagué.

Four months after the Colombians had first asked for technical help, the US Geological Survey finally proposed to install six telemetered seismographs, which would register earthquakes directly at a pick-up station and thus cut out the need to fetch daily readings from the old meters nearer the volcano. But the Americans argued about who should pay and how much. Eventually the costs were reduced to $US10,000 and two earthquake experts were ready to leave on 7 November, armed with a single telemetered seismograph.

Politics then entered the fray. On 6 November, the Colombian President, Belisario Betancour, ordered an assault on rebels who had recently captured the Law Courts in Bogotá. In the ensuing battle, 100 people, including eleven judges, were killed. The American authorities did not feel able to expose their colleagues to such disturbances, and advised the two geologists to stay safely at home. The assault also postponed publication of the new hazard map from

12 to 15 November. This delay could have been an important element in the tragedy that was soon to happen. The commentary that finally accompanied the map indicated that Armero, Honda and Mariquita were the most threatened towns. The map also showed that the people of Armero would have to travel more than one kilometre to safety. But, since nobody had designated or organized a refuge for them, it would have been really hard to evacuate Armero. On the other hand, INGEOMINAS had claimed that an evacuation could be done in two hours – not, of course, counting the time that it would take to send out alerts and mobilize the evacuees.

On 10 November, the volcano started to give off continuous earth tremors, but not as much as before the large eruption on 11 September. However, no analyses of earthquake data had been issued since 10 October, and INGEOMINAS was now even beginning to think that these seismographs were costing too much to run. On 12 November a group of scientists visited the Arenas crater and saw nothing to suggest that the second most lethal eruption of the twentieth century was about to occur.

Mud, Wednesday, 13 November

At 3.06 p.m. on 13 November 1985, a powerful explosion scattered rain-sodden ash as much as 50km northeast of Ruiz. The police, Red Cross and Civil Defence in Caldas and Tolima Provinces were soon told. Settlements near the rivers draining from the volcano were warned to expect floods and mudflows. Red Cross officials were told to 'sound the alarm – if it proved necessary'. But it seems that nobody told them how they should decide this.

At 5 p.m., ash began to shower down on Armero. At the same time, the Tolima Emergency Committee began its scheduled meeting in Ibagué. They were not particularly worried by this fresh outburst from Ruiz. The falling ash, however, was worrying the citizens of Armero, where the emergency services had already been alerted. The mayor and the priest both broadcast over Radio Armero. The gist of their reassuring messages was: 'Keep calm, there is nothing to worry about.' The radio and the church public address system kept on repeating this injunction.

Nevertheless, at 7 p.m., the Red Cross in Ibagué radioed to their representatives in Armero to order the evacuation of the town. But the ash had just stopped falling on Armero. The eruption seemed to be over. Instead, torrents of rather ashy rain soon began drenching down. An evacuation would probably have seemed both pointless and unpleasant. At 7.30 p.m., before any action had been taken, the Red Cross told the committee meeting in Ibagué that conditions had returned to 'normal' in Tolima Province, because ash was no longer falling there. But, of course, the problem was elsewhere, out of sight on the ice-clad summit of Ruiz.

Nevado del Ruiz was just taunting its victims. A national TV station inadvertently joined in the game. It broadcast news of the eruption, but let it be understood that there was no cause for alarm. This reassuring message was chiefly directed at the city of Manizales – and, indeed, it proved to be correct there. But the clear inference was that level-headed people living anywhere around the volcano had no need to panic.

No sooner did everything seem to be settling down again than the situation on the summit changed radically. Very few people realized it. The volcano sprang into real action. At 9.08 p.m. on 13 November, Nevado del Ruiz erupted molten rock for the first time. The preliminaries were over. Scientists monitoring the volcano saw that the glowing ash 'lighted up the raincloud over Ruiz like a lamp'. They alerted Manizales at once. Explosions scattered the molten fragments all over the ice-cap and ash rose in a steaming column 8km above the crater. Hotter than 900°C as it left the crater, the ash could easily start melting the ice. At 9.30 p.m., an even bigger eruption released half a dozen nuées ardentes in quick succession. Hot ash and pumice went on showering the ice-cap for the next two hours. It was not a big eruption as violent eruptions go. Ruiz threw out only about 0.006km^3 of molten rock, which melted less than 0.02km^3 of water from one tenth of the ice-cap. It was enough to form 0.06km^3 of mudflows. More than enough to do a lot of damage if the mudflows could get up speed in some of the steep valleys. They could – and they did.

The mudflows were not just babbling brooks of dirty water, or trails of gently oozing sludge. They were deep, fast-moving, powerful and lethal torrents of destruction. Vast currents of meltwater swooshed from the summit into the neighbouring valley-heads. They gathered up ton after ton of newly erupted hot ash, pumice, molten rock, rain, ice, snow, meltwater, loose rocks and huge boulders torn from the volcano, rain-sodden soil, shrubs, trees and grass, which all combined into several lethal mudflows with the rough consistency of fresh concrete.

One mudflow ran westwards down the River Cauca and submerged Chinchiná, 50km away, at 10.40 p.m. In spite of the prompt 'red alert' warnings issued between 9.30 p.m. and 10.30 p.m. on several radio stations by the director of Civil Defence of Caldas Province, the mudflow arrived in Chinchiná before the town could be completely evacuated. It destroyed three bridges and 200 homes and killed 1,927 people. If they had moved only 75m up the valleyside, they would have lived. Other mudflows sped down the River Gualí and the River Lagunillas. But the really lethal mudflow formed about 9.30 p.m. at the head of the River Azufrado, the main tributary of the River Lagunillas. 'It was the Azufrado that brought everything down and finished the little town downstream.' The mudflow was soon roaring down the steep, narrow valley, glowing yellow in the darkness and making an enormous din. A man living on the valley-side was terrified to hear it – and immensely relieved to see it pass him by. 'It was a supremely horrifying thing; we thought that our time had come . . . you couldn't talk to anyone 50cm away, because you couldn't hear.' The mudflow was held up from time to time by bridges, and then it would rush on again in great surges as soon as they gave way. Its discharge rates averaged about 25,000m^3 per second, but, 10km from its source, the discharge reached as much as 48,000m^3 per second. Its front was 30m high and it was advancing at an average speed of 36km an hour. The mudflow followed the River Azufrado valley into the River Lagunillas, where it gained added vigour when it burst the dam at Cirpe that had caused the mayor of Armero so much worry.

Meanwhile, the ashy rain went on drenching Armero. Most people stayed indoors. There was a soccer match on TV. It was getting near bedtime. The mayor and the priest were right: it was important to keep calm. And, anyway, where could anyone go? It was better to look on the bright side. It was much more comfortable to stay cosily at home than to pack everything up, wake up the children, and start trekking out into the dead of night, with nowhere definite to go, simply because a few scientists, who thought they knew better than the mayor and the priest, said that Ruiz, 60km away, was going to destroy the town, when it had been erupting for almost a year without causing the slightest damage anywhere . . .

Between 9.45 p.m. and 10 p.m., officials in Ibagué tried once again to order the evacuation of Armero, but it was hard to make contact because of the storm. Then, between 10.15 p.m. and 10.30 p.m., Civil Defence officers in Murillo and Ambalema radioed to their colleagues in Armero, telling them to evacuate the town. The police, the fire brigade, the Red Cross, and the Civil Defence in Armero probably all knew by 10.30 p.m. that the mudflow was rushing towards them. But no systematic evacuation order seems to have reached the citizens. It is hard to find out what exactly happened. Most of those who knew were dead within the hour.

Certainly, some individuals tried to warn their fellow-citizens. Afterwards, one survivor said: 'I talked to a young man from the Red Cross who was caught by the mud and almost killed. He was very badly wounded . . . He said that they realized that the volcano had exploded and had gone out to warn the people.' Some families had a chance to escape because their friends had telephoned to say that the mudflow was on its way. One survivor, who had been telephoned at 10 p.m. said that

> one of the firemen in Armero went out into the streets blowing a whistle and setting off the alarm, alerting the people. But the people didn't want to come out of their houses. They said it was a lie, because the priest from Armero . . . said that nothing had happened and [we had] not to be alarmed.

Armero, 11.35 p.m., Wednesday, 13 November

Preceded by waters released from the Cirpe dam, the hot mudflow, with its powerful armoury of boulders, surged out from the River Lagunillas canyon and turned across the plain towards Armero. It was 60km from where it had started.

The mayor of Armero, Ramón Antonio Rodríguez, was talking on two-way radio to someone in Ibagué. Suddenly, he said, 'Wait a minute, I think the town is getting flooded!' These were his last reported words. Radio Armero was playing cheery music when the mudflow arrived. It covered the town in several surges, each lasting less than an hour. It cut off the electricity supply. There was utter chaos. The mud did carry a fortunate few to salvation in Guayabal, 8km away, but most of the citizens of Armero died within a few minutes.

The most murderous components of the mudflow were the thousands and thousands of boulders that it had torn from the valley-floors on its journey down from Ruiz. Now, it hurled these boulders at Armero, smashing even concrete structures like matchwood, and shearing them off at ground level. Its surging waves swept up wooden buildings, cars and trees, and tossed them about like flotsam on a stormy sea. Each new fragment ripped from Armero increased its destructive power. The swirling mudflow levelled most of the town without difficulty, and crushed and battered most of its citizens to death. The mud itself drowned or asphyxiated many of those whom the boulders and masonry had spared. Many survivors had broken limbs and open wounds that became so badly infected that they soon joined the quickly mounting death-toll.

José Luis Restrepo was a Colombian geology student, who had come to Armero on a field trip. He gave the most detailed account of what happened in Barry Voight's analysis of the disaster:

[At 7 p.m.] it was raining heavily. We took shelter in the hotel, had dinner, then the weather settled down, it got hot, then a group of us went to look for a bar to play billiards and when we returned [at 10.50 p.m.], the ash started falling . . . we woke the geology professor up and our colleagues, and when the professor saw [the size of] the particles, he informed us that we should pack because we were leaving . . . We didn't hear any kind of alarm, even when the ash was falling and we were in the hotel . . . we turned on the radio . . . The mayor was talking and he said not to worry, that it was a rain of ash, that they had not reported anything from the Nevado, [and] to stay calm in our houses. There was a local station [Radio Armero] and we were listening to it, when suddenly it went off the air . . . [about fifteen seconds later], the electric power went out and that's when we started hearing the noise in the air, like something toppling, falling, and we didn't hear anything else, no alarm . . . The priest from Armero had supposedly spoken on a loudspeaker [around 6 p.m.] and had said the same thing: that there was no need to leave Armero . . . When we went out, the cars were swaying and running people down . . . there was total darkness, the only light [was] provided by cars . . . we were running and [were] about to reach the corner when a river of water came down the streets . . . we turned around, screaming, towards the hotel, because the waters were already dragging beds along, overturning cars, sweeping people away . . . [we] went back to the hotel, a three-storey building with a terrace, built of cement and very sturdy

Armero destroyed.

... Suddenly, I heard bangs, and looking towards the rear of the hotel I saw [something] like foam, coming down out of the darkness ... It was [a wall] of mud approaching the hotel, and sure enough, it crashed against the rear of the hotel and started crushing walls ... And then the ceiling slab fractured and ... the entire building was destroyed and broken into pieces. Since the building was made of cement, I thought that it would resist, but [the boulder-filled mud] was coming in such an overwhelming way, like a wall of tractors, razing the city, razing everything ... [Then] the university bus, that was in a parking lot next to the hotel, was higher than us [on a wave of mud] and on fire, and it exploded, so I covered my face, thinking, 'this is where I die a horrible death' ... There was a little girl who I thought was decapitated, but ... her head was buried in the mud ... A lady told me, 'look, that girl moved a leg'. Then I moved toward her and my legs sank into the mud, which was hot but not burning, and I started to get the little girl out, but when I saw her hair was caught, that seemed to me the most unfair thing in the whole world ...

All night long, ash was falling. At 4.30 a.m. or 5.00 a.m., more or less, the noise increased again, then we thought that another mudflow was coming. And, sure enough, towards the side you could see something shining that was moving ... And [then] it started to be light, and that's when we lost control, because we saw that horrible sea of mud, which was so gigantic . . . there were people buried, calling out, calling for help, and if you tried to go to them, you would sink into the mud . . . so now you must start counting time as before Armero, and after Armero . . . it's like living and being born again.

Epilogue

The scene that greeted rescuers on 14 November 1985 was one of indescribable horror. It would have needed a heart of steel not to be moved to tears by the scenes in what was left of the town. The mud had swept most of Armero away. Only the foundations of the town centre could be detected under 5m of slime. Here and there, tangled clumps of wrecked buildings, trees, cars and corpses stood out above the stinking grey plain. Trapped cows moaned. Dogs ate mutilated bodies. Injured survivors, who had been swept along by the swirling mud, lay in agony in the wreckage. Their frantic efforts to escape seemed to suck them deeper and deeper into the morass. Nobody could cross the slimy mud to help them until wooden catwalks were eventually laid out. But, by then, many had died, exhausted by their struggles. The sludge and wreckage trapped little Omaira Sánchez for three days as rescuers fought to extract her. Then the muddy waters oozed over her face while a television cameraman filmed her death.

Omaira Sánchez.

Some who survived the mudflow.

Cesar Payan lost his wife and daughters to the mudflow. The surging mass ripped one child from his arms and then carried him far beyond Armero. He recovered consciousness next day about 10km from the town. To his astonishment, he saw his three-year-old youngest daughter struggling in the mud about 100m away. He got to her, put her on his back, and swam through the sludge as best he could to the nearest dry land. At 4 p.m. on 14 November, a helicopter arrived with Red Cross officials. They told him that they would take the little girl to Ambalema for urgent medical attention . . . Perhaps she died. Perhaps she got lost. Perhaps she was kidnapped. Perhaps she was sold. But Cesar Payan never saw his daughter again. They say that he was not the only one.

The cost of the damage was estimated at over $US1,000 million. In fact, the eruption cost the Colombian economy about $US7,700 million – one fifth of the country's Gross National Product. Roads, bridges, electricity cables and telephone lines were cut. The mudflow damaged, or totally destroyed, two hospitals, 50 schools, 58 industrial plants 343 commercial establishments, 5,092 houses, 3,400 hectares of agricultural land, 60 per cent of the livestock, 30 per cent of the rice crop in the area and half a million bags of coffee. The mistakes had been costly, too. Altogether, about 23,000 people and 15,000 animals perished, 4,470 people were injured, and 7,700 were made homeless. Only 100 houses out of 5,000 in Armero remained intact on a small knoll in the northern part of the town. The cemetery was undamaged.

After the disaster, of course, aid of all kinds poured into the area. There was equipment galore afterwards. Everyone of importance could express their most sincere concern. There were abundant photo-opportunities. There was also much research to be done.

As *Epoca* commented in December 1985, 'Where there was life and the hope of production, now there is an ocean of mud, a mute witness to the fury that nature has released.' Nature may have released the fury, but human beings had let it become lethal. With hindsight, it is clear that the scientists' warnings had not been clear or forceful enough, non-experts had been wrong, and the authorities had waited until the last possible moment before they took action, in the vain hope that the emergency would go away. Fearing a false alarm, unrest, enormous expense and criticism, or ridicule, nobody wanted to order an evacuation. They gambled and they lost. The National Government itself offered little guidance; much devolved onto the regional authorities, and it seems that those in Tolima Province, where the disaster struck hardest, were less able than their colleagues in Caldas Province. In any case, both provinces were too poorly prepared, too poorly funded, and too poorly equipped from the outset to face up to such an emergency. After months of official scepticism and delay, the crisis also climaxed far too swiftly for any coherent plan of evacuation to be implemented. But, during the afternoon and early evening of 13 November, any kind of evacuation – even a badly organized flight – could have saved thousands of lives. The people, however, did not truly perceive the real threat to their own lives. They did not realize that death was rushing to meet them.

Nowadays, Nevado del Ruiz is closely monitored from the newly established Colombian Volcanological Observatory. Its every whim is analysed. Too late for its 23,000 victims. The horse has already bolted once, but it is far from certain that the stable door has been closed. Warning systems and evacuation procedures still apparently need to be streamlined. The next mudflow could still rush down the mountain canyons far faster than the threatened people could be saved. Other eruptions and mudflows are inevitable. How many people will Ruiz kill next time?

15

Lake Nyos, 1986

Not many lakes explode – not even in Africa. On the evening of 21 August 1986, a toxic mass of carbon dioxide suddenly spurted from Lake Nyos and asphyxiated about 1,742 people, and many more birds and animals, before they realized what was happening. Lake Nyos? Lake Nyos? Earth scientists soon learnt where Lake Nyos was – especially when vicious conflicts about the origin of the gas soon separated the experts into two bitterly opposed camps. Many do not believe that it was a real volcanic eruption at all.

Lake Nyos is in the Grassfields, an isolated part of the North-West Province of Cameroon, near the Nigerian border. The lake covers an area of about 1.5km^2 and lies at a height of 1,091m. It is set some 200m into the surrounding rugged granite hills, but, in the wet season especially, the excess waters escape over a low spillway into a valley floored with volcanic rocks, running north towards Nyos village. This was the path taken by the gas when it left the lake.

There are about thirty similar lakes in the district. The soils around them are quite fertile, the climate is good for agriculture – and lakes commonly attract settlements. But, rather curiously, the density of population around these lakes is only about one third of that in North-West Province as a whole. Since the disaster, however, several local Bantu legends have come to light which tell of evil and, indeed, exploding lakes in the area. The very name of Lake Njupi, near Lake Nyos, itself means 'bad'. Folk memories of real events, imperfectly preserved in such legends, may have been strong enough to dissuade local people from getting too close to these lakes. It so happens, also, that Nyos village, the site of the biggest death-toll in 1986, was founded at a local crossroads as recently as 1958 and it was peopled largely by immigrant Fulanis, who did not have these legends. But then, of course, legends are only quoted when, with hindsight, they seem to have some scientific relevance.

Lake Nyos was formed about 400 years ago by a volcanic explosion that was much larger than that of 1986. Its companions in the district were probably all formed in the same way. Molten volcanic rock, rising from the depths, met water filtering down from the land surface. The heat suddenly changed the

Lake Nyos.

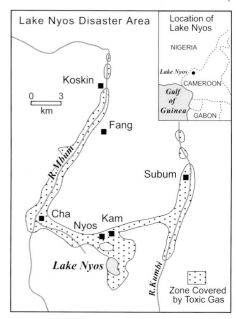

The Lake Nyos disaster area.

water to steam in the cracks between the rocks. The result was a great explosion which shattered a chimney up through the rocks and left a rounded hollow in the land surface. Some of the shattered rocks, including volcanic fragments, were thrown out onto the land; the remaining fragments fell back and choked the chimney. All this probably took less than a day, and perhaps less than an hour. The area gets over 2.5m of rain a year, so that it would not take long for the waters to fill the funnel-shaped hollow at the surface up to the level of the northern spillway, and form a lake 208m deep. Meanwhile volcanic gases, and especially carbon dioxide, could escape from the molten rocks still lying deep below and filter up towards the floor of the lake through the chimney choked with fragments. Did the carbon dioxide rise *suddenly* and burst through the lake in a gas eruption? Or did the gas accumulate *slowly* and dissolve in the lower layers of water in the lake – to be released when these layers somehow overturned? This is the problem that made experts lose their composure. What exactly happened then at Lake Nyos?

A Catastrophic Release of Gas, Thursday, 21 August 1986

A rather cloudy mixture of carbon dioxide and water droplets left the lake. It did not merely bubble out. It was expelled forcibly from the southern floor of Lake Nyos, as if from a jet, at a speed of about 100km an hour and it enveloped houses 120m above its shores. Once it escaped, the cloud spread more gently beyond the lake, and lost most of its water droplets as it did so. Probably almost 1km^3 of almost pure carbon dioxide was expelled. The gas is one and a half times denser than air, so the more concentrated it is, the further it can spread away from its source. It hugged the ground in a mass 40m thick as it travelled downslope under gravity at speeds between 20km and 50km an hour. When it lost its water droplets, this mass became invisible and deadly. But the carbon dioxide did not readily mix with the air, which meant that it stayed in concentration for a long time and over long distances. Human beings are asphyxiated if they breathe concentrations of more than 20–30 per cent of carbon dioxide in the air for more than ten minutes. Along the valley-floors, this lethal concentration persisted for 23km from Lake Nyos.

There was almost no warning. A local healer had apparently been notified on 19 August that herb leaves had turned red near the lake. It is possible that some gas had bubbled out of the lake at that time. Otherwise, this gas escaped suddenly and almost unannounced.

At 4 p.m. on 21 August, some herdsmen noticed strange gurgling noises coming from Lake Nyos, and its waters were fuming slightly. At about 8 p.m. some villagers in Cha, 6km away, heard a loud noise and a blind lady felt an earth tremor. Two or three further 'detonations' followed between 9.30 p.m. and 10 p.m.

According to Mr Malanjaï, water began to spurt from the surface of Lake Nyos at about 8.30 p.m. It formed a steamy-looking cloud that rose from the lake and spread up the steep slopes around its shores. The waters 'swooshed and boomed, pinged and popped', so that he and his neighbours thought that another gunfight had broken out between two of the local ethnic groups. At about 10 p.m. the edge of the cloud enveloped Mr Malanjaï's house, which stood 120m above the lake. 'When I stood up . . . my head hurt.' He went to the women's house and saw that his children had come outside and fallen down. He put them to bed and invited a very confused neighbour to shelter in his house. Neither man fully lost consciousness, although it was 1 a.m. before the cloud began to clear.

Kalus Keituh had a very similar experience that evening at his home in Upper Nyos village, 250m above the southwestern shore of the lake. He also saw water spurt from the southern part of Lake Nyos, 'like water that has burst through a pipe. When it started flowing upwards it was red; when it got further up it turned white.' Mr Keituh and his neighbour, Mr Pakalé, watched the cloud of droplets and gas spread up beyond the southwestern shore of the lake. Its edge covered the house and cattle belonging to Mr Pakalé, who lived down the hill, about 100m above the lake. Mr Pakalé rushed home. Mr Keituh watched him take a kerosene bush lantern: 'he was walking inside that smoke, inside the power of the lake'. (There was, therefore, enough oxygen available on the fringe of the cloud to enable Mr Pakalé to breathe and keep his lamp burning.) Mr Keituh looked on helplessly from above, and he eventually went to bed about 1 a.m. when the gas stopped escaping.

He got up at five o'clock next morning and went down to see his neighbour. Mr Pakalé told him that raindrops from the cloud had burnt his skin, but there had been a greater tragedy. A wife and three of his children were still alive, but one child and all his cows had died. All the survivors were confused throughout the day.

Mr Keituh immediately helped Mr Pakalé bury his child. As they were returning home, they met some people on the road and asked them if they had any idea of what had happened. A child told them that he had just come from Nyos village. 'Things were no better there,' he said. An understatement. Things in Nyos were far, far worse than 'no better'. About 600 people in the village were dead; only six were still alive. There was a similar death-toll in the nearby village of Kam.

The mass of concentrated carbon dioxide began its lethal journey from the northern spillway of Lake Nyos at about 11.30 p.m. on 21 August 1986. It must have reached Nyos village before midnight. Most of the inhabitants were caught unawares. Many died in their beds. In the darkness, those who were still awake hardly realized what was happening. The few survivors said that they had heard birds fluttering and strong winds rustling the trees. Some said they had smelt rotten eggs, (hydrogen sulphide), or gunpowder (sulphur dioxide), which is known locally as the odour of death. The toxic carbon dioxide lingered long enough to kill most of those who lost consciousness in Nyos and Kam. Their animals and chickens died with them. Lack of oxygen would have made most victims highly confused before they lost consciousness, as if they had been anaesthetized. Some tried to remove their clothing, or threw themselves about their houses as they struggled for breath. Some had run outside and a few even reached the edge of the bush. Some seem to have bled from their mouths and a small number were blistered by burns or scalds. One 24-year-old survivor only recovered consciousness at 7 a.m. next morning in Nyos. He was able to revive his father, but everyone else around them was dead.

Nyos village lies 900m high on a watershed between two river–valley systems. Part of the carbon dioxide swept northwestwards through Cha village, where 58 died and about 130 survived. At Cha, the cloud turned northwards into the River Mbum valley where it was eventually diluted by a southerly breeze. But the gas was still strong enough to kill a few people near Koskin, 23km from Lake Nyos. The other branch of the lethal mass travelled northeastwards into the flat-floored valley of the River Kumbi and spread upstream towards Bwabwa and downstream for 3km or 4km beyond Subum, up to 15km from the lake. In Subum, around half of the population of about 800 were killed. In all, the carbon dioxide covered $34.6km^2$ before the air diluted the mass enough to rob it of its toxic identity. In all, an estimated 1,742 people and 6,000 head of cattle were asphyxiated.

Joseph Nkwain survived in Subum. He was awakened about midnight by heat, followed by a noise like an aeroplane, as if he were dreaming. Then his skin became very hot and something made a 'dry smell'.

> I could not speak. I became unconscious. I could not open my mouth because then I smelt something terrible . . . I heard my daughter snoring in a terrible way, very abnormal . . . When crossing to my daughter's bed . . . I collapsed and fell.

I was there till nine o'clock in the [Friday] morning . . . until a friend of mine came and knocked at my door . . . I was surprised to see that my trousers were red, had some stains like honey. I saw some . . . starchy mess on my body. My arms had some wounds . . . I didn't really know how I got these wounds . . . I opened the door . . . I wanted to speak, my breath would not come out . . . My daughter was already dead . . . I went into my daughter's bed, thinking that she was still sleeping. I slept till it was 4.30 p.m. in the afternoon . . . on Friday. [Then] I managed to go over to my neighbours' houses. They were all dead . . . I decided to leave . . . [because] most of my family was in Wum . . . I got my motorcycle . . . A friend whose father had died left with me [for] Wum . . . As I rode . . . through Nyos I didn't see any sign of any living thing . . . [When I got to Wum], I was unable to walk, even to talk . . . my body was completely weak.

By the time Joseph Nkwain rode through Cha that evening, the gas had dissipated. But at six o'clock on Friday morning, a male nurse had suddenly lost consciousness as he rode his moped into Cha. The deadly, invisible gas was still lurking in the lower parts of the village. He came to, gasping for breath, about ninety minutes later. He felt tired and drunk, with a headache and a cough.

Meanwhile, Lake Nyos now looked different. Helicopter pilot Dean Yeoman, from the regional capital, Bamenda, knew the lake well. On 22 August its colour had changed to 'bright orange', with slimy black streaks that seemed to be raffia-palm stalks brought up from the lake floor. Water had also obviously swept up from the southern part of the lake and had stripped a small

Survivors in the hospital at Cha.

area of the western shore completely down to the bare rock. Others reported that there was a round, dull-red patch, about 200m across, in the southern part of the lake. On 22 August, hot water also discharged from Soda Spring, just north of the lake, and prevented villagers from Upper Nyos from crossing the stream there.

A few days later, an Italian team of investigators found that the lake waters at a depth of 2m had a temperature of 30°C, instead of their usual August temperature of 23°C. They thought that the extra heat must have come from hot waters (or steam) erupted with the carbon dioxide. The lake did not return to 23°C until 15 September.

Full and Frank Exchanges of Views

There were further gas emissions, on a much smaller scale, during the last two weeks of December 1986 and in early January 1987. Reddish spots were seen several times on Lake Nyos and three explosions from it were heard on 30 December. Soda Springs also turned reddish for a time at the end of the year, and again on 20 June 1987. But the gas caused no more deaths.

Thereafter, Lake Nyos was quiet. Far more noise has since been generated by the specialists arguing about the 'gas release'. Apart from personality clashes, there were two main reasons for this. Firstly there were only two or three precedents upon which the experts could rely; and secondly, analysis of the eye-witness accounts of events at Lake Nyos – which might have made up for the scarcity of studied precedents – may have run into unexpected linguistic difficulties.

In fact, there had been a precedent at Lake Nyos itself. An 'eruption' apparently took place from Lake Nyos in the early morning of 16 October 1977. But the news failed to reach the international scientific community before the events of 1986 killed any likely eye-witnesses. The second precedent is only taken as a true precedent by those who believe that the gas was ejected from Lake Nyos by a 'real' volcanic eruption. On 20 February 1979, carbon dioxide suddenly erupted from a crater (which contained no lake) on the Diëng Plateau in the active volcanic region of central Java. About 140 people were asphyxiated as they fled. This eruption was studied by a French team of experts.

The third, and most widely accepted, precedent occurred on 15 August 1984 in northwestern Cameroon, about 100km from Lake Nyos. Carbon dioxide suddenly emerged from Lake Monoun and gassed thirty-four people. An American team of investigators concluded that the gas had been dissolved for a long time under pressure in the lower, colder layers of the lake. The layers had probably been disturbed and overturned by a landslide, an earthquake or even by abnormally heavy rains. When the lower layers reached the surface where pressures were much less, the gas would be released and bubble out, just as champagne froths when it is uncorked. The Americans naturally thought that the same thing had happened at Lake Nyos almost exactly two years later.

Livestock gassed near Lake Nyos.

This was not just a problem of academic analysis. To know what is likely to happen in the future, it is vital – literally vital – to understand what has happened in the past. If the gas had really erupted and burst out suddenly from Lake Nyos, the chances are that another eruption would not occur for, say, many decades or centuries. But it would be hard to predict. Other sudden eruptions, however, could occur from any one of the thirty similar lakes in the neighbourhood at any time – not to mention others in France, Germany or the USA, for example. On the other hand, if the carbon dioxide had exuded slowly and dissolved and become concentrated in the lower layers of the lake, then the increases in gas content could be monitored and controlled. The gases could then be released gradually by slowly piping the lower waters to the surface from time to time.

Before the end of the autumn, more investigative missions had scrutinized the enigma than there had been gas emissions. Expert opinions divided on national lines. Some French, Italians and Swiss plumped for a volcanic eruption; the Americans, Germans, Japanese and, eventually, the British decided that the lake waters had overturned and released the gas. The Cameroon government and UNESCO organized an international conference on the catastrophe at Yaoundé, the Cameroon capital, on 16–20 March 1987. It generated more heat than light. Outspoken scientists spoke out. The protagonists fired salvoes from their scientific bunkers. Listeners were not enlightened. In 1989–90, the varied conclusions from these scientific investigations were published in two complete issues of the *Journal of Volcanology and Geothermal Research*. Most experts favoured the idea that the gas had been released when the lower layers of the lake had somehow been brought to the surface, rather than coming from a true volcanic eruption.

Partly because the measurable 'scientific' evidence seemed so ambiguous, eye-witness accounts of the extraordinary event at Lake Nyos became unusually important. But trained scientists did not reach the lake until a few days, or a few weeks, later, by which time memories of an already confusing event *may* have been further muddled. There was undoubtedly a linguistic barrier to be overcome. The varied peoples in the Grassfields area speak about thirty different languages. They communicate with each other, and with out-siders, in pidgin English – using English words, with the linguistic concepts and structures of their native tongues. These do not always correspond with those of English. For instance, pale colours are 'white', dark colours are 'black', and the remainder are 'red'. An important aspect of the volcanic eruption theory is that the iron-rich lake waters changed to red when they were oxidized. Perhaps the local testimony was unreliable on this point. However, several French speakers also said that the lake had developed a red patch after the gas emission. There is no doubt that when they saw 'rouge', they saw 'red'.

Some of the survivors claimed to have smelt rotten eggs (hydrogen sulphide) or gunpowder (sulphur dioxide). These gases are often ejected by eruptions, but would not have been expelled if the lake waters had merely overturned. Those who believed that the lake had overturned then suggested that the victims had only imagined that they had smelt hydrogen sulphide and sulphur dioxide as they were losing consciousness. The victims had suffered from what the experts called 'olfactory hallucinations'. The supporters of the volcanic eruption theory replied that such hallucinations had never even been mentioned before in the medical or scientific literature.

Over 800 people were interviewed in the hospitals at Wum and Nkambe: 72 per cent had 'body pains', 31 per cent had a cough, and 26 per cent had headaches – common effects of inhaling carbon dioxide. But 19 per cent had superficial 'burns' that are harder to explain. Perhaps the convulsing victims had fallen onto fires, or onto boiling water as they had lost consciousness. But they could equally well have been injured by hot gas or steam, from a real vol-canic eruption cloud. Of course, if the cloud *was* hot, then it must have come from a volcanic eruption, because droplets from overturned layers of lake water would have been cold.

It was also suggested that the first people on the scene may have put ideas into the heads of the local people, by the very questions they asked. The locals, willing to please, may then have claimed to have, indeed, smelt the smells and heard the noises that they were questioned about. Naturally, the interviewers vigorously denied doing anything of the kind. In any case, people in the village of Issu had complained of headaches and smells of rotten eggs before they had been told of the disaster at nearby Lake Nyos.

There is at least one feature that points to a volcanic eruption which does not depend on linguistics, hallucinations or leading questions. The gas rose 120m above the southern part of the lake only. Mixed with steam and water droplets, the carbon dioxide was expelled in such a concentrated and narrow jet that it stripped a small area of the shore bare of soil and vegetation. But gas released from water layers that had been newly brought to the surface would spread more or less uniformly and hug the ground, simply because carbon dioxide is denser than air. Nevertheless, after a decade of research, the scientific and national controversy continues. Non-experts can do little more than wave the national flags they fancy.

Postscript

The survivors were displaced and the affected villages were deserted after the catastrophe and plans were made to turn the district into a national park. Within a decade, a life-size geophysical experiment began on Lake Nyos, after trials on Lake Monoun. The aim was to siphon water continuously from the lower layers of the lake up to the surface through a polyethylene pipe some 205m long and 14cm across. The carbon dioxide dissolved in these lower layers would then slowly bubble out from the water when it reached the lower pressures near the surface of the lake. A large, sudden and disastrous release of gas would, therefore, be prevented. Gas was successfully removed from Lake Nyos by this method on 25 March 1995. It is calculated that ten similar pipes could remove the carbon dioxide dissolved in the deep waters within five years. Thus, if the layers of the lake were to turn over again, there would presumably be no lethal consequences. However, those who believed that there had been a real eruption of volcanic gas in 1986 contended that such siphoning would only lull the local people into a false sense of security, because it could in no way prevent another explosive emission. Time will tell – perhaps – who is right. But further deaths around similar lakes in Cameroon, or in other parts of the world, could well occur before the scientific dispute is resolved and the means of preventing further similar disasters can be developed. In any case, the lethal gas came from a volcanic chimney that was itself formed relatively recently by a violent explosion. A repetition of such an eruption, with the prospect of deaths, must always be a distinct possibility.

In the meantime, Lake Nyos poses another – and potentially far greater – threat. The 40m-high natural dam holding back the waters at the northern spillway is composed of easily eroded volcanic fragments. This dam *could well* give way – even before the next gas release. The waters of Lake Nyos would then flood well-populated valleys in neighbouring Nigeria and threaten some 30,000 lives. No measures have yet been taken to strengthen this fragile barrier.

16

Pinatubo, 1991

Pinatubo unleashed the second largest eruption of the twentieth century and its climax coincided with a typhoon. The handling to this crisis shows that the thousands of victims of past eruptions did not die entirely in vain.

A Surprise

Early in 1991, Philippine earth scientists were keeping a watchful eye on their five most dangerous volcanoes: Bulusan, Canlaon, Hibok-Hibok; and especially Mayon, one of the most graceful volcanoes on the face of the globe, and nasty little Taal that explodes violently from a lake from time to time. The Philippines also had sixteen other active volcanoes which could, of course, wake up at any moment.

Pinatubo was one of these. But it seemed unlikely to join the threatening five, because it had been quiet since before the Spaniard, Ruy Lopez de Villalobos, named the Philippines in honour of the future King Felipe II of Spain in 1543. Pinatubo, indeed, had quite modest claims to fame, and although, at 1,745m, it was one of the highest peaks in the Zambales range in central Luzon, it was rather hidden by the mountains around it. There was, however, an attractive view of the summit from Clark US Air Base, about 25km away to the east. But scarcely known volcanoes have a habit of suddenly springing back into life, and, in spite of all the recent advances in technology and monitoring, they have provided the twentieth century with some of its biggest volcanic surprises – and some of its most violent eruptions. Katmaï in 1912, Mount Lamington in 1951, Bezymianny in 1956 are amongst the most impressive members of this club. Pinatubo took its place of honour in the company in 1991.

The eruption of Pinatubo was a disaster averted – in fact, remarkably well averted. Amongst all the eruptions of the twentieth century, it exploded a volume of material that was second only to the eruption of Katmaï in Alaska in 1912. Katmaï killed nobody, because no humans lived in the district. But in 1991, about half a million people lived within easy striking distance of Pinatubo, including about 16,000 Americans at Clark US Air Base. Pinatubo could easily have produced the most lethal eruption of the century. But surveillance, political will, evacuation of the threatened population and, indeed, the logical behaviour of the volcano itself prevented the catastrophe. Earth

Pinatubo in eruption.

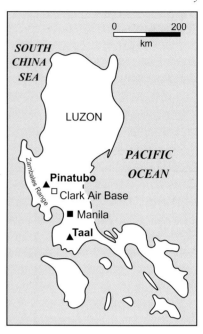

The location of Pinatubo.

scientists put Pinatubo under constant surveillance as soon as it started to grumble, and the eruption became the first of its size to be monitored from start to finish. They also quickly studied the geological history of the volcano and drew up hazard maps that pinpointed the most threatened areas around it. There was close co-operation and understanding between the earth scientists, the American and Philippine military authorities, and the Philippine administration – especially in Civil Defence and the disaster co-ordinating councils. Unlike in many countries, the administrative infrastructure already existed to deal with the crisis and therefore tasks could be distributed as soon as they had been defined. The people were made well aware of the dangers they faced, thereby reducing inertia and scepticism. Thus a well co-ordinated and efficient evacuation of the threatened population could be staged as the eruption increased in power. The technical, social, financial and administrative means were available to carry out this evacuation with due speed. Many, therefore, profited from the dire lessons of the tragedy of Armero that will haunt volcano-watchers for decades to come.

Pinatubo also behaved in a logical and an understandable way and helped the forecasters by cranking up its assault in orderly stages from the first steam emission on 2 April 1991 to the immense climax of the eruption ten and a half weeks later. Its small explosions *en route* even came at the right time to convince many sceptics and encourage the evacuations to refugee camps. On the other hand, all was not entirely plain sailing. Pinatubo gave clear indications that it was about to unleash a big eruption only during the first two weeks of June, when events developed at such a pace that the forecasters were scarcely more than one step ahead of the volcano as the danger grew. There

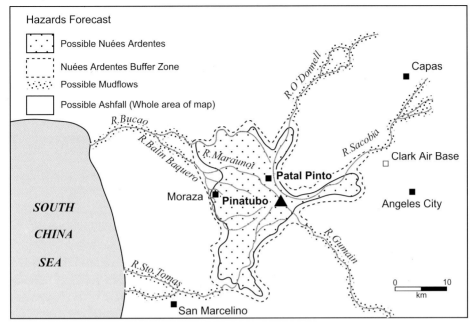

Likely hazards forecast for the eruption of Pinatubo.

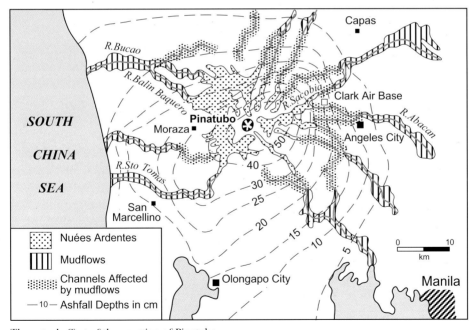

The actual effect of the eruption of Pinatubo.

was also the little matter of Typhoon Yunya, which complicated the prepara-
tions as Pinatubo reached its paroxysm in mid-June. In spite of these supplementary problems, the human reaction to the eruption represented a rare
and laudable triumph in limiting the deaths that it might have caused.
Nevertheless, the deaths of several hundred people show that such eruptions
have not yet met their master . . .

   Those who suffered most from the eruption were the Aetas. Pinatubo had
been the home of these semi-nomadic peoples for at least 400 years, ever since
the steep, thickly forested flanks of the volcano had offered them isolation
and protection from the incoming Spaniards. To the Aetas, Pinatubo means
'to make grow' – a place where crops would grow easily. The Aetas grew
bananas, coffee and root-crops on changing plots in the forest, and they supplemented their diet by hunting and fishing. The Aetas believed, that
Pinatubo was the home of Apo Namalyari, the Great Protector and Provider.
To those who knew Pinatubo best, the mountain was benevolent – and far
from repellent or fearsome. The Aetas also thought that their crops would be
more abundant whenever the fissures near the summit gave off more steam
than usual. But they had no folk memories of eruptions, although some of the
older people recalled that steam had sometimes exploded from these fissures.
Many of the Aetas were organized into the Lubos na Alyansa ng mga Katu-
tubong Ayta ng Sambales (the Negrito People's Alliance of Zambales). The
acronym, LAKAS, means 'power'; and the alliance aimed to protect the culture
of the Aetas from modern encroachments. However, several Catholic and
Protestant missionaries were operating amongst the Aetas, including the
Franciscan Missionaries of Mary. It was one of these missionaries, Sister Emma
Fondevilla, who was first to break the news of the eruption of Pinatubo to the
outside world.

   Many geological and sociological studies of the eruption were to have
been published as a professional paper of the US Geological Survey. But,
regrettably, the USGS declined to handle the work because it would cost too
much, although so many chapters were devoted to forecasting, preventing
and limiting volcanic dangers that it was almost a manual for saving lives in
future volcanic crises. Fortunately more enlightened views prevailed at the
Philippine Institute of Volcanology and Seismology, in Quezon City, and at the
University of Washington Press, in Seattle. Together they published the studies
in 1996 as *Fire and Mud: Eruptions and Lahars of Mount Pinatubo, Philippines*,
under the joint editorship of Christopher G. Newhall and Raymundo S.
Punongbayan.

Preliminaries

It may have been a large earthquake on 16 July 1990, centred about 100km
northeast of Pinatubo, that allowed molten rock to start rising again and eventually spurred the volcano into action. On 3 August 1990, the Aetas heard

The shroud of ash from Pinatubo.

some rumbling on Pinatubo; there was a landslide near the summit, and the cracked ground began to steam. The missionary, Sister Emma Fondevilla, reported the disturbance to the Philippine Institute of Volcanology and Seismology (PHIVOLCS) in Quezon City. On 5 August the experts inspected the site and at first concluded that the features were not related to volcanic activity. However, before August was out, there were five earthquakes near Pinatubo. Then there was a lull until 15 March 1991 when the Aetas again felt rumbling earth tremors. All these little events, however, were no more than hints that Pinatubo could be up to something.

Clarification came on Tuesday, 2 April 1991 when the villagers of Patal Pinto saw steam and ash exploding from a fissure, about 1.5km long, high on the northern slopes of Pinatubo. There was a smell of sulphur in the air and fine ash dusted hamlets 10km away. The following day, Sister Emma Fondevilla returned to PHIVOLCS in Quezon City with this more disturbing news. With help from the Philippine Air Force and Civil Defence, PHIVOLCS set up the first of a series of seismographs, which promptly registered over 200 small earthquakes during the next twenty-four hours. PHIVOLCS at once declared a danger zone, 10km around the summit of Pinatubo, and recommended that villages within that radius should be evacuated. Thus on Friday, 5 April, the Department of Social Welfare brought 5,000 Aetas into refugee camps. The Philippine experts also contacted their American counterparts, and three members of the US Geological Survey arrived with an array of monitoring equipment on 23 April. The speed of all these reactions, and the monitoring that followed, made a sharp contrast with the inertia that had prevailed for months after Nevado del Ruiz had first erupted.

Pinatubo under Surveillance

Monitoring Pinatubo started in earnest during the last week in April. On 26 April, PHIVOLCS and the American geologists set up a Pinatubo Volcano Observatory at Clark US Air Base, where facilities, communications and helicopters were available. By 13 May, seven telemetered seismic stations were relaying between 30 and 180 earthquakes a day to the observatory. They provided vital information as the eruption developed – especially when bad weather or ash clouds masked the volcano itself. At the time, the American and Philippine governments were re-negotiating their agreement over American bases, but this proved no handicap to international scientific collaboration. Indeed, the experts could get on with their work on the base in relative isolation whilst PHIVOLCS in Quezon City dealt with the increasing number of questions from journalists.

The earth scientists immediately set out to shed light on Pinatubo's dark – and almost unknown – past. They had to establish its previous pattern of behaviour, in order to forecast what it might do next and when it might erupt, as well as to draw up maps of the areas most likely to be threatened. In 1977, radio-carbon dating had indicated that Pinatubo had had three very violent eruptions during the past few thousand years. This was why Pinatubo had been placed in the group of twenty-one active Philippine volcanoes in 1988. The further investigations in May 1991 were not at all reassuring. Pinatubo had had a turbulent history. Its broad base was just over a million years old, but the mountain itself was much younger. Half a dozen huge eruptions had built up the volcano within the last 35,000 years. Each time, falling ash, nuées ardentes and volcanic mudflows had spread at least 20km from the crest of Pinatubo. The eruptions were apparently getting less violent as time went on, but the intervals between them had become shorter. Pinatubo had last erupted about 500 years ago – just before the Spanish settlement – and had buried pottery dated to between the thirteenth and fifteenth centuries. A dome of viscous lava had then oozed from the volcanic chimney at the end of this eruption. It now formed the summit of Pinatubo, and it was soon to be shattered to smithereens.

The volcanic events during early May were not on this scale. The earthquakes continued near Pinatubo, the fissure went on steaming, and, now and again, small explosions scattered a thin layer of cool ash over the volcano. It hardly seemed to be the reawakening of a volcanic giant.

But, then, on Monday 13 May, the observers discovered that Pinatubo was giving off sulphur dioxide. The gas was apparently escaping from molten rock which, therefore, could well be rising beneath the volcano. Pinatubo might

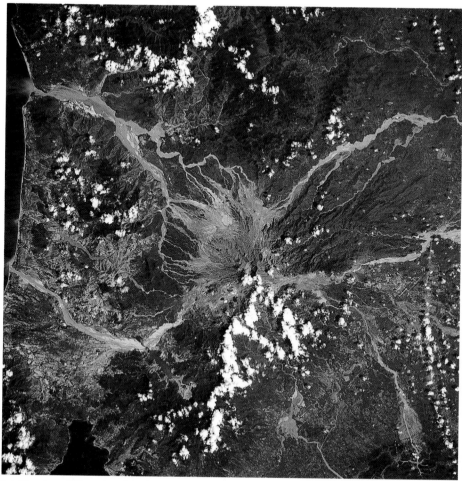

Satellite view of Pinatubo after the eruption.

be preparing something much worse, and the observers immediately warned the Civil Defence and military authorities. The monitoring was already paying off, for none of these developments was obvious from the lowlands. On 13 May also, PHIVOLCS issued a system of five alerts to publicize the degrees of danger. Alert-Level 1 was defined by small earthquakes near the volcano and emissions of steam, although no eruption was imminent. Pinatubo had been at this level during April. Alert-Level 2 was defined by moderate earthquakes, with some evidence of rising molten rock, as, for example, from escaping sulphur dioxide. It suggested that molten rock might erupt at some ill-defined date. Pinatubo had reached this level on 13 May. The other three alert-levels might be attained as the crisis developed. Thereafter, PHIVOLCS issued these alert-levels daily, along with 'state of the volcano' bulletins. In addition, on 23 May the scientists completed their first hazard map showing where ashfalls, nuées ardentes and mudflows were likely to spread around Pinatubo. PHIVOLCS sent copies of the map and the daily alerts and bulletins to

President Corazón Aquino, National Disaster organizations, local civil and military authorities, as well as to radio, television and the newspapers. Thus all those who wanted to know what Pinatubo was doing, and what it might do next, could easily find out.

Meanwhile, throughout late May, more earthquakes became concentrated at between 2km and 6km deep, about 5km northwest of Pinatubo. There were 1,800 earthquakes between 7 May and 1 June 1991. They happened each time that the rising molten rock elbowed a little further upward through the earth's crust. The molten rock was releasing more and more sulphur dioxide – the emissions increased tenfold between 13 May and 28 May. And Pinatubo was still steaming, and sometimes exploding fine ash as well.

However, the volcano seemed so far away from the surrounding lowlands that sceptics found it hard to imagine that their homes would soon be in real danger. A vivid film replaced the need for vivid imaginations. After Nevado del Ruiz had devastated Armero, the famous French students of volcanoes, Maurice and Katia Krafft, had made a graphic film called *Understanding Volcanic Hazards*. It was shown to President Aquino and to as many government, military, religious and community opinion-formers as possible. Local newspapers and television took up the story. The threatened people then realized what sort of death awaited them and the hazard map showed them where it might meet them. Only hardened sceptics remained unconvinced. Even so, at the end of May there was still a chance that all the signals might be false alarms and that the great eruption would not take place.

Eruptions and Evacuations

On Saturday, 1 June, Pinatubo itself raised the stakes. The earthquakes became concentrated 5km directly below the steaming area just northwest of the summit. The rising molten rock was now pushing upward in one place – as if it had found the easiest path to the surface. It blocked the fissures through which sulphur dioxide had been escaping: emissions on 5 June fell to only 5 per cent of what they had been on 28 May. At 7.39 p.m. on 3 June, Pinatubo began a series of small ash explosions coupled with yet more earthquakes. The volcano itself had also started to bulge a little. (But the main volcanic news of 3 June was that a nuée ardente had killed Maurice and Katia Krafft as they were studying the eruption of Unzen in Japan.)

On 5 June, the bulging and the increased earthquakes and explosions incited PHIVOLCS to declare Alert-Level 3, suggesting that an eruption of molten rock was possible within two weeks. About 10,000 Aetas were taken to refugee camps – including some who had returned home after their first evacuation on 5 April. On Friday, 7 June there were 1,500 earthquakes under Pinatubo, and it was bulging even more. About 5 p.m. an explosion sent a column of steam and – still cool – ash about 8km above the volcano. PHIVOLCS promptly issued Alert-Level 4, indicating that an eruption of molten rock was possible within twenty-four hours, and they extended the danger zone to a radius of 20km from the crest.

Molten Rock Reaches the Surface

Late on 7 June 1991, nine and a half weeks after the first explosions of steam, molten rock reached the surface of Pinatubo. Not at the summit. Not in an explosion. Lava like molten glass oozed out and formed a little dome about one kilometre northwest of the crest in the headwaters of the River Maraunot. This dome was to last less than a week. On Monday 9 June, masses of sulphur dioxide started to escape again, and the first small nuées ardentes tumbled 4km down-valley. At 5.15 a.m. that day, PHIVOLCS issued their first Alert-Level 5: 'eruption in progress'. Evacuation plans came sharply into focus. Mayors in the lowland towns sent transport to evacuate people living in the 20km danger zone. Pinatubo issued its own warning with a larger eruption of ash. The Aetas, with their goods and animals, waited on the roadsides for the buses and lorries that would take them to the refugee camps. But their departure was not without its problems. Some Aetas got on the wrong buses because they could not read the signs, and were then so embarrassed that they returned home to put their trust in Apo Namalyari. It seems that nobody had explained what they had to do. Other Aetas were still loath to leave their homes, their crops, or their water-buffaloes. However, many were lucky enough to change their minds when the eruption grew more violent. Soon a total of 25,000 were housed in the refugee camps. The stubborn or misguided few who remained in the danger areas had not long to live.

On Monday, 10 June, the Americans took their first step towards abandoning Clark Air Base. All their aircraft and 14,500 American servicemen, servicewomen and their families left the air base in a motorcade for the US Naval Base at Subic Bay. General MacArthur must have turned in his grave. Only three helicopters, 1,500 Americans and 1,500 Philippine military personnel stayed behind to ensure maintenance, while PHIVOLCS moved their observatory to the far eastern edge of Clark Air Base. The still sceptical mayor of nearby Angeles City declared that the Americans were over-reacting and causing panic.

The Climax of the Eruption

Events then began to unfold at an accelerating pace. At 8.51 a.m. on Wednesday, 12 June, Pinatubo celebrated Philippine Independence Day with a violent eruption that sent columns of ash surging like a huge firework display some 20km into the air. The sky darkened, ash showered down to the southwest of the volcano, and nuées ardentes devastated some of the villages that had already been evacuated. The first lives had been saved . . . but the first few lives had also been lost amongst those who had refused to leave. About 600 more Americans left Clark Air Base.

The authorities quickly evacuated people living within a 30km radius of the crest of Pinatubo. The total number of evacuees rose to 58,000 – plus those who had left the air base. There was less scepticism now. At 8.41 a.m. on 13 June, another great explosion raised a column that reached 25km high. Then there followed twenty-eight hours without explosions, although the earthquakes continued unabated. In the clear morning sky of 14 June, Pinatubo displayed its old summit for the last time.

At 1.09 p.m., a violent explosion broke the eruptive truce and a billowing column soared 21km into the air in fifteen minutes. A typhoon was also approaching. Rumour had it that a huge blast, like that at Mount St Helens, would soon devastate Olongapo City, southwest of Pinatubo. The typhoon came; the blast did not. A series of thirteen huge explosions, at shorter and shorter intervals, occupied the next twenty-four hours. Yet more ash showered down – again mainly to the southwest. Nuées ardentes devastated the main valleys radiating from Pinatubo and destroyed all but one of the seismographs that were taking the quaking pulse of the volcano.

Then the weather made a vain attempt to steal the show. At 11 a.m. on Saturday, 15 June, Typhoon Yunya passed within 100km to the northeast of Pinatubo as it tracked across central Luzon. By then it had weakened into a tropical storm, but the gales still spread fine, swirling rain-drenched ash over an unusually wide area. Eventually, it lay as much as 5cm deep over $4,000km^2$ and 1cm deep over $7,500km^2$. Darkness fell again all around Pinatubo. There were incessant thunderstorms and lashing rains. Ash, with lumps of pumice 4cm across, began to fall on Clark Air Base. At 3 p.m. on 15 June, all its remaining occupants and the Pinatubo Observatory staff decamped through the gloom to take refuge at Pamponga Agricultural College, 38km east of the volcano. At 3.39 p.m., as the observers retreated, there began an eruptive convulsion of rare ferocity, which lasted for nine hours and yielded 90 per cent of all the volcanic materials that Pinatubo expelled. Great cauliflower columns of ash, gas and steam towered up to 34km skywards and soon stretched 400km across the stratosphere. Although Katmaï had erupted more molten materials in 1912, this was probably the most powerful volcanic outburst of the twentieth century. At 4.30 p.m., the whole summit of Pinatubo started to sink, amidst a rumble of earthquakes, into the subterranean gap left by the erupted molten rock. At 8 p.m. on 15 June, PHIVOLCS increased the evacuation zone to a radius of 40km around Pinatubo, where 375,000 people were living. This zone included Olongapo City, whose mayor consulted PHIVOLCS. But they decided against an evacuation, because, by then, the earthquakes were already decreasing, which indicated that the worst of the crisis might be coming to an end. So it proved.

The convulsion stopped at 10.30 p.m. on that eventful Saturday. The memorial to the eruption was a huge crater – a *caldera* – 2.5km across, that now crowned Pinatubo. It was centred about one kilometre north of the old

Ash at the eastern end of Clark Air Base on 15 June 1991.

summit. The crest of the volcano, which had stood 1,745m above sea-level at midday on 15 June, rose no more than 1,480m at midnight. Ash and pumice, 100m or more thick, had completely choked all the valley-heads radiating down the flanks of Pinatubo. The mantle had even blocked the upper valley of the River Sacobia and diverted it across a ridge into the River Abacan, whose vastly increased discharge was soon flooding through Angeles City. The views of its sceptical mayor were not recorded. (It was an explosion within the still-hot ash and pumice that enabled the Upper Sacobia to resume its old path on 4 April 1992.) In all, rain and wet ash drenched a darkened area covering 340,000km². Rooftops collapsed under the heavy ash layers; crops were smothered; roads, pipes and canals were clogged. Manila Airport had to close. Fine ash fell a few days later across the South China Sea on Vietnam and Cambodia.

The Waning Eruption

Pinatubo quickly calmed down after these excesses. Eruptions declined from an average of three or four a day until mid-July, to one a day at the end of August, and they stopped on 4 September 1991. PHIVOLCS then reduced the designated danger zone to a radius of 10km with an Alert-Level 3, which they dropped to Alert-Level 2 on 4 December 1991. But Pinatubo continued to tease its monitors. A dome of viscous lava began to grow in the great crater in July 1992 and PHIVOLCS again had to issue an Alert-Level 5 on 14 July which lasted until 2 December 1992, and another Alert-Level 3 from 11

February 1994 until 6 June 1994. But, generally, the activity of Pinatubo was declining.

Pinatubo had ejected 17 megatonnes of sulphur dioxide, at least 500 megatonnes of steam or water, between 3 and 16 megatonnes of chlorine and between 42 and 234 megatonnes of carbon dioxide. In total, Pinatubo erupted between 8.4km^3 and 10.4km^3 of volcanic fragments. Nuées ardentes accounted for between 5km^3 and 6km^3 of these fragments and they covered about 400km^2 and surged 16km from the crest. Between 3.4km^3 and 4.4km^3 of dust, ash and pumice were hurled into the air and fell over a vast area of Luzon and much of the South China Sea. Pinatubo expelled ten times as much volcanic material as Mount St Helens and 1,500 times as much as the fatal eruption of Nevado del Ruiz, but still only two-thirds as much as the longer, but far less explosive, eruption of Laki in 1783.

The eruption directly caused between 200 and 300 deaths, although succeeding events increased the official death toll to 1,202.

Aftermath

ROOFS

Typhoon Yunya made the climax of the eruption of Pinatubo particularly unpleasant. It also drenched the erupted ash. Roofs commonly collapse when ash accumulates upon them like snow. But wet ash is heavier and more dangerous than snow and that from Pinatubo proved to be 25 per cent heavier than its dry equivalent. During the climax of the eruption, the deluge of wet ash and heavy rain, with lightning and swirling gales, did not provide a congenial environment for rooftop shovelling. People stayed indoors and listened to the galvanized steel roofs caving in around them. The result was that, to the southwest of the volcano in particular, up to 15cm of wet ash accumulated and one third of the roofs collapsed. Houses fared best because their walls or pillars were less than 5m apart and thus supported the roof-spans effectively. Where the walls or pillars were more than 5m apart, the roofs were five times as vulnerable. Thus the heavy ash created havoc in public buildings, and the roofs of 98 hospitals and health centres, 18 public markets, and 83 administrative buildings, as well as many schools and hangars, were damaged or destroyed. Luckily they were largely unoccupied at the time. But collapsing roofs provided the biggest single cause of death during the eruption. Figures vary, but they killed between 180 and 280 people, and injured a similar number who had believed that they were sheltering in safe places.

AIRCRAFT

The dust, ash and gas that reached high altitudes could well have produced a similar death-toll, because it is very hard for pilots to distinguish between normal clouds and the much more dangerous clouds of volcanic aerosols. From 12 April onwards, the Philippine authorities issued over a dozen traffic warnings – 'notices to airmen' – about the eruption. These warnings were not always heeded, probably because pilots and airline companies did not then fully appreciate the gravity of the threats that the volcanic clouds might present. Less than three hours after the eruption on 12 June, three planes entered the volcanic cloud, although they were within sight of the eruption and less than 200km from the volcano. Then, within twenty-four hours of the climax of the eruption on 15 June, no fewer than thirteen passenger aircraft flew into the cloud over the South China Sea, between 700km and 1,750km from Pinatubo. Some planes had lucky escapes. In several cases, the cloud choked the jets, the engines lost power and the aircraft lost height – but managed to recover before they crashed. The cloud coated other engines with sulphate deposits and, altogether, ten engines were damaged beyond repair. The cloud also cracked and abraded windows and paintwork. All the aircraft would have suffered much greater damage – and could have crashed – if they had flown closer to Pinatubo, where the cloud still held its larger particles. As a result of these narrow escapes, the airline companies and volcanic observers now communicate faster and co-operate more closely whenever a volcano releases a dangerous high-altitude cloud. There is a lot of money to save – as well as lives. The eruption of Pinatubo probably cost aviation at least $US100 million.

STRATOSPHERIC EFFECTS

The dust cloud that inconvenienced the civil airliners spread quickly westwards. At 8 p.m. on 15 June, it had already covered 300,000km^2, and was advancing in a broad, high-altitude lobe towards Ho Chi Minh City in Vietnam. The coarser particles, winnowed from the cloud, fell into the South China Sea and eventually covered nearly 400,000km^2 of its floor. The layer was 6cm thick near Luzon, but only 1mm thick off the Vietnamese coast. All this marine deposition was probably harmless, although it may have inconvenienced the sea-floor dwellers.

The cloud that remained airborne was more remarkable. Water, dust and sulphur dioxide soon combined into the largest sulphuric acid aerosol since Krakatau erupted in 1883. Within three weeks, the aerosol had spread round the earth in a broad belt stretching between latitudes 30° north and 10° south. It covered the whole globe within twelve months. It lasted longest – at least until the end of 1993 – in the northern hemisphere. There, in spite of the effects of global warming, the average temperatures actually fell by 0.5°C. The aerosol thus probably reduced temperatures by at least 1°C. (However, unlike the effects of the Laki eruption in 1783, the following winters tended to be warmer than average. It was the cooler summers of 1991–3 that lowered the global averages.) Pinatubo seemed to be to blame for the cool and wet Canadian summer of 1992 (when pack-ice in Hudson Bay did not always melt), abnormally early snowfalls in September and October 1992 in Alaska, Scotland, Switzerland and Russia, and stormy summers and autumns over much of Europe and North America in 1993.

The aerosol also delivered the familiar array of fine sunsets, glowing twilights and pale, hazy suns, but never, it seems, as fine as those caused by Krakatau. Perhaps the world is now more blasé? However, the world is perhaps less blasé over the ozone layer. In 1992, the aerosol from Pinatubo apparently helped increase the hole in the ozone layer in the southern hemisphere to an unprecedented area of 27 million km^2. The ozone was vanishing as never before – or, at least, since measurements had been taken, which might not be the same thing.

REFUGEES AND RESETTLEMENT

The Aetas suffered most from the eruption. They lost the home of their God, Apo Namalyari, their homelands, their homes, their crops, their animals and sometimes their relatives. But most of the 30,000 Aetas were saved by the prompt evacuations. This was when their other troubles started. As the danger grew, some groups had to be moved from camp to camp until they could be housed in more permanent 'relocation sites'. The Aeta refugees were confused and disorientated, and baffled by the wide open spaces of the lowlands, while in the camps, they were too cold at night and too hot during the day. The hastily organized supplies of drinking water and the waste disposal arrangements proved inadequate for the crowds. The Aetas then succumbed to diseases, from which they had previously been isolated, before they could all be immunized. And there seems to have been a – perhaps inevitable – lack of total rapport between the Aetas and the health workers. The unhappy result was that illnesses in the refugee camps killed more people than the ash and pumice that Pinatubo had erupted. Of 349 deaths recorded in these camps during the first twelve weeks following the eruption, measles killed 108 people, diarrhoea killed 101, and acute respiratory infections killed 77, while illnesses related to malnutrition accounted for most of the remainder. By the end of December 1991 the Office of Civil Defence had registered 537 deaths from disease in the camps, and 94 per cent were Aetas. The Aeta children proved to be the most vulnerable of all and over 150 of them had already died before the second week in August. The unexpected length of the crisis made the problems much worse than might have been expected.

Mudflows

Pinatubo erupted masses of loose ash and pumice that smothered its steep flanks, destroyed much of its forests, and lay between 50m and 200m deep in

A mudflow from Pinatubo.

the valleys, waiting for the monsoon rains. The focus of danger then switched from the crest of Pinatubo to its flanks – and much closer to the large and vulnerable population on the surrounding plains. Erosion is fastest where heavy, intense rainfall forms swift, flooding streams that run down a steep land surface blanketed by loose fragments which have no protecting and binding mantle of trees or even grassland. Suddenly, the flanks of Pinatubo had acquired the ingredients of extremely rapid erosion; and changes that would normally have taken thousands of years happened in the space of a few rainy days. After each monsoonal storm, the streams picked up so much ash and pumice that they soon changed into mudflows.

   The mudflows carried finer fragments than those from Nevado del Ruiz, and were smaller than the glacier bursts from Öraefajökull, but there were many more of them. With peak discharges of $1,000m^3$ per second, the mudflows swept down-valley at speeds of 30km an hour. Once they reached the much gentler slopes of the plains, they could no longer transport their great load of fragments. They choked the stream channels, spread sideways,

MGA DAPAT GAWIN UPANG MAIWASAN ANG PAGIGING BIKTIMA NG MUDFLOW:

1. Iwasan ang mga lugar na malapit sa mga maaaring daanan ng mudflow sa tuwing umuulan ng malakas at ibabaw ng Mt. Pinatubo at mga bulubundukin na malapit dito;

2. Kung nakatira sa mababang lugar, lumikas kaagad sa mataas na lugar; tandaan na ang pinatutunguhan ng mudflow ay yaong kadalasan na ring binabaha sa panahon ng tag-ulan, ngunit dapat ring isaisip na dahil sa pagbabaw ng mga ilog at sapa na dinaluyan na ng mga bagay-bagay mula sa Mt. Pinatubo sa mga naunang pagputok nito, posibleng mas lumawak pa ang abutin ng mudflow kaysa sa mga dati nang binabaha sa panahon ng tag-ulan;

3. Maaari ring gumawa ng sariling "bundok" na puwedeng tunguhan kung may bantang mudflow. Ang mga buhanging dulot ng pagsabog ng Mt. Pinatubo noong Hunyo 14-15 ay maaaring itambak ng mga magkakapit-bahay sa taas na apat (4) na metro o higit pa sa pinakamataas na lugar na maaaring tambakan sa kanilang barangay. Ang tuktok nito ay dapat patagin upang magsilbing "evacuation center" sa oras ng panganib;

4. May pagkakataon ding maaaring gumawa ng "barriers" o sagabal sa maaaring daanan ng mudflow, ngunit dapat isaisip na ang mudflow ay mabilis at maaaring may puwersa;

5. Ang mga magkakapit-bahay ay dapat magkaroon ng tanod sa isang nalalapit na mataas na lugar at siya ang mamamahala sa anumang "alarm system" (tulad ng sirena o kampana) na maghuhudyat ng anumang panganib na maaaring idulot ng mudflow;

6. Laging maghanda ng flashlight o de bateryang radyo;

7. Palagiang makinig sa radyo sa mahahalagang balita, at babala mula sa mga nakaaalam na mga awtoridad;

8. Manatiling mahinahon sa lahat ng sandali at huwag padala sa mga maling balita o tsismis.

'What you should do to avoid becoming a victim of a mudflow.'

WALANG DAPAT IKABAHALA KUNG TAYO AY MAG-IINGAT AT MAGKAKAISA.

broke embankments and dikes, swept through village after village and deposited as much as 5m of sludgy ash and pumice. They covered more than 400km^2 of the plains without difficulty – and they may eventually swamp over 1,000km^2 – for there are few hills, or even hummocks, to impede them; or to provide natural refuges for the people.

No fewer than 200 mudflows raced down the valleys on the eastern flanks of Pinatubo during the rainy season in the last five months of 1991. By the close of 1993, they had brought down some 1.9km^3 of ash and pumice to the plains, and had caused about 100 deaths. The dangers, and the deaths, have continued ever since, and are likely to threaten the lowland populations around Pinatubo well into the twenty-first century, until new forests have grown and stabilized the ash and pumice. No mudflows on a comparable scale have ever been recorded, although there have been even larger examples on many volcanoes – including Pinatubo itself – in the geological past. It is a symbol of the effectiveness of the Philippine warning and evacuation systems that the hundreds of mudflows that invaded a densely populated area have not caused one twentieth of the disastrous Colombian death-toll in 1985. Of course, lessons had been learnt from Armero, and the Philippine mudflows were rather easier to predict because they were unleashed by rainfall, which can be forecast more precisely than eruptions. Nevertheless, efficient planning was still needed, because the evacuation times – between receipt of the warning and the arrival of the mudflow – usually ranged only between 30 and 45 minutes. There was little scope for dithering indecision – the people needed to be well prepared.

The authorities and experts together developed a system of warnings and alerts that have saved thousands of lives. They distributed long-range warnings, including brochures, videos and maps of the threatened areas. They held seminars to heighten the villagers' perceptions of the dangers they faced, and issued a graphic poster clearly describing what to do when the warnings came.

PHIVOLCS devised three mudflow Alert-Levels as a general background to these warnings. Alert-Level 1 means that rain is falling in the Pinatubo area. Alert-Level 2 means that intense rain (10mm or more) has fallen for thirty minutes in that area. Alert-Level 3 means that mudflows have been observed. These alerts formed the basis of the short-range warnings, which the Office of Civil Defence sent out to a hierarchy of co-ordinating councils, who then transmitted them to those in danger through village captains, priests or the police, using radio announcements, loud speakers, sirens, church bells or gunshots.

Of course, the early evacuations, in particular, were not without problems. Many villagers thought that the dangers had ended with the eruption. Several false alarms merely increased scepticism, which subsided only when a few villages were buried in 5m of mud. It was also hard to establish a code of practice that would cater for everyone. Some people believed that the mudflows would never reach them; some preferred their own rooftops to a refugee camp; some had handicapped relatives; some pushed women and children aside, whilst others threw them unceremoniously into the evacuation lorries; and some wanted to bring their ducks. But thousands of people have been safely evacuated, often several times, and thousands of lives have been saved.

The people have tried to live with their tormentor. For example, the authorities have encouraged villagers to pile up permanent, flat-topped hummocks, 4m high, near their homes, where they can take refuge when the mud comes. But, of course, their livelihoods would still be in danger. Where the mud was over 2m thick, crops and livestock were killed and homes were made largely uninhabitable. The survivors then had to start afresh, often elsewhere. But if the mud was no more than 50cm thick, the villagers could scrape it away, or plough it into the soil underneath and continue their farming, especially because their homes would still be intact, if rather dirty.

The villagers have also come to terms with the seasonal nature of the threat. Instead of relying on slowly maturing crops that might be destroyed before the harvest, farmers have planted quickly ripening produce, such as tomatoes, peanuts, cassava or sweet potatoes, that can be harvested before the late summer rains bring the threat of destruction.

Economic Costs of the Eruption

The eruption put the brakes on the developing economy of lowland central Luzon. The damage to crops, communications and property cost $US374 million in 1991 and a further $US69 million in 1992. During those two years alone, aid to the refugees cost nearly $US100 million; and over $US150 million was spent trying to control mudflows. Over 8,000 houses were destroyed and another 75,000 suffered severe damage. About 650,000 people were thrown out of work for several weeks and some two million people were closely affected. The Americans abandoned Subic Bay Base in November 1992, and Clark Air Base the following month, thereby causing unemployment amongst those who had variously serviced these bases.

The eruption and the subsequent mudflows played havoc with roads, bridges, water-supply and irrigation and flood-control systems. About 700 schools were destroyed and 236,000 pupils and 7,000 teachers were displaced. Mudflows have affected at least 42 per cent of the croplands around Pinatubo. For example, about 86,000 hectares of especially vulnerable low-lying rice-fields were destroyed and 775,000 poultry and farm animals were killed. About 500 industrial firms suffered losses, notably in the food-processing and furniture-making sectors.

Massive social disruption was inevitable. In October 1993, for instance, 159 evacuation centres were still sheltering 55,000 people and providing an additional population of 1.3 million with food, clothing or work. The people from many destroyed villages were often relocated in entirely new settlements. But the authorities committed the serious error of constructing the public buildings and roads before the houses – which did not encourage the gratitude of the refugees. Many people preferred to return to take their chance in their battered villages – and have, in fact, proved remarkably successful, especially where they can grow new, quickly ripening crops.

On the other hand, there is a danger that those who continue to live in refugee camps or new settlements will become so dependent on aid that they will be unable to fend for themselves ever again. It is hard to decide when humanitarian aid starts to encourage a culture of welfare dependency amongst its recipients. The wealthy also always seem to be afraid that the poor will forever make demands on their charity. Aid will always have to be accurately targeted to the best schemes for economic and social revival while the mudflow threat continues.

The events surrounding the eruption of Pinatubo show that science is making a little progress towards limiting the worst excesses of volcanoes – although it is a long way from being able to stop an eruption. However, all the economic and social problems and costs involved seem trivial in comparison with the 20,000 or perhaps 50,000 lives that expert advice, political will, and prompt and well-organized evacuations combined to save. The biggest volcanic disaster of the twentieth century thus did not take place.

17

Conclusion

Causes of Death

The end of the eruption is not the end of the problems in the devastated areas. Indescribable chaos often prevails for weeks. Survivors have to be comforted, fed, housed, or given medical aid. The dead have to be buried, if the volcano has not done so already. There is much more to do than count the bodies. Until recently, there was no legal requirement to register the dead; and population statistics were known only very imperfectly, either before or after the disaster. Hence the quoted numbers of eruption victims could only really be estimates – which had every chance of being exaggerated in the heat of the moment. Thereafter, constant repetition has bestowed a false air of certitude upon them. In the chaos, too, autopsies to determine the exact causes of death were hardly ever carried out, although more detailed medical information might have helped save lives during subsequent eruptions.

Some volcanic eruptions are almost benign, others have been famously lethal, and, in several cases, their secondary effects have caused more devastation than the materials expelled from the crater. The killers kill in many different ways. There is certainly no correlation between the volume of volcanic material erupted and the deathtoll that can ensue. Surprise and the density of the surrounding population are much more important factors. It is commonly assumed that lava is the most dangerous substance that volcanoes produce. It is not – apart from a few wholly exceptional cases in the geological past. The largest lava outpouring of historic time, from the Laki fissure in 1783, directly killed nobody at all. Neither did the much smaller flows from Etna in 1669, or those from Parícutin between 1943 and 1952. Lava-flows generally issue from rather moderate eruptions and cover relatively small areas, where damage to fixed property and crops far outweighs the number of casualties. But lava-flows can be frightening; and they even gave nightmares to the beleaguered Catanians in 1669. However, except where lavas remain molten near the volcanic chimney, most people could run – or even walk – away from advancing flows.

Life goes on . . . Local villagers venture out after the eruption of Pinatubo.

The moderate explosions of ash and cinders that often accompany emissions of lava-flows also rarely cause fatalities. For instance, over a dozen such eruptions in Lanzarote between 1730 and 1736 provoked not a single death, although fine ash blanketed the island. However, columns of ash often cause thunderstorms. Thus it happened that the only three victims attributed directly to the eruption of Parícutin had the bad luck to be struck by lightning. Amongst all these moderate ash explosions, the death toll at Monte Nuovo in 1538 was quite exceptionally high. The victims paid an unusually severe penalty for believing that the eruption was over. Its very last blast caught and killed them as they were climbing up the new cone. However, when the next eruption comes in this densely populated area around Pozzuoli, there might be many more casualties unless a timely evacuation is organized. The gas release from Lake Nyos in 1986 exemplifies the most insidious and lethal of moderate eruptions. Whether it was a true eruption or not, it came as a total surprise, and the gas which killed 1,742 people emerged from a volcanic chimney that was formed only 400 years ago. It serves as a dire warning to those living near a multitude of similar lakes elsewhere.

The more violent eruptions have a greater array of lethal weaponry at their disposal that affects much wider areas which are themselves often densely populated because of the renowned fertility of weathered volcanic soils. Violent eruptions can cause deaths directly by ashfalls and nuées ardentes, and, indirectly, by mudflows, tsunamis, fires, famines, and even social disturbances. Ash, dust and pumice often accumulate so thickly that rooftops collapse under their weight, and kill or injure hundreds, or maybe thousands, of people. But the greatest effects of ashfalls are remarkably contrasting. In the short term, ash can blanket the countryside to such an extent that all vegetation and crops are destroyed and animals starve. In the past, when communications were painfully slow, famine would decimate the population before any likely aid could arrive. The long-term effects of ashfalls are quite different. The ash adds valuable nutrients to the soil, and vastly increases crop yields in the following years. Those that survive the ashy deluge can, therefore, look forward to a rosier future. It is hard to say how many lives the ashfalls from Vesuvius claimed in AD 79. Those from Öraefajökull and Coseguina would certainly also have claimed more victims had they not occurred in sparsely populated regions. However, ashfalls do not only cause physical hardship and injury. The accompanying total darkness adds a certain, but unquantifiable, dimension of psychological distress, especially in countries where portents are both sought and feared as a part of everyday life. The worst effects of ashfalls can best be avoided by leaving the stricken area, or by taking shelter in a strong building.

Nuées ardentes have an altogether higher index of ferocity. They are the most effective direct killers in the volcanic repertoire: they appear suddenly, travel fast, and take few prisoners. Nuées ardentes can claim their victims in many different ways. They can be gassed, scalded, burnt, asphyxiated, or felled by blast or falling masonry. The muscles of many victims are contorted as if they had been suddenly petrified as they were fighting. Many die from oedema of the lungs or throat, or from shock lung (respiratory distress syndrome) when they inhale the searing air and dust. Death comes from a whole gamut of causes, and the bodies end up charred, twisted, and sometimes even mummified by the heat. The nuée ardente that wrecked Saint-Pierre on 8 May 1902 claimed a record total of 27,000 victims in the city alone. Death was almost instantaneous. Few of those who had 'swallowed the fire' lasted for more than an hour or so, and only about sixty-nine survived. The only practical way to withstand such an onslaught might be to shelter under a wet blanket in a deep cellar and breathe as little as possible during the two or three minutes that it takes the nuée to pass over. Easier said than done. This tactic itself presupposes that the nuée gives adequate notice of its impending arrival. They are not usually so obliging.

The indirect consequences of volcanic eruptions – mudflows, tsunamis, fires, famines and social disturbances – at least give short-term signals of their advent. Nevertheless, warnings have often proved inadequate in the past, which is why they can be sometimes far more lethal than the direct effects of eruptions. Evacuation of the whole population seems to be the only solution when mudflows or tsunamis threaten. Mudflows pose their greatest dangers in valleys radiating from volcanoes. Nevado del Ruiz created the historical record by killing some 23,000 people. The mud asphyxiated or drowned many, but perhaps the majority were crushed by masonry, cars or trees as the mud dragged them through Armero. Many of those who did not sink into the mud soon developed tetanus and gangrene from their cut and broken limbs. They died even before rescuers could find ways of crossing the sea of slimy mud surrounding them. Because mudflows only usually travel between 30km and 50km an hour, and mainly affect valley-floors, it is possible to evacuate threatened areas – provided adequate warning systems are already in place, as events at Pinatubo have demonstrated since 1991. Glacier-bursts, the wetter equivalents of mudflows, could be greater killers because they are often larger and travel much faster. Fortunately, their impact is mainly restricted to thinly populated areas of Iceland. Hence, although its eruptions are more powerful, Öraefajökull has never yet emulated Nevado del Ruiz.

The only mitigating factor about tsunamis is that they are usually limited to the lowest 30m along the affected seaboard. Unfortunately, this is precisely where the most densely peopled coastal settlements are generally located. But, with adequate warning, it is quite possible to escape to higher ground. Most of the victims of tsunamis drown, of course, but falling masonry, trees or cars, for instance, can also kill significant numbers. The waves might throw a lucky few onto the shore – but they seem more often to suck unlucky thousands out to sea. The eruption of Krakatau claims the largest number of volcanic tsunami deaths in recorded history, with 32,000 victims.

For all the talk of 'fire' during volcanic eruptions, real fires are fairly rare, and most cause few fatalities. The largest number of victims in modern times probably resulted from the blaze that spread from the distilleries in

Saint-Pierre on 8 May 1902, but it is impossible even to guess how many of the injured died as a result.

In the past, several volcanic eruptions have caused notable famines. Many communities were already subsisting at such a precariously low level that any disaster could precipitate a famine, especially in isolated areas where any aid would probably arrive too late to save the starving. The most severe famine in recorded history occurred when at least 44,000 people died after the Indonesian volcano, Tambora, erupted in 1815. However, the much more moderate eruption of Laki in 1783 precipitated the Icelandic 'Haze Famine' that killed one-fifth of the population of the country. Presumably, international aid would now prevent a recurrence on such a scale today – especially if the disaster happened in a strategically important country.

Finally, volcanic eruptions have an undoubted psychological influence on the people living near them. Side-effects can be both personal and social, and it is hard to know how to alleviate, or to avoid traumas, or to assess how many people are permanently affected by them. For instance, perhaps a hundred or more villagers are said to have died of grief when the lavas from Parícutin forced them to abandon their homes and ancestral lands. Quarrels over land ownership then also caused deaths at intervals during the next fifty years. Events in Sicily in 1669 provided another twist to the variety of human reactions to volcanic crises. When people fled from Etna to Catania, they were so terrified that they looked as 'wild as thieves'. After sessions of rough justice, those who 'looked guilty' were hanged. They thus became the only – albeit indirect – victims of that eruption.

Return to Normal

As the crisis abates, things begin 'to return to normal'. For some. Sometimes. The stricken area has to be repaired, and the survivors who are bereaved and bereft of homes and livelihood have to be comforted. States, communities or individuals respond to the enormous challenge.

Attitudes after a volcanic eruption naturally differ from those prevailing beforehand. Before a disaster, the authorities are afraid of taking decisions, because they cannot accurately foresee the outcome, and – above all – they do not want to be held responsible for errors of judgment. After a disaster, on the other hand, they know the result. They have free rein to take decisions, propose new initiatives, award development grants, send aid and equipment, show appropriate concern, and to be quoted and photographed in suitably tragic situations. In essence, they can be seen to be doing something. Following the admirable example of the Emperor Titus, they can promise recovery, renovation, reconstruction – or re-*anything* – knowing full well that the survivors will be grateful, and that the world media will be impressed. Some cynics might claim that there is more than pure altruism in such behaviour . . . But a disaster can also sometimes provide the catalyst for real and vigorous action, especially if the people themselves call for effective preventive or palliative measures. The political will to carry them out might then grow out of such demands. Thus, some threatened countries have developed disaster-limitation programmes. Organization has certainly limited the deaths around Pinatubo since 1991. But, sadly, other countries – facing at least comparable dangers – have done no such thing. In the past, of course, any planning was rare, and depended almost totally on the motivation, or whims, of the individuals in power.

Many survivors of eruptions show amazing resilience. Nostalgia is also a powerful sentiment. People return 'home'. Lost cities are therefore rare. The Romans abandoned Pompeii and Herculaneum when Vesuvius buried them in ash and pumice, but the Emperor Titus, who had already helped the survivors, might have revived these towns if he had lived longer himself. Even there, 1,500 years later, settlements had proliferated around Vesuvius, including Resina-Ercolano that had been unwittingly built right on top of Herculaneum. Tripergole was left buried under Monte Nuovo in 1538, but the Spanish Viceroy reconstructed neighbouring Pozzuoli. San Juan and Parícutin were abandoned beneath the advancing lava-flows in 1944, and the inhabitants were resettled elsewhere, partly in accordance with the current Mexican views on land reform. But these are exceptional cases. Determination to conquer the effects of the eruption is far more common. Catania has been rebuilt time after time, whenever the Etnean lava-flows have overwhelmed the city. The towns along the Soenda Straits in Java and Sumatra were also rebuilt after the sea-waves from Krakatau had swept them away; and even a rather sad substitute for old Saint-Pierre grew up again after Montagne Pelée had flattened 'the Pearl of the West Indies' in 1902. Poor agricultural communities also react positively to the aftermath of a volcanic crisis. On Lanzarote, for example, the peasants developed new and ingenious techniques of cultivation to make the very best use of the fresh blanket of ash. Similarly, when the eruption of Laki destroyed a score of farming hamlets, nearly every one was reconstructed, in spite of a terrible famine. And much of the devastated area around Mount St Helens has become a laboratory for studies of biological regeneration.

Critics, naturally, could claim that such reconstructions are foolhardy, because the people are deliberately putting themselves back in danger. In all logic, these critics are right, but humanity's struggle against nature is not always dominated by logic; and it must be said that there are more dangerous places to live in than Saint-Pierre or Catania.

Large and destructive eruptions occur, on average, once every ten years or so. Nowadays, many volcanoes that seem likely to cause death and damage are kept under close surveillance, but several apparently extinct volcanoes have nevertheless erupted violently within the past few decades. When the next lethal eruption happens, will the threatened population be adequately warned, and will they react properly to the warnings, will they be saved, or will they join the victims of the past? The answers to these questions could depend, for instance, upon the accuracy of the specialists' forecasts, upon the resolve and ability of the authorities to do something about the eruption, and upon the eagerness of the people to respond. Nature proposes; humanity disposes, but only if humanity respects the rules of nature. As this account shows, the volcano always wins.

Eruptions and Their Victims

79	Vesuvius, Italy	*c.* 5,000
1538	Monte Nuovo, Italy	24
1669	Etna, Italy	[? 'thieves' hanged] 0
1727	Öraefajökull, Iceland	*c.* 200?
1730	Lanzarote, Canary Islands	0
1783	Laki, Iceland	[famine] 9,367
1835	Coseguïna, Nicaragua	7
1883	Krakatau, Indonesia	36,417
1902	Montagne Pelée, Martinique	28,600
1943	Parícutin, Mexico	3
1980	Mount St Helens, USA	57
1985	Nevado del Ruiz, Colombia	*c.* 23,000
1986	Lake Nyos, Cameroon	1,742
1991	Pinatubo, Philippines	1,202
	Stromboli, Italy – 2,500 years of activity	[very few]

Sources and Further Reading

General Books

Blong, R.J. *Volcanic Hazards*, Academic Press, Sydney, 1984

Bullard, F.M. *Volcanoes of the Earth*, University of Texas, Austin, Texas, 2nd edn, 1984

Chester, D. *Volcanoes and Society*, Edward Arnold, London, 1993

Decker, R.W. and Decker, B. *Volcanoes*, W.H. Freeman, San Francisco, 2nd edn, 1989

MacDonald, G.A. *Volcanoes*, Prentice-Hall, Englewood Cliffs, New Jersey, 1972

McGuire, W., Kilburn, C.J.R. and Murray, J. (eds) *Monitoring Active Volcanoes*, UCL Press, London, 1995

Scarpa, R. and Tilling, R.I. (eds) *Monitoring and Mitigation of Volcano Hazards*, Springer, Berlin, 1996

Scarth, A. *Volcanoes*, UCL Press, London, 1994

Scarth, A. *Savage Earth*, HarperCollins, London, 1997

Sheets, P.D. and Grayson, D.K. (eds) *Volcanic Activity and Human Ecology*, Academic Press, New York, 1979

Williams, H. and McBirney, A.R. *Volcanology*, Freeman, San Francisco, 1979

Vesuvius

Gasparini, P. and Musella, S. *Un Viaggio al Vesuvio*, Liguori, Naples, 1991

Hamilton, Sir W. *Campi Phlegraei, Observations on the Volcanoes of the Two Sicilies*, Fabris, Naples, 2 vols, 1776 and 1779

Hamilton, Sir W. 'An account of the eruption of Mount Vesuvius in 1767', *Philosophical Transactions of the Royal Society of London*, vol. 58, 1–12, 1768

Hamilton, Sir. W. 'An account of the late Eruption of Mount Vesuvius', *Philosophical Transactions of the Royal Society of London*, vol. 85, 73–116, 1795

Pliny the Younger, *Letters and Panegyricus*, Loeb Classical Library, Harvard University Press, Harvard, Letters 16 and 20 (to Tacitus)

Sigurdsson, H., Carey, S., Cornell, W. and Pescatore, T. 'The eruption of Vesuvius in AD 79', *National Geographic Research*, vol. 1, 332–387, 1985

Sigurdsson, H., Cashdollar, S. and Sparks, R.S.J. 'The eruption of Vesuvius in AD 79: reconstruction from historical and volcanological evidence', *American Journal of Archaeology*, vol. 86, 39–51, 1982

Monte Nuovo

Barberi, F. and Carapezza, M.L. 'The Campi Flegrei case history', in R. Scarpa and R.I. Tilling (eds) *Monitoring and Mitigation of Volcano Hazards*, Springer, Berlin, 771–786, 1996

Barberi, F., Corrado, G., Innocenti, F. and Luongo, G. 'Phlegraean Fields 1982–1984: brief chronicle of a volcano emergency in a densely populated area, *Bulletin of Volcanology*, vol. 47, 175–185, 1984

Di Vito, M., Lirer, L., Mastrolorenzo, G. and Roland, G. 'The Monte Nuovo eruption (Campi Flegrei, Italy)', *Bulletin of Volcanology*, vol. 49, 608–615, 1987

Dvorak, J.J. and Gasparini, P. 'History of earthquakes and vertical ground movement in Campi Flegrei Caldera, Southern Italy: comparison of precursory events to the AD 1538 eruption of Monte Nuovo and of activity since 1968', *Journal of Volcanology and Geothermal Research*, vol. 48, 77–92, 1991

Hamilton, Sir W. 'Remarks upon the nature of the soil of Naples and its neighbourhood', *Philosophical Transactions of the Royal Society of London*, vol. 61, 1–43, 1771

Hamilton, Sir W. *Campi Phlegraei, Observations on the Volcanoes of the Two Sicilies*, Fabris, Naples, 2 vols, 1776 and 1779

Miccio, S. *Vita di Don Pietro da Toledo*, Archivio Storico Italiano, vol. 9, 1846 [first published Rome, 1600]

Parascandola, A. 'Il Monte Nuovo ed il Lago Lucrino', *Bollettino della Società dei Naturalisti in Napoli*, vol. 55, 152–264, 1946

Etna

Borelli, I.A. 'Historia et Meteorologia incendii Aetnei anni 1669', *In Academia Pisana*, Officina Dominici Ferri, Pisa, 1670

Chester, D.K., Duncan, A.M., Guest, J.E. and Kilburn, C.R.J. *Mount Etna: The Anatomy of a Volcano*, Chapman and Hall, London, 1985

De Fiore, O. 'Manoscritti inediti su fenomeni vulcanici dell' Italia meridionale, Pt III: Relazione sull' eruzione dell' Etna nel 1669'. *Rend. e Memorie della Acad. Sci. lett. ed arte degli zelante*, Acireale, ser. 3, vol. 7, 187–195, 1912

Ferrara, F. *Descrizione dell'Etna, con la storia delle eruzioni ed il catalogo dei prodotti*, La Data, Palermo, 1818

Forsyth, P.Y. 'In the wake of Etna, 44BC', *Classical Antiquity*, vol. 7(1), 49–57, 1988

Recupero, G. *Storia naturale e generale dell'Etna*, Stamperia Regia Università, Catania, 2 vols, 1815

Romano, R. and Sturiale, C. 'The historical eruptions of Mt. Etna', *Mem. Società Geologica Italiana*, vol. 23, 75–97, 1982

Sartorius von Waltershausen, W. *Der Aetna*, Engelman, Leipzig, 2 vols, 1880

Anon. '"Some inquisitive English merchants". An answer to some inquiries concerning the eruptions of Mount Aetna, An. 1669', *Philosophical Transactions of the Royal Society of London*, vol. 14, 1028–1034, 1669

Tanguy, J.C. and Patanè, G. *L'Etna et le monde des volcans*, Diderot Multimédia, Paris, 1996

Winchilsea, Earl of 'A true and exact relation of the late prodigious earthquake and eruption of Mount Aetna, or Monte Gibello, as it came in a letter written to His Majesty from Naples, by the Right Honourable, the Earl of Winchilsea, His Majesty's late Ambassador at Constantinople, who in his return from thence, visiting Catania in the Island of Sicily, was an eyewitness of that dreadful spectacle', T. Newcomb, *Savoy*, London, 29pp, 1669

The sources of the quotations from the classical authors are as follows: Pindar, *Pythian Odes*, I: 21–28; Lucretius, *On the Nature of Things*, VI: 641–646; Strabo, *The Geographies*, VI: 2.8; Virgil, *Aeneid*, III: 571–582; Ovid, *Metamorphosis*, V: 346–358; Virgil, *Georgics*, I: 466–473; Pliny the Elder, *Natural History*, II: 28; Plutarch, *Life of Julius Caesar*, LXIX: 3–4; Tibullus, *Elegies II*, 5: 75–76; Suetonius, *Augustus*, 81.2; and Shakespeare, *Hamlet*, Act I, Scene I: 114–116. My translations from Greek or Latin were based on those editions in the Loeb Classical Library, Harvard University Press, Cambridge, Massachusetts

Öraefajökull

Henderson, E. *Iceland, or a Journal of a Residence in that Island during the Years 1814–1815*, Edinburgh, 1818

Thórarinsson, S. 'The Öraefajökull eruption of 1362', *Acta Naturalia Islandica*, vol. 2(2), 1–98, 1958

Lanzarote

Carracedo, J.C. and Rodríguez Badiola, E. *Lanzarote, La Erupción Volcánica de 1730*, C.S.I.C. Servicio de Publicaciones, Excmo. Cabildo Insular de Lanzarote, 1991

Carracedo, J.C., Rodríguez Badiola, E. and Soler, V. 'The 1730–1736 eruption of Lanzarote, Canary Islands: a long, high-magnitude basaltic fissure eruption', *Journal of Volcanology and Geothermal Research*, vol. 53, 239–250, 1992

Real Audiencia de Canarias, 'Copia de las Ordones y providencias dadas para el alivio de los Vezinos de la Isla de Lanzarote en su dilatado padezer a causa del prodigioso Volcán, que en ella rebentó el primer dia de Septiembre del año immediato pasado de 1730, y continúa hasta el dia de la fecha . . . Canaria y Abril 4 de 1731', *Legajo 89, Gracia y Justicia*, Archivo General de Simancas, Spain, 1731

Von Buch, L. (trans. C. Boulanger,) *Description physique des îles Canaries*, Levrault, Paris, 1836

Laki

Cullum, Revd Sir J. 'An account of a remarkable frost on 23rd of June 1783', *Philosophical Transactions of the Royal Society of London*, vol. 74, 416–418, 1784

Franklin, B., 'Meteorological imaginations and conjectures', *Mem. Lit. Philos. Soc.*, Manchester, vol. 2, 373–377, 1784

Grattan, J. and Brayshay, M. 'An amazing and portentous summer: environmental and social responses in Britain to the 1783 eruption of an Iceland volcano', *Geographical Journal*, vol. 161, 125–133, 1995

Grattan, J. and Charman, D.J. 'Non-climatic factors and the environmental impact of volcanic volatiles: implication of the Laki fissure eruption of AD 1783', *The Holocene*, vol. 4, 101–106, 1994

Jackson, E.L. 'The Laki eruption of 1783: impacts on population and settlement in Iceland', *Geography*, vol. 67, 42–50, 1982

Kington, J.A. *The Weather Patterns for the 1780s over Europe*, Cambridge University Press, Cambridge, 1988

Leeds Intelligencer, 15 July 1783; 29 July 1783

Mourgue de Montredon, M. 'Sur l'origine et sur la nature des Vapeurs qui ont régné dans l'Atmosphère pendant l'été de 1783', *Mémoires de l'Académie Royale des Sciences*, Paris, 754–773, Année MDCCLXXXI (published 1784)

Rabartin, R. and Rocher, P. 'Les Volcans, le climat, et la révolution Française', *L'Association Volcanologique Européenne*, Paris, Mémoire No. 1, 1993

Steingrímsson, J., 'Fullkomid skrif um Sídueld (A complete description of the Sída volcanic fire dated November 24 1788 at Prestbakki)', in *Safn til Sögu Islands*, vol. 4, Copenhagen, 1–57, 1907–1915 (1788)

Thórarinsson, S. 'The Lakagígar eruption of 1783', *Bulletin volcanologique*, vol. 33, 910–929, 1970

Thordarson, T. *The eruptive sequence and eruption behaviour of the Skaftár Fires (Laki), 1783–85, Iceland: characteristics and distribution of eruption products* (Master Thesis, The University of Texas at Arlington, Texas), University Microfilm International, Ann Arbor, Michigan, 1990

Thordarson, T. *The Laki eruptions of 1783–85: Tephra deposits and course of events*, University of Iceland Special Publication F90018, 1991

Thordarson, T. and Self, S. 'The Laki (Skaftár Fires) and Grímsvötn eruptions in 1783–1785', *Bulletin of Volcanology*, vol. 55, 233–263, 1993

Thordarson, T. *Volatile release and atmospheric effects of basaltic fissure eruptions* (Ph.D Thesis, University of Hawaii at Manoa, Oahu, Hawaii), University Microfilm International, Ann Arbor, Michigan, 1995

White, G. *The Natural History of Selborne*, Penguin, Harmondsworth (reprinted 1977 from the 1789 edition)

Wood, C.A. 'Climatic effects of the 1783 Laki eruption', in C.R. Harington (ed.) *The Year without a Summer?* Canadian Museum of Nature, Ottawa, 58–77, 1992

Cosegüina

Caldcleugh, A. 'Some account of the volcanic eruption of Cosegüina in the Bay of Fonseca, commonly called the Bay of Conchagua on the western coast of Central America', *Philosophical Transactions of the Royal Society of London*, vol. 1, 27–30, 1836

Galindo, J. 'On the eruption of the volcano Cosigüina, in Nicaragua, 17th January, 1835', *Journal of the Royal Geographical Society*, vol. 1, 387–392, 1835

Self, S., Rampino, M.R. and Carr, M.J. 'A reappraisal of the 1835 eruption of Cosigüina and its atmospheric impact', *Bulletin of Volcanology*, vol. 52, 57–65, 1989

Stephens, J.L. *Incidents of Travel in Central America, Chiapas and Yucatan*, Century, London, 1988 [first published 1841]

Williams, H. 'The great eruption of Cosegüina, Nicaragua, *University of California Publications in Geological Sciences*, vol. 29, 21–46, 1952

Krakatau

Carey, S., Sigurdsson, H., Mandeville, C. and Bronto, S. 'Pyroclastic flows and surges over water: an example from the 1883 Krakatau eruption', *Bulletin of Volcanology*, vol. 57, 493–511, 1996

Furneaux, R. *Krakatoa*, Prentice-Hall, Englewood Cliffs, New Jersey, 1964

Simkin, T. and Fiske, R.S. *Krakatau 1883: The Volcanic Eruption and its Effects*, Smithsonian Institution Press, Washington, DC, 1983

Symons, G.J. (ed.) *The Eruption of Krakatau and Subsequent Phenomena: reports of the Krakatau Committee of the Royal Society*, Trübner, London, 1888

Verbeek, R.D.M. *Krakatau*, Landsdrukkerij, Batavia, 1885 [French edition, 1886]

Montagne Pelée

Adélaïde-Merlande, J. and Hervieu, J.P. *Les Volcans dans l'histoire des Antilles*, Karthala, Paris, 1997

Anderson, T. and Flett, J.S. 'Report on the eruption of the Soufrière in St Vincent, in 1902, and on a visit to Montagne Pelée in Martinique', *Philosophical Transactions of the Royal Society of London*, Part I, seri. A200, 353–553, 1903

Ariès, P., Daney, C. and Berté, E. *Catastrophe à la Martinique*, Herscher, Paris, 1981

Berté, E. 'Récit et observations d'un témoin', *La Géographie*, September 1902, 25–38

Boudon, G. and Gourgaud, A. (eds) 'Mount Pelée', *Journal of Volcanology and Geothermal Research*, vol. 38, 1989

Chrétien, S. and Brousse, R. *La Montagne Pelée se réveille*, Societé Nouvelle des Editions Boubée, Paris, 1988

Coeur Créole (Canon L. Lambolez) *Saint-Pierre Martinique, 1635–1902*, Annales des Antilles Françaises – Journal et Album de la Martinique. Livre d'or de la Charité, Berger-Levrault, Paris, 1905

Contour, S. *Saint-Pierre (Martinique) Tome II: La Catastrophe et ses suites*, Editions Caribéennes, Paris, 1989

Freeman, E.W. 'The awful doom of St Pierre', *Pearson's Magazine*, vol. 14, 313–325, September 1902

Heilprin, A. *Mont Pelée and the Tragedy of Martinique*, Lippincott, Philadelphia, 1903

Lacroix, A. *La Montagne Pelée et ses éruptions*, Masson, Paris, 1904

Tanguy, J.C. 'The 1902–1905 eruptions of Montagne Pelée, Martinique: anatomy and retrospection', *Journal of Volcanology and Geothermal Research*, vol. 60, 87–107, 1994

Tauriac, M. *Martinique: Les Années Créoles*, Omnibus, Paris, 1996

Ursulet, L., *Le Désastre de 1902 à la Martinique*, L'Harmattan, Paris, 1997

Parícutin

Atl, Dr *Como nace y crece un volcán?: El Parícutin, México*, Stylo, México City, 1950

Foshag, W.F. 'The life and death of a volcano', *Geographical Magazine (London)*, vol. 17, 159–168, 1954

Foshag, W.F. and González-Reyna, J.R. 'Birth and development of Parícutin volcano, Mexico', *US Geological Survey Bulletin*, vol. 965D, 355–489, 1956

Luhr, J.F. and Simkin, T. (eds) *Parícutin. The Volcano Born in a Mexican Cornfield*, Geoscience Press, Phoenix, Arizona, 1993

Nolan, M.L. 'Impact of Parícutin on five communities', in P.D. Sheets and D.K. Grayson (eds) *Volcanic Activity and Human Ecology*, Academic Press, New York, 293–338, 1979

Mount St Helens

Baxter, P.J. 'Medical effects of volcanic eruptions', *Bulletin of Volcanology*, vol. 32, 532–544, 1990

Corcoran, T. *Mount St Helens: The Story Behind the Scenery*, K.C. Publications, Las Vegas, Nevada, 1985

Foxworthy, B.L. and Hill, M. (eds) *Volcanic eruptions of 1980 at Mount St Helens. The First 100 Days*, US Geological Survey Professional Paper 1249, 1982

Harris, S.L. *Fire and Ice: The Cascade Volcanoes*, The Mountaineers and Pacific Search Books, Seattle, Washington, 2nd edn, 1980

Harris, S.L. *Fire Mountains of the West*, Mountain Press, Missoula, Montana, 1988

Lipman, P.W. and Mullineaux, D.R. (eds) *The 1980 Eruptions of Mount St Helens, Washington*, US Geological Survey Professional Paper 1250, 1981

Nevado Del Ruiz

Acosta, J. 'Relation de l'éruption boueuse sortie du volcan de Ruiz et de la catastrophe de Lagunilla dans la République de Nouvelle Grenade'. *Comptes Rendus de l'Académie des Sciences, Paris*, vol. 22, 709–710, 1846

Hall, M.L. 'Chronology of the principal scientific and governmental actions leading up to the November 13, 1985 eruption of Nevado del Ruiz, Columbia', *Journal of Volcanology and Geothermal Research*, vol. 42, 101–115, 1990

Mileti, D.S., Bolton, P.A., Fernandez, G. and Updike, R.G. *The Eruption of Nevado del Ruiz Volcano, Colombia, South America, November 13, 1985*. National Academy Press, Natural Disaster Series, vol. 4, Washington, DC, 1991

Podesta, B. and Giesecke, M. *El Nevado del Ruiz y el Riesgo Volcánico en América Latina*, Centre Regional de Sismología para América del Sur, CERESIS, Lima, Peru, 1990

Simón, P. *Noticias Historiales de las Conquistas de Tierra Firme en las Indias Occidentales*, Casa Editorial de Medardo Rios, Bogotá, Colombia, (first published 1625), 1892

Voight, B. 'The 1985 Nevado del Ruiz volcano catastrophe: anatomy and retrospection', *Journal of Volcanology and Geothermal Research*, vol. 42, 151–188, 1990 and *Journal of Volcanology and Geothermal Research*, vol. 44, 349–386, 1990

Voight, B. 'The management of volcano emergencies: Nevado del Ruiz', in R. Scarpa and R.I. Tilling (eds) *Monitoring and Mitigation of Volcano Hazards*, Springer, Berlin, 719–770, 1996

Williams, S.N. (ed.) Nevado del Ruiz Volcano, Columbia, I, *Journal of Volcanology and Geothermal Research*, vol. 41, 1990 and II, *Journal of Volcanology and Geothermal Research*, vol. 42, 1990

Lake Nyos

Baxter, P.J. and Kapila, M. 'Acute health impact of the gas release at Lake Nyos, Cameroon, 1986', *Journal of Volcanology and Geothermal Research*, vol. 39, 265–275, 1989

Freeth, S.J. 'The anecdotal evidence: did it help or hinder investigation of the Lake Nyos gas disaster?' *Journal of Volcanology and Geothermal Research*, vol. 42, 373–380, 1990

Leenhardt, D. *La Catastrophe du Lac Nyos au Cameroun*, L'Harmattan, Paris, 1995

LeGuern, F., Shanklin, E. and Tebor, S. 'Witness accounts of the catastrophic event of August 1986 at Lake Nyos (Cameroon)', *Journal of Volcanology and Geothermal Research*, vol. 57, 174–184, 1992

Sigvaldson, G.E. 'International conference on Lake Nyos disaster, Yaoundé, Cameroun 16–20 March 1987: conclusions and recommendations', *Journal of Volcanology and Geothermal Research*, vol. 39, 97–108, 1989

Tazieff, H. 'Mechanisms of the Nyos carbon dioxide disaster and the so-called phreatic steam eruptions', *Journal of Volcanology and Geothermal Research*, vol. 39, 109–116, 1989

Pinatubo

Newhall, C.G. and Punongbayan, R.S. (eds) *Fire and Mud: Eruptions and Lahars of Mount Pinatubo, Philippines*, Philippine Institute of Volcanology and Seismology, Quezon City, Philippines and University of Washington Press, Seattle, 1996

Conclusion

Tanguy, J.C., Ribière, C., Scarth, A. and Tjetjep, W.S. 'Victims from volcanic eruptions: a revised database', *Bulletin of Volcanology*, vol. 60, 137–144, 1998

Index

Illustration Acknowledgements

Royal Tropical Institute, Amsterdam: 152, 153. The Associated Press Ltd: 249. Circus World Museum, Baraboo, Wisconsin: 177. Museo Archeologico Nazionale, Naples/The Bridgeman Art Library, London & New York: 24. By permission of the British Library: 20, 42. © John V. Christiansen/Earth Images: 220, 221. Heilprin, *The Tower of Pelée*, Philadelphia & London, 1904: 185. NASA: 261. By courtesy of the National Portrait Gallery, London: 23. Anthony Newton: 206. Perret, *The Eruption of Mount Pelée 1929–1932*, London 1935: 161. Planet Earth Pictures: 84 (© Thomas Dressler), 190, 226, 274 (© Bourseillier & Durieux). Popperfoto 240, 241, 242. © Dieter & Mary Plage/Oxford Scientific Films: 147. Alwyn Scarth: 16, 25, 32, 39, 40, 46, 53, 54, 65, 86, 91, 94, 100, 102, 166, 176, 172, 179, 182, 224, 254. Simpson, *Eruption of Krakatoa*, London, 1888: 134, 139. Smithsonian Institution Archives: 195. Jean-Claude Tanguy: titlepage, 12, 17, 56, 60, 73, 122, 150, 156, 269. Thorvaldur Thordarson: 104, 109. Carmen Thyssen-Bornemisza Collection: 45. U.S.G.S.: 213, 210, 222, 223, 244, 251, 259, 265. U.S. National Archives and Records Administration: 198, 200, 202. David Williams/David Williams Picture Library: 76, 80, 81.